TEACHING
AS A
MORAL CRAFT

Teaching
as a
Moral Craft

ALAN R. TOM
Washington University

Longman
New York & London

Teaching as a Moral Craft

Longman Inc., 1560 Broadway, New York, N.Y. 10036
Associated companies, branches, and representatives
throughout the world.

Portions of Chapters 2 and 3 initially appeared in "The
reform of teacher education through research: A futile
quest." *Teachers College Record* 82 (1980) 1:15-29.
Portions of Chapters 4 and 5 initially appeared in
"Teaching as a moral craft: A metaphor for teaching
and teacher education." *Curriculum Inquiry* 10 (1980)
3:317-323.

Developmental Editor: Nicole Benevento
Editorial and Design Supervisor: James Fields
Production/Manufacturing Supervisor: Ferne Y. Kawahara

Library of Congress Cataloging in Publication Data

Tom, Alan R., 1937–
  Teaching as a moral craft.

  Bibliography: p.
  Includes index.
  1. Teaching. 2. Education—Aims and objectives.
3. Moral education. I. Title.
LB1025.2.T63 1984   371.1'02   83-17520
ISBN 0-582-28307-8

Manufactured in the United States of America
Printing: 9 8 7 6 5 4 3 2 1 Year: 92 91 90 89 88 87 86 85 84

CONTENTS

ACKNOWLEDGMENTS

No scholar works alone. In the case of this book there are several people who deserve special mention. Tom Fox not only urged me to write the book but also suggested that my experience in using the moral craft metaphor (Part III) would make the book more interesting and useful to practitioners. Kevin Ryan offered overall encouragement and provided thoughtful comments on the manuscript. Also reading the manuscript in its entirety was Ken Zeichner, whose careful attention to the logic of my argument enabled me to rethink many aspects of the book.

Over the last several years a number of people have offered critical comment on papers and articles that eventually grew into this book. Besides my colleagues at Washington University, these people include: Bob Floden, Michael Connelly, Harry Broudy, Margaret Buchmann, B. O. Smith, John Palmer, Francis Schrag, David Wright, Guy Larkins, John Mergendoller, N. L. Gage, Bob Houston. I appreciate the thoughts and reactions of these people.

Through the entire preparation of the manuscript Nicki Benevento gave wise editorial counsel, and Becky Torstrick and Marian Schick led me through the mysteries of word processing. Lastly, to my wife, Abbie, and my boys Michael and Jason, I promise a few more evenings and weekends at home.

INTRODUCTION

A PRELIMINARY ASSUMPTION

Every educator—be he* a K-12 teacher, supervisor, administrator, or college professor—is guided in his day-to-day professional activity by an idea about the nature of teaching. Frequently, the concept may be implicit or its influence may go largely unrecognized, but no educator can operate without making assumptions about the goals and exigencies of his profession. How I introduce novices to a career of teaching, how you develop a curriculum for your fourth-grade class, or how you attempt to enhance an experienced English teacher's writing instruction reflects ideas and assumptions about what teaching means.

In recent years, several scholars have tried to demonstrate the links between particular views of teaching and some realm of educational practice. Brauner, for instance, argues that for each of the six teacher-training approaches widely used over the past 175 years there originally was "a distinctive view of teaching." Such a view "seems to carry with it a special notion of how to train people" (1978, p. 162). In addition to our current atheoretic view of teaching, which leads to an immersion approach to training, Brauner identifies five earlier views and their related approaches to teacher training: monitorial method (mechanical training), object teaching (demonstrative training), Herbartianism (programmed training), the

---

*Rather than use such awkward constructions as "his or her" or "s/he," I have chosen to alternate between using masculine and feminine pronouns. Later in the book, I employ the commonly used terms "craftsmen" and "fisherman" to refer to both genders.

Montessori method (diagnostic training), and experimentalism (supervisory training). In a similar way Hartnett and Naish (1980) contend that current teacher education programs are rooted in one or more of the following perspectives: ideological, technological, craft, or critical. Each perspective has a particular orientation toward education, epistemology, and professional legitimation, and each illustrates my claim that an educator's concept of teaching shapes his daily practice.

Scratching below the surface of accepted practice reveals a variety of ideas about teaching, though for any particular era and culture one or two tend to predominate. We are socialized into these dominant conceptions by our professional training and our early work experience, and, as a result, personal inquiry into the ultimate potency and effectiveness of these ideas tends to be abandoned as a teacher gains experience. However, without attention to the linkages between our conception of teaching and our daily practice, our professional lives can become ritualized, that is, our teaching activities can become grounded in a rigid adherence to current practice or tradition. A major goal of this book is to analyze the potency and efficacy of the concepts of teaching that socialize the teachers of the 1980s and to promote a new interpretation based on viewing teaching as a moral craft.

OVERVIEW OF THE BOOK'S ORGANIZATION

The first part of the text describes and critiques the concept of teaching that has dominated professional educators' thinking for more than half a century: teaching as an applied science. At root, the applied science concept of teaching is a belief that behavioral and social scientific research can produce generalizations, principles—even laws—that the teacher can "apply" to help resolve a specific teaching problem. In Chapter 1, I use historical vignettes to illustrate the persistence of the applied science metaphor and to examine this metaphor's widespread influence on curriculum development, research on teaching, and teacher education. Yet, work grounded in the applied science metaphor—especially research on teaching—has been, at best, inconclusive and, at worst, barren. I discuss specific reasons for this disappointing result in Chapter 2. Chapter 3 shows why the applied science concept of teaching inadequately represents the phenomenon of teaching and gives attention to three faulty assumptions commonly made by teacher effectiveness researchers. Some form of metaphoric representation of teaching is useful, but the content of this metaphor must accord more with the situational and normative dimensions of teaching than does the applied science conception.

In Part II, I introduce and develop a new metaphor—teaching as a moral craft. Chapter 4 emphasizes the various senses in which teaching is a moral activity, while Chapter 5 examines the craft basis of teaching. The synthesis of the moral and craft components of teaching results in the moral craft metaphor and leads us to view the teacher as a moral craftsman. In Chapter 6 I compare the moral craft concept of teaching with other common images of teaching, such as teaching as a fine art (see, for example, Eisner 1979, chap. 9; Rives 1979; Rubin 1981), teaching as an applied science (Brophy & Evertson 1976; Freeman 1930; Resnick & Ford 1981), and teaching as a craft (Cohen 1977; Lortie 1975). The overall purpose of Part II, therefore, is to explicate the moral craft metaphor, illustrate how this metaphor leads to perceiving the teacher as a moral craftsman, and compare and contrast the moral craft image of teaching with such other metaphors for teaching as art, applied science, and craft.

Part III is devoted to applying the moral craft metaphor to issues of educational research and practice. In the introduction I discuss several cautions that must be considered in using the moral craft metaphor in educational research and practice. These cautions address my limited experience with the moral craft metaphor, the tendency for a root metaphor such as moral craft not to entail a specific course of action, and the difficulty in applying any metaphor to the ongoing events of teaching. With these problems in mind, I describe my attempts to implement the moral craft metaphor. In Chapter 7 I describe my efforts at working directly with teachers to improve instruction and offer case examples for preservice teacher education, in-service teacher education, and classroom supervision. Perhaps insights from my experience can be applied to other situations familiar to the reader. Chapter 8 examines the implications of the moral craft metaphor for research on teaching and for one area of policy-making, program accreditation. Throughout Part III I try to be realistic about the problems involved in applying the moral craft metaphor to educational research and practice.

PURPOSE AND AUDIENCE

That each part of the book has a unifying theme and that the book as a whole is an argument for a particular way of conceptualizing teaching differentiates this book from many texts. A more common approach is for an author to include as many theoretical ideas from a field as possible and to leave the synthesis of these ideas—and often their application to practice—to the reader. Coverage of a field has become the sine qua non of textbook publishing.

The problem with many of these encyclopedic texts is twofold. On the one hand, coverage-oriented texts tend to overwhelm students. In response to one of these "compilation of ideas" texts, one of my supervision students recently observed: "I am an experienced supervisor, but I am getting more and more confused by all these theories, each of which seems to be reasonable when I read about it." Moreover, these textbooks miss out on a major opportunity to help students assimilate material. Rather than integrate the diverse ideas into a framework or a coherent point of view, the typical text presents the material in a series of loosely related topics that often reflect scholars' specialized concerns.

An alternative to the coverage-oriented text is one that is selective in its presentation of ideas and tries to tie the ideas to a framework or point of view. In this way a text acts as a model of what is involved in identifying the root issues in a field, considering the interconnections among these issues, and relating these issues to one's role as a practicing professional. Such a focused and framework-based book can deepen the student's understanding of a field and lead him to rethink his role as a practicing professional.

My book aims to enlighten the student about the weaknesses of the applied science view of teaching and offers the alternative metaphor of teaching as a moral craft. The book is addressed to experienced teachers and to those who work with experienced teachers, such as department heads, supervisors, curriculum consultants, principals, and advisors. A related audience is preservice teacher educators since these people are responsible for introducing novices to the practice of teaching. But I also examine the implications for research of the moral craft metaphor; consequently, another readership for the book is people preparing to be educational researchers and instructors in research courses for teachers. Contemporary research on teaching, with its base in the applied science metaphor, has become sterile and badly needs redirection toward a more defensible view of teaching. This text, therefore, is useful for graduate courses in instructional supervision, staff development, curriculum, teacher education, and research on teaching.

A PERSONAL NOTE

All too often authors reveal so little about themselves that readers may well think a typewriter wrote the book. Such anonymity is a mistake—particularly in a field such as teaching where human purposes are centrally involved. Not only do readers deserve to know an author's background and predispositions in order to be alerted to biases that may be built into a book but the author can also profit by reminding himself of his predilections, many of which have become second nature over the years.

While my experience prior to becoming a college professor reflects a typical career path for a professor of education, my university-level experience is somewhat unusual and has strongly influenced the way I think and write about teaching.

After deciding not to complete a doctorate in European history, I took the education courses needed for social studies certification and did a one-semester internship during the fall of 1962 in a small city in central Wisconsin. Then I taught for a year and a half in a Chicago suburb before returning to graduate school to obtain a doctoral degree in curriculum and instruction. Along with my course work I spent considerable time supervising student teachers.

This relatively conventional career path abruptly changed when I took my first college-level job at Washington University in 1966. For the next three years, I spent most of my time in the schools working in a federally funded project designed to implement the "new" social studies curricula. I worked with twelve social studies teachers to select from the newly produced social studies curricula those materials we wanted to pilot in six St. Louis area school districts. While the typical assistant professor of education spends the initial years of his career being socialized into an academic perspective, I spent my formative years talking and working with teachers who were attempting to make basic curricular changes. These three years of intense involvement with a small group of teachers gave me insight into a variety of practical issues, for example, the normative dimension of curricular decision making, the politics of day-to-day school operation, the vagaries of federal funding priorities, and the conceptual gulf between school and university faculty.

In an effort to convey some of my practical learnings to a wider audience, as well as to meet the scholarly expectations of a research-oriented university, I started writing about practical issues at the conclusion of my involvement in a project or program development experience. Over the years I have written about selecting (Tom 1970) and implementing (Tom and Applegate 1969; Tom 1973a, 1973b) curricula at the end of the social studies project, the prospects for the clinical professorship after holding such an appointment (Tom 1974a), the problems with school-university cooperation at the conclusion of a Triple-T project (Tom 1973c), the issues involved in pass-fail grading of student teaching after our department faced this policy question (Tom 1974b), and the accreditation of teacher education programs subsequent to our institution's visit by a team from the National Council for Accreditation of Teacher Education (NCATE) (Tom 1980a, 1980b, 1981, 1983).

I believe that the thread that holds all of my scholarship together is my desire to make sense out of events that I have experienced. I write with a concern for the problems of practice, with my core research question frequently taking the form: Is it possible for our thinking about this area of practice to be refined, even reformulated, and the area of practice thereby improved? I am rarely satisfied with merely trying to understand particular phenomena; I usually want to press ahead and propose changes.

After the conclusion of the social studies project, I participated in a Triple-T project, a federally funded program the goals of which were bold but nebulous (Provus 1975). At Washington University we experimented with clinical professor roles and ultimately developed a field-based elementary program that had considerable impact on the current formulations of our elementary and secondary teacher education programs. A lasting effect of the Triple-T experience was the uneasy feeling that my own ideas on teacher education were inadequately developed, a deficiency I hoped to remedy at some future time.

With the end of the massive influx of federal funds into the educational system during Lyndon Johnson's administration, I assumed a position that in larger institutions would have been called Director of Student Teaching. In this role and subsequently as coordinator of the secondary education program, I worked with a group of faculty to alter our relatively traditional teacher-education programs to make them more field-oriented and integrated (a professional semester of correlated methods course work and student teaching is the core of both our elementary and secondary programs). In a sense, one personal reason for writing this book is to satisfy myself that our changes in teacher-education programming actually do have reasonable intellectual underpinnings. Like many practitioners, I often make modifications in practice without having a clearly developed rationale for these changes, partly because the scope of the rationale is unclear to me at the beginning of a change effort and partly because I generally lack the time to both create new programs and concurrently ground them intellectually.

By now the reader should be well aware of my concern for the problems of practice, my tendency to use scholarship in a retrospective way, and my desire to improve upon current practice. As a result, I question the widely held belief that the problems of practice can best be studied by reconceptualizing them in terms of disciplinary perspectives derived from the social and behavioral sciences. Again and again we have been admonished by a great variety of scholars that if only we would apply social and behavioral science methodologies to teaching we could generate theory to guide teaching practice (for example Dunkin & Biddle 1974; Gage 1978; Kerlinger 1968; Schaefer 1967).

On the contrary, I came to believe that practice ought to inform theory, that theory in a professional field such as teaching should arise from the rigorous study of the problems and dilemmas of practice (Atkin 1973). Of course it would be an error to replace the simplistic theory-guides-practice orientation with the equally simplistic view that practice governs theory. In reality, theory generated out of the rigorous study of practice ought to inform our subsequent teaching practice. The relationship between practice and theory should be cyclical and interactive (deCastell & Freeman 1978). But I believe that the starting point for the development of educational theory ought to be the educational situation, not the canons of disciplinary inquiry.

CONCERNS ABOUT THE LITERATURE ON TEACHING

During my twenty years in teaching, I have come to see that much of the literature on teaching and related topics is replete with undefined terms, dogmatic in nature, and inattentive to assumptions. Each of these flaws can be illustrated with examples drawn from the literature on teaching and teacher education.

Many of the key terms used in the professional literature on teaching and teacher education are carelessly defined. No topic in teacher education receives more discussion than the reputed gap between theory and practice, yet few authors ever bother to define *theory*. The reader, therefore, does not know if theory is being used to refer to unrealistic advice, to empirically based generalizations and/or lawlike statements, or to desirable principles of practice. A single author may well use the term theory in all three ways without ever making clear when a shift has occurred to a new meaning. Other educational terms are part of our daily language so that the necessity for technical definitions may not be recognized; here we find such terms as *needs, teaching, curriculum, learning, growth,* and so forth. Our inability to understand one another further complicates the task of building a cumulative literature, a result not only of the careless use of language but also of our tolerance of this carelessness. While precision in our use of language will by no means resolve all educational issues under dispute, such precision will at least help us clarify where we disagree (Kilbourn 1982).

To clarify the nature of our disagreements is a modest goal. Many practitioners aspire to the more grandiose goal of resolving all our vexing problems of practice. Such a passion leads, I believe, to a high degree of dogmatism, which is expressed in a variety of ways, including the refusal to ground practice-oriented inquiry in relevant literature and the widespread assumption that certain ways of guiding teacher preparation are categorically superior to others. For example, the NCATE *Standards for Accreditation of Teacher Education* (1979) attempts to impose on everyone the traditional teacher-education curriculum, even though there is little evidence to suggest the superiority of any particular approach to teacher preparation (Tom 1980a, 1980b). While educational researchers are adept at pointing out the rigidities of practitioners, they too can be dogmatic, especially in believing that the problems of practice can be ameliorated by the judicious application of research findings.

The liabilities of dogmatism cannot be overestimated. The literature on teaching frequently lacks analytic power because of its reliance on conviction and categorical statement. At the same time, strong statements of conviction, which could lead to a productive dialogue with those who hold conflicting orientations, tend to be ignored by all but the already converted. Perhaps the most damaging impact of dogmatism, however, is the way it can mask assumptions that underlie proposed educational solutions.

Inattention to assumptions is a serious deficiency in the literature on teaching and teacher education. This literature is full of grandiose plans and solutions and attacks on these very same plans and solutions; underlying intellectual issues and assumptions are ignored. Performance-based teacher education is a case in point. Some authors tout performance-based teacher education while others attempt to eradicate it. Little exploration occurs of such underlying issues as the research base for performance-based teacher education or the adequacy of viewing the teaching act as divisible into many individual operations that can be readily integrated into meaningful wholes. It is much easier to throw around such terms as accountability, competence, antihumanistic, or narrow minded than it is to probe the underpinnings of performance-based teacher education.

Because teaching is so complex and value laden, our assumptions should constantly undergo examination and reassessment. How many times has each one of us started an article or a paper on teaching or teacher education only to discover that the author has taken for granted exactly what we believe to be the key issue at dispute? Constant attention to underlying issues can, I hope, make our discussions of teaching more penetrating and ultimately more relevant to the improvement of educational practice.

I hope to minimize the problems of imprecise language, dogmatism, and lack of attention to assumptions. In part, I hope to avoid these difficulties by careful use of language, especially avoiding the use of undefined terms.

Avoiding dogmatism is particularly difficult in a text that attempts to interpret a set of phenomena in a new way. On the one hand, simple statements of my position are pedagogically useful because such categorical statements make clear how my analysis of a topic differs from the commonly accepted analysis. However, to exclude relevant qualifications of these absolute statements is intellectually misleading, if not dishonest, even though such omissions probably make my analysis more comprehensible to the reader. To the best of my ability I will try to maintain a balanced presentation so that my analysis is simple enough to be clear yet not so categorical as to fail to reflect the complexity of teaching phenomena.

Oversimplification is but one aspect of dogmatism; dogmatism also involves excessive commitment to certain ideas. The line between warranted and excessive commitment is hard to see, especially in regard to one's own convictions. In the end, the reader must judge whether the information and analysis marshalled to support my convictions provide an adequate "warrant" for these ideas.

Judging one's success in ferreting out his own assumptions and evaluating these assumptions is somewhat easier for an author to do. But the actual task of identifying and analyzing the assumptions is quite difficult, especially for phenomena as complex as teaching. One must be knowledgeable in many different areas since teaching can be viewed from so many perspectives. For example, one should be conversant with research on teaching (especially research derived from the dominant psychological paradigm); various approaches to teacher preparation; contrasting ways analytic philosophers have construed the concept of teaching; day-to-day activities of teachers; and the interaction between teachers and supervisors and administrators. In addition to being conversant with these areas, the author interested in detecting and analyzing assumptions needs to be able to explore relevant epistemological issues, to see both the normative and empirical bases of teaching activity, to comprehend the impact on teaching of locating this activity in a bureaucratic organization.

The need to be familiar with many different substantive areas and to be prepared to probe the depths of these areas literally overwhelms me. Can I do justice to all the assumptions which need to be explored? The enormity of this task has forced me to go far beyond my training as a social studies teacher and curriculum specialist. In this endeavor I have been greatly aided by working for the last seventeen years in a relatively small department of education (less than twenty faculty) which offers a broad scope of programs (undergraduate through doctorate). In my department there is ample opportunity to do a wide variety of teaching and scholarly activities; indeed our size in relation to the scope of our activities practically prevents us from becoming specialists. The net effect on me is that I have developed a broad set of analytic and practical skills, hopefully in sufficient depth that I can avoid the overspecialized and shallow analysis which is all too common in our literature.

TEACHING: WHY FOCUS ON IT?

The reader may wonder why I have chosen to emphasize the concept of teaching, particularly in a book designed for supervisors and administrators as well as for teacher educators and researchers on teaching. Even if the audience were to be restricted to researchers and teacher educators, there are other concepts that seem to be as centrally important to the teacher's role—for example, learning, curriculum, subject matter, evaluation, student, and so forth. Indeed, Schwab (1973) argues that "defensible educational thought must take account of four commonplaces of *equal* rank: the learner, the teacher, the milieu, and the subject matter" (pp. 508–09). He believes that none of these commonplaces can be omitted without also omitting a vital aspect of educational thought. Further, Schwab gives examples of the distortions that result when we let one of the commonplaces dominate the others. The proper relationship of the four commonplaces to one another is coordinacy, not super-ordination-subordination. Gowin (1981) has developed the four coordinate commonplaces into a theory of educating.

Schwab's analysis is cogent and insightful. To overemphasize any of the four commonplaces—the learner, the teacher, the milieu, or subject matter—is to risk creating curricula that are seriously flawed, such as the structure-of-the-disciplines curricula of the 1960s, the social-change-oriented curricula employed in many totalitarian countries, or those student-centered curricula grounded in the idea that all subject matter is of equal worth. The major point on which I differ with Schwab is that instead of using the term *curriculum* to draw the four commonplaces together, I use the term *teaching*.

The four commonplaces do intersect at teaching. Institutional-ized teaching brings together teacher and student to study certain content within a particular milieu—the classroom—which in turn is related to other more comprehensive social milieus. Focusing on teaching, therefore, permits us to look at the commonplaces not as separate entities but rather in dynamic relationship with one an-other. Another advantage of using *teaching* as a focal point for examining the four commonplaces is that we are able to organize and present our analysis in a framework consistent with the day-by-day experience of the classroom teacher. So much educational inquiry has little practical impact because its interpretation is meaningless to the classroom teacher.

Teaching, as I will use the term, is not only a dynamic activity, but it is also a comprehensive term. Although some researchers see teaching as merely the most efficient means to reach specified ends, teaching in reality is a much more complex activity. Teaching involves a subtle moral relationship between teacher and student, an attempt to bring important content to the awareness of a student, and the ability to analyze situations and to use instructional skills appropriate to these situations. In brief, teaching is seen here as a moral craft.

·PART I·

TEACHING
AS AN
APPLIED SCIENCE

Seventy years ago E. L. Thorndike looked forward and saw a glorious future for the field of education:

> Education, like history, economics, sociology, and the other sciences of man, is just beginning to give promise of quantitative knowledge, of descriptions of facts as numerically defined amounts, and of relations or laws in terms of rigid, unambiguous equations. The changes that take place in intellect and character are coming to be measured with the same general technique, and, we may hope, with the same passion for clearness and precision, which has served the physical sciences for the last two hundred years. (1912, p. 289)

Thorndike believed that we were on the threshold of developing a "science of education" (p. 289).

If education were to become a science, then teaching—apparently a triadic relationship among a teacher, a student, and something to be taught—could be viewed as an applied science. As the teacher "applied" himself to help the student learn content, the newly discovered scientific facts and laws would greatly ease the teacher's job. While some educators might object that the common-sense judgment of a first-rate teacher without this scientific knowledge is preferable to a stupid or incompetent teacher possessing this knowledge, Thorndike reminds us that "the work of science [is] to get good work done by those of us who are rather mediocre.... We should all prefer to have for our children a stupid doctor of today, who nevertheless understood the use of antiseptics and antitoxins, than Galen or Hippocrates, though in respect to common-sense there would be no choice" (p. 299). Thorndike's confidence that scientific facts and laws could lift today's run-of-the-mill teachers past the achievements of a Socrates or a Pestalozzi is a powerful image. It is easy to see how the promise of a science of education, and the undergirding metaphor of teaching as an applied science, has captivated the attention of educational scholars throughout the twentieth century.

Part I elaborates and critiques the applied science conception of teaching, a conception clearly articulated at least a half century ago (for example, see Freeman 1930). In Chapter 1, historical vignettes are used to illustrate the origin of the scientific study of education and its persistence in the form of teacher effectiveness research, even though minimal progress has been made toward an applied science of education. Chapter 2 examines the research strategies used by teacher effectiveness researchers and explores the specific problems associated with four of these research strategies. Since these problems are so severe, Chapter 3 looks at even more fundamental issues, especially the overly simplified view many teacher effectiveness researchers have about how teaching directly produces learning. In addition, Chapter 3 contains an analysis of two other widely held assumptions: that teaching is a natural phenomenon and that teaching is a technical activity in which each teaching problem theoretically has a one-best-solution.

After reading Part I, I believe the reader will see that there are serious flaws in the applied science conception of teaching that underlies the long-pursued science of education. Attempts to overcome these flaws by proposing a new conception of teaching is the core of Part II. But before elaborating this new conception—teaching as a moral craft—we must first examine in some detail why the dominant conception—teaching as an applied science—is an inadequate representation of teaching.

·1·

SEARCHING FOR
THE ONE
BEST WAY

The contemporary fascination with building a scientific basis for teaching has roots that extend back into the nineteenth century. It is important to touch upon this history, partly to illustrate the durability of the so-called teacher effectiveness approach—despite very limited results—and partly to illustrate the impact of this approach on such varied areas as research on teaching, curriculum development, and teacher education. In addition, historical snapshots of instances of the teacher effectiveness orientation can serve as concrete reference points for my analysis in the next chapter of the futility of building a science of education through the empirical study of teaching.

What I have chosen to do is to write four historical vignettes, three of major educators who pursued the elusive goal of a science of teaching and one of a major reform effort based on the "scientific" findings derived from the study of teaching. In chronological order, the vignettes focus on Joseph Mayer Rice, W. W. Charters, A. S. Barr, and performance-based teacher education. These are not necessarily the most important people or movements in the twentieth-century drive for a science of teaching; no such list, for example, could exclude E. L. Thorndike (Jonçich 1968).

But these four people/movements do give an overview of the drive toward a science of teaching because they represent both varying time periods and differing thrusts toward the scientific study of teaching. Joseph Mayer Rice, for example, was at the height of his professional activity in the 1890s and early 1900s, and he sought above all else to convince the skeptical mainstream of educators that the quality of teaching should be measured by its results, that is, by

15

the amount of student learning. By the post–World War I period, when W. W. Charters was professionally influential, the achievement of results (student learning) was assumed by many educators to be *the* indicator of educational quality. This conceptual battle won, Charters turned his enormous energies to the systematization of curriculum development through applying the technique of activity analysis to a variety of occupations. He was particularly interested in the improvement of teaching so he attempted through the judgment of experts to identify specific teaching methods effective in producing student learning. Charters' concern for specificity was shared by his contemporary, A. S. Barr, as the latter attempted to make supervision as objective as possible. Unlike Charters, however, Barr was not satisfied with validating teaching methods through expert judgment; Barr wanted to establish experimentally that certain teacher behaviors were more likely than others to be linked with student achievement. But by his career's end in 1960, Barr had concluded that effective teaching does not have an entirely behavioral basis. Ironically, the alleged behavioral basis of effective teaching shortly thereafter became the foundation of a major reform effort in teacher education. Performance-based teacher education, the logical culmination of the scientific study of teaching initiated by Rice and his contemporaries, has persisted for fifteen years despite the absence of a substantial and enduring research base linking particular teacher behaviors with increased student learning.

While the study of teacher effectiveness is so well established today that it persists in spite of its inability to generate significant findings, this approach to the examination of teaching was a minority viewpoint in the 1890s, the decade in which Joseph Mayer Rice burst upon the educational scene. A physician turned journalist and educator, Rice advocated a revolutionary way to study the quality of teaching: the empirical examination of the results of this teaching.

JOSEPH MAYER RICE

Joseph Mayer Rice was an extraordinary man. His work is simultaneously seen as beginning the progressive movement in education (Cremin 1962) and as beginning the twentieth-century movement for the empirical study of education (Scates 1947). He wrote muckraking attacks in the *Forum* on political corruption and repressive teaching practices (Rice 1893) while his classic study titled "The Futility of the Spelling Grind" was apparently the first comparative experiment ever conducted in schools and published (Stanley 1966). Though his role as an early progressive is interesting, it was his commitment to using empirical data for determining the best approach to spelling that initiated the twentieth-century search for the one best way of teaching, that is, the most efficient and potent teaching approaches (Kliebard 1982b).

Rice believed that opinion and philosophy had too long been used to address two key questions in education: "What results should be accomplished?" and "How much time should be devoted to a subject?" (Rice 1914, p. 5). As a result, there were no agreed upon answers to these issues, merely a variety of philosophical positions. To move ahead, the issue must be reformulated so that instead of asking "What results should be accomplished?" we ask "What results can be accomplished?" Posed now in a testable form, the issue can be answered by "subjecting children taught under different systems to one and the same test...and comparing the results" (p. 7). The results obtained by the most successful teachers in the country would become the level expected of all teachers, and a careful examination of the successful teachers might help us "discover certain fundamental laws of teaching which may be applied by all" (p. 12).

Rice, however, was no detached scholar. He passionately believed that "progressive" educators, with their commitment to stimulating youngsters and to extending the curriculum beyond the three Rs, were able to broaden the education of children without sacrificing achievement in the three Rs. Rice decided that the best way to force the traditionalists in charge of "mechanical" schools to adopt a progressive curriculum was to prove through a comparative study that progressive approaches to instruction in the three Rs did not produce less learning in these areas than did the drill-like teaching common in mechanical schools. In a more general sense he felt that his study of the results of instruction would help establish a scientific basis for elementary education.

His first attempt at comparative testing began in 1895 and concerned the subject of spelling. Before he had finished in 1897, Rice had developed three versions of his spelling test and had examined almost 33,000 children. The results were hard to interpret because the range in achievement was small and because the differences that did exist were distributed across such factors as type of school, social class, and teaching methods. Some classrooms from "mechanical" schools fared better than "progressive" classrooms, but the reverse was also true; it was not even possible to distinguish the schools attended "by the children of cultured parents from those representing the foreign laboring element" (Rice 1914, p. 77). Similarly, variable results were obtained across such instructional methods as oral spelling, placement of words in sentences as opposed to columns, and so forth. Rice, thus, concluded there was "no direct relation between methods and results" but rather that the results are determined by the ability of the teacher who employs the methods (p. 88). Indeed his failure to find systematic differences in relation to any factor besides student intelligence led him to observe that "nothing can take the place of that personal power which distinguishes the successful from the unsuccessful teacher" (p. 99).

The one recommendation Rice believed his data supported was the need to limit the time devoted to spelling. Regardless of whether ten minutes or forty minutes were spent each day on spelling, the results on the spelling tests were essentially the same. These findings caused Rice to conclude that "waste" could be eliminated by devoting less time to spelling drill and that children should be spared the "old-fashioned spelling grind" (Rice 1914, p. 78).

Since Rice failed to prove his major point—that instruction in the three Rs was as good in "progressive" schools as in "mechanical" ones—one might expect his findings and recommendations to go largely unnoticed. However, even before his research on spelling was published in the *Forum* (Rice 1897), he received an invitation to conduct a "round table" on the three Rs at the February 1897 meeting of the NEA Department of Superintendence. At the round table session, Rice introduced his finding that children who had studied spelling forty minutes a day had not done any better than students who had devoted only ten minutes a day to spelling. According to Ayres:

> The presentation of these data threw that assemblage into consternation, dismay, and indignant protest.... The educators there present, and the pedagogical experts, who reported the deliberations of the meeting in the educational press, characterized as silly, dangerous, and from every viewpoint reprehensible the attempt to test the efficiency of the teacher by finding out what the pupils could do. With striking unanimity they voiced the conviction that any attempt to evaluate the teaching of spelling in terms of the ability of the pupils to spell was essentially impossible and based on a profound misconception of the function of education. (1912, p. 300)

That the value of teaching could be measured by the specific content learned by students was an idea not readily accepted in 1897. Monroe notes that the last decade of the nineteenth century was a time of commitment to particular theories and methods of teaching (1952, p. 62). Despite much talk about a science of education, science was more likely to be viewed as a deductive process than as an empirical study. For example, the Herbartian method was viewed as scientific in the sense that its five formal steps followed from certain "laws of teaching." The validity of the Herbartian method came from its a priori principles, not from the results achieved through its use. Similarly, the teaching-as-an-art proponents did not believe their position needed empirical verification. Also opposed to the measurement of results were the advocates of faculty psychology. They believed that such faculties as memory and reasoning needed to be developed through rigorous and disciplined study, especially in the three Rs. Since the ultimate purpose of spelling from a faculty psychology perspective is not so much to teach children to spell as it is to develop their minds, any attempt to reduce the time allocated to this subject would obviously be disastrous.

Fifteen years later, however, the same association of school superintendents, again gathered in convention, could choose among forty-eight addresses and discussions on the topic of tests and measurements for educational efficiency. Leonard Ayres, a proponent of educational efficiency, proudly observed: "The basal proposition underlying this entire mass of discussion was that the effectiveness of the schools, the methods, and the teachers must be measured in terms of the results secured" (1912, p. 301). Efficiency in education was indeed a bandwagon movement in 1912. That was the year after the appearance of Frederick W. Taylor's influential book, *The Principles of Scientific Management*, a book whose impact on education has been enormous (Callahan 1962). Perhaps to remind educators who had laid the foundation for the efficiency movement in education, Rice dusted off his studies published in the *Forum* between 1896 and 1904, wrote a brief introduction, including a quote by E. L. Thorndike that Rice had conducted "the first of a series of studies of the actual results of school work," and published the compilation in 1913. *Scientific Management in Education* was his last major publication in the field of education.

While Thorndike credited Rice with being a pioneer in the empirical study of education, he also gently criticized Rice for jumping rather hastily to strongly stated conclusions (1910, p. 130). Other critics were more harsh, noting that certain important terms were not carefully defined, words on the various forms of the test were not of equal difficulty, and the experimental situation was poorly controlled. After analyzing these and other objections, W. F. Tidyman concluded that Rice's work "offers little of direct, positive value to pedagogical theory and practice" (1915, p. 400). By coincidence, 1915, the year that Tidyman published his evaluation of Rice's work, was the year that Rice, then age 58, chose to retire. He spent the last nineteen years of his life writing philosophical works and ruminating about his unrecognized role as a leader in educational research. His death in 1934 went unnoticed in the educational press, even ignored by the *Forum* in which he had published so often. Only a brief obituary in the *New York Times* marked his passing.

While Rice's professional contemporaries had little respect for his specific findings, many of them did believe he was an important historical figure. E. L. Thorndike's estimate of his pioneer role in directing education toward the measurement of results has already been noted. Tidyman, while attacking Rice's findings, did acknowledge that his study of spelling performed a "monumental service to education" because it "raised questions and stimulated experimentation and criticism of existing practices" (1915, p. 400). More recent estimates of Rice's contribution concur with, and possibly extend, those of a half century ago. Stanley credits Rice with "nudging us toward causal inference and away from dead-end description" (1966, p. 138), and Borrowman notes it is "customary to designate Joseph M. Rice's study of 'The Futility of the Spelling Grind' as the beginning of the empirical study of the science of education" (1956, p. 166).

That Rice played a significant role in reorienting the science of education away from the deductive approach of the Herbartians and others toward an inductive, empirical approach is a major accomplishment, especially since he was outside the educational establishment. A physician by training, Rice spent most of his educational career as a journalist (1890–1907), with his mid-career years being devoted to the editorship of the *Forum* (1897–1907). During his waning active years (from 1907 until his retirement in 1915), he increasingly lost contact with the movement he helped start: the empirical study of the science of teaching. This alienation occurred in part because the empirical movement became increasingly quantitative and statistical, and Rice lacked a knowledge of statistics. Another important factor was Rice's failure to secure a university appointment at a time when virtually all of the important proponents of the empirical study of education held such appointments. Additional complicating factors were Rice's lack of financial resources and lack of contacts with the new generation of investigators (Noble 1970, p. 304). An articulate and creative outsider had helped turn educational thought on its head, but the scientific movement Rice helped create passed him by.

W. W. CHARTERS

In contrast to Joseph Mayer Rice's role as an outsider, W. W. Charters was a lifelong member of the educational establishment. Starting in 1894 as a teacher of all subjects at a rural school in Rockford,

Ontario, he held a succession of appointments as principal of a model school (1899–1901), principal and supervisor of practice teaching at a normal school (1904–1907), and professor of education at six universities (1907–1942) (Waples 1953). He, along with Franklin Bobbitt, pioneered the development of a new field of specialization: curriculum. While Bobbitt was interested primarily in reforming the curricula of the elementary and secondary school, Charters, perhaps because of his normal school teaching experience, was interested throughout his career in teacher training.

Not until 1918, however, did Charters turn his attention to determining efficient methods of instruction, a concern which was to culminate eleven years later in the publication of the Commonwealth Study (Kirschner 1965, pp. 52–55). Like many of his contemporaries, he was concerned that teaching was not as efficient as it might be. While this problem might be attributed to a lack of trained teachers, an absence of inventiveness, or a low level of teacher effort, Charters felt the real problem was that teachers were taught principles of education with the assumption that they could invent methods of teaching on their own. "This belief," notes Charters, "is erroneous. To apply principles is immeasurably more difficult than to learn them" (1918a, p. 218).

What is needed is a way for an administrator and his research staff to collect, validate, and disseminate to teachers information about "excellent methods of teaching" (Charters 1918b, p. 238). According to Charters this activity involves four processes. First is diagnosis of difficulties. A classroom expert or a select committee of teachers analyzes classroom management and the subjects in the course of study to uncover teaching difficulties. Once teaching difficulties are identified, questionnaires can be given to experienced teachers who will provide "curative measures" currently being used (p. 240). The curative measures then need to be grouped with the appropriate teaching difficulty. Third is the testing and evaluation of the groups of curative measures, some of which are "more efficient than others" (p. 241). Ideally, a group of curative measures would be compared under controlled conditions to discover the "best method to use to get certain results under given conditions" (p. 241). While education had made some progress in this direction, Charters believed we could not yet rely on the laboratory study of educational methods to tell us which method was most efficient. In the meantime we must choose the less scientific path of submitting the groups of curative measures to teachers who are qualified to judge their efficiency. This judgment can be based either on past experience with the teaching difficulty or on classroom trial of the various methods. The last step in the process is the duplication and distribution of the best method for each type of teaching difficulty, making sure that "the number of copies printed should be enough to supply each teacher and to leave enough on hand for future use" (p. 242).

The four steps of diagnosing difficulties—identifying difficulties teachers have, collecting possible curative methods, evaluating the relative efficiency of these methods, and publishing the "best methods"—was Charters' first attempt at constructing a curriculum for teacher education. While his ideas did evolve, partly in response to his critics and partly in response to his own curriculum development experience, this initial effort in 1918 reveals several patterns characteristic of Charters' work. Curriculum construction should focus on specifics, not generalities; a year later he was to recommend that the specifics be stated in behavioral terms (Kirschner 1965, p. 72). Second, curriculum construction should never stray far from the realities with which it is to deal, and practitioners are to be involved in so far as possible. Third, while science through controlled experimentation would one day produce "the right answer to everything," for now we must rely on the judgment of experts to determine the most effective methods (Charters 1951, p. 33). In short, curricular planning should be specific, stay close to job realities, and be validated through expert judgment.

In 1919 Charters moved to the Carnegie Institute of Technology to become Director of the Research Bureau for Retail Training. At Carnegie he applied his ideas to the problem of training secretaries, department store clerks, and others in business occupations. In the jargon of the time, he was engaging in "activity analysis," a technique derived from the ideas of the efficiency expert Frederick W. Taylor and popularized by Franklin Bobbitt. According to Bobbitt, we need only go to the classroom, study the teacher, and "list the two hundred or five hundred or five thousand tasks which the competent teacher accomplishes in his work. The *abilities* to perform these tasks, then, are the fundamental teacher-training objectives—the abilities to do the jobs are the objectives. There are no others" (1924, p. 188). By 1924 Charters, now at the University of Pittsburgh, was ready to apply activity analysis, or functional analysis as he preferred to call it, to teacher training. His ideas were completely developed, though they were remarkably similar to the original conception in 1918.

Curriculum building in teacher training required two forms of analysis: for teacher traits and for teacher functions. He believed that trait analysis was necessary because teaching personality was a necessary ingredient of teaching success. Beginning teachers are more likely to fail, he argued, because of "lack of critical traits of personality than they do through lack of information" (Charters 1924, p. 338). Since each teaching position calls for somewhat different traits, it is necessary to develop a separate cluster of traits for primary teachers, intermediate teachers, English teachers, physical education teachers, and so forth. Once the traits for a position are identified, a teacher-in-training can receive direct or indirect instruction in each appropriate trait. For example, if the trait is accuracy, then the student can be given specific assignments in which accuracy is the major goal (direct instruction) or the student can be required to be accurate in all the work he does (indirect instruction).

The second line of attack was a functional analysis of the teacher's job. Unlike trait analysis, whose importance to training Charters felt compelled to defend, functional analysis needed no defense. Functional analysis was the temper of the time. As a result, Charters focused his discussion on explicating the four steps of functional analysis. First, we must discover "what the teacher has to do in the particular type of position for which he is preparing" (Charters 1924, p. 339). This analysis can be done either by securing a complete list of duties (duty analysis) or by discovering what teachers have difficulty doing (difficulty analysis). Once the duties or difficulties are collected and grouped, the second step is to collect methods of performing the duties or of overcoming the difficulties. These methods can be gathered from the literature of the field and from the experience of expert teachers.

To guarantee that these successful methods are not mere rules of thumb, a third step is necessary: each method must be related to the principle implied by that method. This connection between theory and method is made by posing the question "Why is this method successful?" In order to answer this question for each method we must "collect and invent the principles of psychology, sociology, etc., that are fundamental to teaching" (Charters 1924, p. 341). The last step involves arranging this material, methods and principles, in teachable form with due regard for the psychology of the teachers-in-training. With the exception of this last step, the four steps of functional analysis bear considerable similarity to the previously described four steps for identifying excellent teaching methods (Charters 1918b).

While Charters' trait and functional analysis may seem elaborate, it is only the first part of the curriculum. In addition to the methods and principles conveyed to the prospective teachers by classroom instruction, there is a critical need to give them "what is known in the business world as 'training on the job'" (Charters 1924, p. 341). This training in education is known as student teaching, and its curriculum is determined entirely by difficulty analysis. In other words the critic teacher and other supervisory personnel stress the problems which the student teacher encounters from day to day.

In 1925 Charters secured a three-year grant for $42,000 from the Commonwealth Fund to develop a new teacher training curriculum. Dean Charles H. Judd invited Charters to move to the University of Chicago, where he and Douglas Waples conducted the study. Unfortunately, Charters and Waples found three years to be too short a time to do both the trait analysis and all four steps of the functional analysis. As a result, instead of a finished teacher education curriculum, the bulk (430 of 650 pages) of the Commonwealth Study (Charters and Waples 1929) is composed of a listing of twenty-five traits and 1,001 activities along with rankings of these activities for importance, difficulty of learning, and desirability of inclusion in preservice training. Moreover, much of the first 220 pages discusses the procedures for deriving the traits and activities. Only two chapters, about seventy pages, deal with the fourth step of functional analysis, that is, with questions of how these lists of twenty-five traits and 1,001 activities might be used by a faculty to revise existing courses or to construct new ones. Step four of functional analysis, therefore, is incomplete, and step three, relating specific teaching activities to fundamental principles, is omitted.

If deriving a curriculum from 1,001 activities seems difficult, then one might be comforted to know that there could easily have been more. When given a choice, Charters was inclined to choose the most specific level of activity because he believed "the goals of teacher education needed to be quite specific" (Tyler 1953, p. 44). Charles H. Judd and Henry C. Morrison "ridiculed this view"; they said Charters was uncritically accepting "the specific atomism of Thorndike, and was expressing a mechanical conception of curriculum development that missed the main point of education, namely, the process of generalizing learning" (p. 44). According to Ralph Tyler, then a doctoral student at Chicago and the statistical supervisor for the study, this criticism by Judd and Morrison caused Charters to raise the level of generality of the activities, thus *reducing* the total number of activities to 1,001. Tyler reports these 1,001 activities were derived from some 1,000,000 activities submitted from the field.

The degree of detail into which activities were subdivided can be best illustrated by sampling from the activities Charters and Waples (1929) finally included in the Commonwealth Study:

> 103. Recalling useful information obtained from reading and
>   experience [under subdivision B: "Teaching Pupils to
>   Study" of Division I: Teachers' Activities Involved in
>   Classroom Instruction] (p. 340)

294. Explaining school regulations [under subdivision B:
"Activities Involving Contact with Pupils" of Division II:
Teachers' Activities Involved in School and Class
Management (Exclusive of Extra-curriculum Activities)]
(p. 354)

667. Securing promotion from school board [under subdivision
A: "Relations with School Board" of Division IV: Activities
Involving Relationships with Personnel of the School Staff]
(p. 412)

While there was considerably less specificity in the listing of traits, each teacher was expected to be cooperative, considerate, forceful, magnetic, and to possess some twenty other traits.

The professional community gave the Commonwealth Study a mixed reception. Most reviewers were sympathetic to the effort, though they frequently pointed out problems. Henry Harap (1929), a prominent curriculum theorist, complained that not enough activities were obtained from "progressive groups" so that use of the activities would lead to perpetuating the status quo. M. E. Haggerty lamented the failure to synthesize the findings into courses and wondered whether "this last and necessary step is not more difficult and baffling than the report reveals" (1929, p. 628).

Perhaps the most devastating critique was delivered by Boyd Bode before the book even appeared; this critique was aimed at the concept of activity analysis. Both in correspondence with Charters and in publication, Bode contended that scientific analysis could never determine the desirability of anything, that is, could not determine objectives (1924; 1927a, chap. 5; Kirschner, 1965, pp. 81–84, 121–45). "Having once determined...that men do certain things, e.g., bricklaying, it is possible to go further and determine in detail just how they do these things. But this is not a process of determining objectives; it is a process of determining how certain objectives, which are arrived at in other ways, are concretely realized" (Bode 1927a, pp. 107–08). Charters attempted to respond to Bode's and similar criticisms by pointing out that his approach to functional analysis did enable one to set objectives because he had judges evaluate which were the most important activities for a teacher to master. Evaluations of importance by expert judges are the best we can do, argued Charters, until "methods of measurement more exact than consensus are available" (1929a, p. 33).

Leaving aside the validity of Bode's attack, we can conclude that Haggerty's doubts concerning the practicality of converting the twenty-five traits and 1,001 activities into a curriculum were well founded. I have discovered only one instance in which extensive use was made of the Commonwealth Study. At Ohio State, the institution to which Charters moved in 1928, a large-scale effort was made to reorganize the teacher education curriculum. This process involved setting objectives for the college of education, organizing these objectives into courses, and relating the activities in the Commonwealth Study to the course objectives. The reform effort started in 1928 and apparently was not completed until 1934 (Bennett 1934; Charters 1929b), yet by 1940 a new reform effort was underway at Ohio State (A. J. Klein 1941).

It may well be significant that when Charters decided in 1934 to explore the extent to which activity analysis was being used, he surveyed leaders in commercial education, not teacher education. Although the results of this survey were very positive, Charters concluded the discussion of the survey results by deploring the failure of educationists to use functional analysis. But his faith in the ultimate victory of science was unshaken: "When scientists have constructed measures for educationists as accurate as those of engineers, teaching wastes will be cut and curriculum engineering will become a routine of curriculum construction" (1939, p. 144).

A. S. BARR

In 1929, the same year that the Commonwealth Study appeared, A. S. Barr published what is generally regarded as one of the first classroom studies of teaching behavior (Medley 1972). Barr aspired to place teaching and, therefore, supervision and teacher education on a scientific basis. While Barr's aspiration was not new—indeed Charters totally shared it—his approach to the issue was innovative. Instead of relying on Charters' approach of soliciting judgments from experts, Barr attempted the direct study of teacher behavior in classrooms.

Barr's predilection to study classrooms apparently resulted from his experience in the early 1920s as director of supervision for the Detroit Public Schools. We do know that while in Detroit, Barr became interested in the "subjective character of current supervisory procedures" (1929, p. 1). He believed that a major cause of this subjectivity was the highly inferential judgments typically made by supervisors. Expressions such as "the pace is slow," "the atmosphere is good," and "the class is responsive" are conclusions or inferences based on observation of specific student and teacher activities. Unfortunately, these general expressions have varying meanings for different people. In addition, each supervisor tends to have his own list of favorite inferential categories; Barr obtained 131 different categories when he polled 106 supervisors (p. 4). Supervision, therefore, is subjective in that little consensus exists either on the meaning or on the importance of any particular category.

To Barr the path was obvious (1929, pp. 11–27). Supervision must be far more specific so inferences were unnecessary, and scientific study of teaching was needed to determine which specific teacher behaviors or characteristics were important to effective instruction. Barr proposed to identify these essential behaviors and characteristics by studying two groups of teachers, one outstanding and the other poor. Such a comparison should yield the behaviors and characteristics common to good teaching as well as those typical of poor teaching. The teachers, forty-seven in each group, were selected through a combination of superintendent nomination, state inspector evaluations, and Barr's own classroom observations. Barr's urban bias was revealed by his decision to restrict nominations for good teachers to cities larger than 4,000 while cities less than 4,000 provided all of the poor teachers. Stenographic reports, observation schedules, interviews, and related procedures were used to gather data on about forty teacher behaviors or characteristics, including posture, student assignments, teacher questions, supervised study, length of pupil responses, the average number of hands raised per question, and so forth.

Barr (1929) made literally hundreds of behavioral comparisons. In some cases he made very specific comparisons, such as the twenty-five most frequently used teacher responses to student answers. The most common response, "all right," was used forty-two times by poor teachers and forty-four times by good teachers; the good teachers' second most popular response, "I, etc.," was used forty times while poor teachers used it only ten times. Sometimes he made more general comparisons. Subject matter organization, for instance, was considerably more textbook oriented for poor teachers (thirty-four to fifteen) while good teachers dominated the category of topical organization (eighty-three to seventeen).

For both specific and general comparisons, differences often did exist, though the behavior of good and bad teachers did not fall neatly into separate categories. Because of this overlapping, Barr concluded that he had not identified any factor that might be viewed as critical, that is, a factor so important no teacher could succeed without it. The best that could be said is that certain behaviors might contribute to teaching success. "Good teaching," Barr concludes, "is probably the result of many small matters well done" (1929, p. 77). In a similar vein Barr ends the chapter on time use of good and bad teachers by stating that "teaching performance is highly variable. . . . Good teachers function successfully within a wide range of time expenditures" (p. 92).

Perhaps to salvage something from the study, Barr reverted to a common line of inquiry in the 1920s: the survey of expert opinion. He submitted a checklist of his findings to 200 social studies experts for their reactions, he analyzed 229 articles on methods of teaching social studies to discover the specific teacher and pupil activities therein recommended, and he examined 339 journal articles for current trends in social studies methodology. These data were categorized, and totals were computed. Any category of practice occurring over 100 times was considered by Barr to be "desirable" and, therefore, "particularly significant" for social studies teaching (p. 97). The ten categories that met this criterion are "aspects of teaching which supervisors may, with safety, take into consideration in their supervision of the social studies" (p. 12).

In contrast to this relatively optimistic conclusion concerning supervision, Barr closes the book by noting the inconclusive outcome of his main line of inquiry: the attempt to distinguish between the behaviors of good and bad teachers. He repeats his earlier finding that there was considerable overlap in the behaviors used by good and poor teachers. His research, therefore, did not uncover any teaching behaviors "*critically* significant" to successful instruction (p. 121). Barr concludes that "the performance of teachers is so variable as to make it next to impossible, in the absence of further evidence, to say that an observed practice is wholly good or wholly bad" (p. 123).

Barr's personal assessment of his 1929 study evolved in an interesting way. In the book itself, his tone is mixed. On the one hand he notes that he found no "wholly good or wholly bad" (p. 123) teacher behaviors, yet Barr did believe that he had identified certain behaviors which were "probably *contributing*...factors in teaching success" (p. 121), and that he had "validated" certain aspects of teaching for the serious attention of supervisors (p. 110). In two supervision texts from the 1930s, Barr summarizes segments of his 1929 findings, neither endorsing nor criticizing these findings (Barr 1931, pp. 142–47; Barr, Burton, & Brueckner 1938, pp. 364–69). However, by 1947 Barr merely footnotes his *Characteristic Differences in the Teaching Performance of Good and Poor Teachers of the Social Studies* and emphasizes puzzling questions about the quest for teacher performances "true for all purposes, persons, and conditions" (Barr, Burton, & Brueckner 1947, p. 336). Fourteen years later he emphatically states that his 1929 study proved "good teachers cannot be separated from poor teachers in terms of specific teacher behaviors (there is an appropriateness aspect to teacher behaviors that must be taken into consideration)" (Barr 1961a, p. ii). By the end of his career, therefore, Barr believed that he had asked the wrong question in 1929; good teaching is not an enterprise independent of purpose and circumstance.

A lifetime of inquiry, including over 100 doctoral dissertations, seems like a large price to pay to find out that the original question needs redefinition. Yet Barr did not despair. His ultimate optimism is well illustrated by a paper directed to those who were to follow in his footsteps (Barr 1958). While he grants that past efforts to measure and predict teaching success have "met with only moderate success," he believes that the problems facing future researchers are soluble (p. 695). What is needed is careful attention to a number of procedural issues, including the need to define the essence of teaching, to overcome problems related to the development and use of data gathering devices, to specify appropriate validating criteria, and to resolve a variety of difficulties with research design. To bring home the point that research on effective teaching ought to be pursued, Barr ends the article with the advice he had offered to many students who had run into research difficulties: "I always say that there is nothing but trouble ahead in all research. If it were not so it wouldn't be research" (p. 699).

It is ironic that Barr's reputation as a researcher rests heavily on his *Characteristic Differences in the Teaching Performance of Good and Poor Teachers of the Social Studies*, a book whose guiding question he subsequently rejected. That his 1929 book is the basis for his research reputation, however, is understandable. With one exception (Barr et al. 1935), Barr never again personally conducted research on teacher effectiveness. Instead he wrote several books and many articles on supervision and on educational research; frequently summarized the status of teaching effectiveness research, including seven times for the *Review of Educational Research*; edited two journals for a total of sixty-four years; and was active in the affairs of the University of Wisconsin and several professional associations. The so-called Wisconsin studies in teaching ability conducted between 1940 and 1960 were really the work of his many graduate students (Barr 1961b). After 1929 his most significant contribution to the field of teacher effectiveness probably was the periodic attempts he made to evaluate the field and redefine its direction (Barr 1939, 1948, 1958).

From the perspective of the last twenty years, Barr's 1929 study seems simplistic. Medley and Mitzel (1963), for example, applaud Barr's attempt to study such a wide variety of behavioral data, but they note that "the value of the study was sharply limited by the poorness of the criterion of effectiveness, which was based on supervisory judgment rather than on effects on pupils" (p. 258). Moreover, Medley and Mitzel criticize Barr for not attending to the reliability of his observational data and for not organizing the categories of behavior in dimensions. Other more recent discussions of teacher effectiveness either ignore Barr's work (Dunkin & Biddle 1974; Gage 1978) or refer to it only for its historical significance (Medley 1972; B.O. Smith 1971). Barr's pioneering attempt to identify the behavioral patterns differentiating effective and ineffective teachers is now forgotten.

Barr himself, as already noted, increasingly came to believe that his original commitment to the behavioral basis of good teaching was naive. While he retained to the very end his lifelong interest in studying effective teaching, he gradually accepted the view that effective teaching could not be reduced to specific behaviors or behavioral patterns. In one of Barr's last papers, he made clear his belief that teaching success did not have a solely behavioral basis: "Acts are not good or bad, effective or ineffective, appropriate or inappropriate in general but in relation to the needs, purposes and conditions that give rise to them" (Barr 1958, p. 696). In an unpublished memo, written to identify a research agenda for his retirement years, Barr (1960) admonished himself to strike out in a new direction: "Can behaviors be considered in isolation or out of context? I think not. Can behaviors be divorced from purposes, persons, and situations? I think not. The tabulation of behaviors out of context may be misleading. I believe this is important. Study this carefully."

PERFORMANCE-BASED TEACHER EDUCATION

A fundamental irony in the history of research on effective teaching is that its half century of barren results was rewarded in the 1970s by making this research a key component of the reform movement known as performance-based teacher education (PBTE). PBTE is an attempt to make teacher effectiveness the central element of the professional component of teacher education, an assertion whose validity is evident from an examination of any one of the commonly accepted definitions of PBTE. Gage and Winne, for example, assert that "PBTE is teacher training in which the prospective or inservice teacher acquires, to a prespecified degree, performance tendencies and capabilities that promote student achievement of educational objectives" (1975, pp. 146–47). According to Gage and Winne, *teacher performance* refers to observable behaviors, nonverbal as well as verbal, and *performance tendencies* can be distinguished from *performance capabilities* because the former includes what the teacher normally does in a teaching situation while the latter includes what the teacher does when working his hardest. The observable teacher behaviors, both tendencies and capabilities, are "selected and defined with reference to their effects on student achievement" (p. 147).

A similar definition is provided by Coker, Medley, and Soar (1980), except that they do not try to distinguish between performance tendencies and performance capabilities. They note that the teacher behaviors or competencies which form "the objectives of the teacher education program" must be "operationally defined" so that their mastery can be readily assessed (p. 131). In addition, before a teacher behavior is to be included in a PBTE program, it must be validated, that is, "evidence [must] be produced to show that teachers who possess it are (on the average) more effective in helping pupils learn than teachers who do not" (p. 131).

The definitions of Coker et al. (1980) and of Gage and Winne (1975), as well as similar ones (Elam 1971; Houston 1974), stress that PBTE has two key components: specific teacher behaviors are to be included, and the validation of these behaviors is accomplished by empirically linking them with student learning. Specifying and empirically validating teacher behaviors are concerns that have a hallowed tradition in research on teaching, concerns that Barr, Charters, and Rice all shared and that Barr addressed in his 1929 study.

Unfortunately, we now know little more than Barr did fifty years ago about which teaching behaviors consistently produce student learning. Medley, though sympathetic to PBTE, is quite candid on this topic:

> The proportion of the content of the teacher education
> curriculum that has been empirically shown to relate to teacher
> effectiveness is so small that if all of what is taught to students in
> preservice programs was eliminated except what research has
> validated there would be nothing left but a few units in methods
> of teaching. (1973, pp. 39–40)

After a careful review of relevant research, Heath and Nielson conclude that the conception, design, and methodology of these studies preclude their use as an empirical basis for PBTE (1974). The authors go one step further and summarize other reviews of the connection between teacher characteristics and student learning; they find that the reviewers of this research generally conclude that "an educationally-significant relationship simply has not been demonstrated" (p. 477). Those who doubt this sad state of affairs should examine the paltry result when a well-known researcher tried to create an empirically based teacher education program (Travers 1975).

However, advocates of PBTE often respond to critiques of the teacher effectiveness research base by claiming that some recent breakthroughs promise to overcome many of the technical short-comings of past research efforts. Since many of the critiques are from the mid-1970s, a brief look at some current research may be wise, not so much to summarize its findings as to assess whether promising new approaches are being developed. Recently, Coker, Medley, and Soar reported results which they consider "startling" because these results "call into question some of our strongest convictions about teaching" (1980, p. 149). In their study, competencies identified by a committee of teachers were correlated with two areas of student growth: cognitive achievement and self-concept. Low-inference measures were used in order to obtain reliable assessments of the specified competencies. The competencies included those commonly thought to be marks of good teaching, such as "involves students in organizing and planning," "gives clear, explicit directions," and "when student not on task, teacher makes contact." The majority of the correlations of teacher behaviors and student outcomes were not significant, and some were even negative. Coker and associates conclude that their study provides little support for "our common assumption that beliefs of teachers or experts about the nature of effective teaching are generally correct" (p. 149). The implication, of course, is that we need teacher effectiveness research to identify the really effective teacher behaviors.

Though Coker et al. (1980) attempt to establish the indis-pensability of teacher effectiveness research, their study has a fundamental design flaw. The study assumes that a linear relation-ship exists between any one competency and student outcomes. That is, Coker et al. postulate that the more a particular competency is used, the more effect this competency will have on student outcomes. But as Wilson et al. pointedly observe: "All competent guitarists can play a G chord, but the most competent guitarist is *not* necessarily the one who plays G chords most frequently" (1981, p. 737). On the contrary Wilson et al. argue that "the competent teacher...is one who employs a particular behavioral competence...most likely to work in a given set of circumstances" (p. 736), a claim Barr made throughout the latter part of his career. Coker, Medley, and Soar (1981) defend the use of the linear assumption by arguing that linearity was assumed by those who developed the competency statements, not by the three evaluators. Even if their contention about the source of the linear assumption is correct, Coker et al. go beyond their data when they claim that "most teacher educators, administrators, or other experts would agree...that...these are behaviors that should characterize effective teachers rather than ineffective ones" (1980, p. 149), without regard for the context in which the behaviors occur. A few teacher educators may agree that increasing, without qualification, the use of certain teacher behaviors will lead to more and more student learning, but most are not so naive.

To be sure, Coker, Medley, and Soar are not the only researchers who toil in the vineyards of teacher effectiveness research. Indeed some interesting work is currently being done in several areas in which there is no assumed linear relationship between increased use of a particular teacher behavior and increased student achievement. While there are suggestive findings, especially concerning direct instruction (for example, Gage 1980; Good 1979; Peterson 1979) and cognitive information processing (for example, Calfee 1981; Shulman 1981), these findings are inconclusive and do not provide a substantial knowledge base for PBTE. Not only does PBTE not yet have a well-established knowledge base but in addition the debate surrounding the findings of Coker et al. (1980) indicates that the field of teacher effectiveness research still has issues in need of considerable clarification.

Nevertheless, in contrast to the typical pessimistic assessment of the effect of research on teacher education, PBTE is an example of practice actually anticipating the results of research. While the Commonwealth Study and other major teacher education studies seem to have had little impact on practice (Monroe 1951), the mere promise of future knowledge on effective teaching behaviors has helped propel us into a massive reform movement. Faced in the early 1970s with the reality that there was little research support for this developing movement, some proponents of PBTE suggested that PBTE programs be used as settings to generate such research findings (Dickson 1975; Kay & Rosner 1973). One overanxious state went so far as to mandate the discovery of competencies:

> By the end of 1974, competencies expected of teaching personnel
> in elementary and secondary schools will be clearly identified.
> Evidence will be available showing relationships between
> teacher competencies and pupil learning. Teacher training
> techniques will be available for use in preservice and inservice
> teacher education programs. (Cited in Andrews 1972, p. 156)

Competencies and related training techniques, of course, do not appear upon command, and most of the research done on PBTE programs does not focus on the connection between competencies and student learning. Instead, this research examines student perceptions of PBTE programs (see, for instance, Adams & Patton 1981;

Dickson 1979; Kilgore 1980), or problems of implementing these programs (see, for instance, Dunn 1980; Lorber 1979). It is not surprising, therefore, that Gall (1979) found that less than 10 in his sample of 255 sets of PBTE training materials had been subjected to rigorous summative evaluation and that such evaluation rarely included the impact of the training materials on student learning.

In the early 1980s, PBTE—without a significant research or materials base—remains a healthy movement. Bolstered by legislative mandates, by a societal press for teacher accountability, and by a results-oriented internal logic, PBTE continues to chug along. The major change in the last ten years is that the advocates of PBTE in the 1980s are more subdued in their estimates of the power of PBTE than were the proponents of PBTE in the early 1970s. But whatever steam has left the PBTE movement seems to have been diverted into teacher competency testing, which increasingly focuses on classroom teaching performance (Sandefur 1982; Vlaanderen 1982). Off to the races.

FOR WHAT WERE THEY SEARCHING?

The belief that we can do a better job of teaching is a theme that permeates the four vignettes. With the possible exception of Rice, who maintained a commitment to progressive educational ideas through much of his career (Kliebard 1982b), *better* tends to be seen as synonymous with increased pedagogical effectiveness. Charters, for example, felt that expert judgment within the context of functional analysis could help resolve the question of what teaching methods and activities were most effective in producing student learning. Barr shared Charters' general orientation, except that Barr, at least early in his career, tried through classroom observation to tie teacher behavior directly to student learning. Though Barr gradually became disenchanted with the behavioral focus of the teacher effectiveness perspective, his original interest in empirically linking teacher behavior to student learning ultimately became the conceptual basis of PBTE. Pedagogical effectiveness, of course, is the core of the PBTE rationale because this approach promises to prepare teachers who produce more student learning than do teachers prepared in programs whose curricula are not research based. Even Rice believed that comparative experiments would prove that the three Rs could be taught as effectively in progressive schools as in so-called mechanical schools. In brief, among practitioners as well as researchers, there is a well-established line of inquiry in which pedagogical effectiveness is the major concern.

The vignettes in this chapter illustrate that the identification of the most effective teaching methods or behaviors has proceeded very slowly. This lack of productivity, however, has had little impact on the commitment of researchers to the goal of pedagogical effectiveness, except perhaps to cause recent teacher effectiveness researchers to be more cautious than earlier ones about the time needed to achieve this goal or about the possibility of discovering laws of teaching (Gage 1978; Good 1979).

Instead of reconsidering the goal—that is, the primacy given to effectiveness—each new generation of researchers has tended to see research design flaws and related methodological weaknesses as the primary cause of the prior generation's slow progress toward the goal of pedagogical effectiveness. So it is that Thorndike and Tidyman criticized Rice for employing inadequate definitions, for using spelling items of unequal difficulty, and for failing to adequately control the experimental situation; that Harap and Haggerty complained Charters did not select enough teaching activities from progressive teachers and did not synthesize the 1,001 activities and the twenty-five traits into courses; that Medley and Mitzel criticized Barr's 1929 study for using supervisory judgment as a criterion of success, for not attending to the reliability of his observational data, and for failing to dimensionalize the categories of behavior; that Heath and Nielson attacked the design and overall methodology of studies commonly cited as a research base for PBTE.

Not all criticism of teacher effectiveness research focuses on the technical shortcomings of this research. Bode, for example, argued that Charters could never derive desirable objectives out of a functional analysis of teaching, and Broudy (1972) raised a number of problems with the concept of PBTE itself, not just with its inadequate knowledge base. Yet such nonmethodological criticisms have been in the minority and have had minimal impact on teacher effectiveness researchers and on the numerous practitioners sympathetic to the teacher effectiveness orientation. In the twentieth century, teaching has been widely viewed as a technical activity.

It is interesting to speculate why Dewey, Counts, Bode, and others who were deeply concerned about the purposes or ends of teaching have had so little impact on the effectiveness perspective. Is it because education has been deeply affected by the business ideology of efficiency, not only early in the twentieth century (Callahan 1962) but also later in the century with the popularity in education of such business-related techniques as management by objectives, performance contracting, and cost containment? Or is it because modern social science, widely accepted as the most appropriate means for studying education, is based on the premise that empirical issues must be rigorously separated from any value decisions involved in identifying the ends of teaching? Or is it because educational issues are increasingly resolved by court orders and legislative decisions, procedures whose ties to educational ends are frequently tenuous? Or perhaps some combination of business efficiency, "objective" social science, and legal mandates has in large part neutralized the impact of those educators who have attended to the ends of education? Such speculation, though fascinating and important to investigate, is beyond the scope of this book.

CONCLUSION

Though the teacher effectiveness perspective remains dominant despite the attacks of ends-oriented critics, I will argue that this perspective is not going to succeed on its own terms. That is, the teacher effectiveness research tradition cannot generate a significant and enduring body of findings on the nature of effective teaching. To make this argument I will turn in the next chapter to an analysis of four research strategies commonly used by teacher effectiveness researchers, including the specific problems encountered by practitioners of these strategies. The problems associated with the four teacher effectiveness strategies are so severe that the last part of the chapter addresses the question of whether the teacher effectiveness tradition can be saved, a question whose answer is unclear.

· 2 ·

IS THERE A
ONE BEST
WAY?

After reading the four vignettes one cannot help but be struck by the enduring optimism of those researchers who have pursued the essence of effective teaching. Whether it be Rice seeking to defeat the advocates of spelling drill through comparative testing, Charters anticipating the day when curriculum engineering would eliminate all waste, Barr planning a new research agenda for his retirement years, or PBTE proponents envisioning the elimination of incompetent teachers, we have witnessed a succession of dreams about victories to be won through the scientific study of pedagogical issues. Today the progression of dreams continues as some contemporary researchers contend either that our competing ideologies about the nature of teaching can be validated (or disproved) by scientific knowledge about teaching (Dunkin & Biddle 1974, p. 29) or that we need not so much "wisdom and broad understanding of the issues that confront us" as we need "deeply structured theories in education that drastically reduce, if not eliminate, the need for wisdom" (Suppes 1974, p. 9).

Practitioners—classroom teachers, teacher educators, supervisors, and so forth—have been a willing audience for these dreams. After all, educational practitioners must make hundreds of decisions daily with little sense whether the results we desire will actually occur. Frequently we do not even know which results we ought to pursue. As we ponder which goals to seek, which among our "unsubstantiated" methods to use, and whether our impact is real or imagined, we have been sustained by the faith that researchers on teaching will one day discover fundamental teaching theories on which we can ground our professional work. Particularly appealing to practitioners is the promise of each new generation of teacher effectiveness researchers that a breakthrough is imminent, that we will soon know which teaching behaviors or methods are most tightly linked to student learning.

Recently, however, many educators have lost faith in our ability to find laws or fundamental regularities in the phenomenon of teaching. Unlike earlier critics who came largely from outside the teacher effectiveness tradition and who argued that this tradition was an overly narrow approach to the study of teaching, many of the current doubters are well-known members of the empirical research establishment. McKeachie, for example, notes that he no longer believes in the educational relevance of the principles of learning about which he used to lecture teachers. He now believes that these principles "apply most clearly to the learning of animals in highly controlled artificial situations" and that meaningful educational learning is both "more robust and more complex" than the situations to which the classic principles apply (1974, pp. 10, 11). In a more general sense, Cronbach argues that "enduring systematic theories about man in society are not likely to be achieved" and that the best that educators and other social scientists can hope for is to "pin down the contemporary facts" and "gain insight into contemporary relationships" (1975, p. 126). Such aspirations for research on teaching are far removed from those held by Rice, Charters, Barr, PBTE proponents, Dunkin and Biddle, and Suppes.

The purpose of this chapter is to explore why McKeachie and Cronbach, as well as other prominent researchers on teaching, have reduced their expectations about what teacher effectiveness research can accomplish. Their deep skepticism about the potency of teacher effectiveness research raises such fundamental questions about this research that their ideas merit careful consideration.

The main body of this chapter examines four strategies for approaching the study of teacher effectiveness: discovering the so-called laws of learning, identifying effective teaching behaviors, uncovering aptitude-treatment interactions, and specifying models of effective instruction such as direct instruction. Careful attention is given to the specific difficulties experienced by the practitioners of each research strategy. The results from these four behaviorally oriented research strategies are at best inconclusive. In Chapter 4, I examine teaching effectiveness research strategies which are cognitively based; interest in these strategies stems in part from disenchantment with behavioristic approaches to teacher effectiveness. Not addressed in this book is another tradition concerned with the scientific study of education; the developmentalist orientation, rooted in the child-study movement led by G. Stanley Hall, focuses more on the scientific study of the student than on the scientific examination of teaching (Kliebard 1982b). Though most modern-day developmentalists believe that their research findings have substantial implications for teaching practice, I have chosen to restrict my attention to researchers interested in deriving a science of education through the empirical study of teaching.

The last section of the chapter examines the question of whether the teaching effectiveness model can be saved. Here I suggest that the various research strategies involve trade-offs and that these trade-offs make it difficult to have an instructional theory that is both accurate and applicable to a wide variety of situations. In addition, those instructional models that attempt to transcend the trade-offs between accuracy and generality have tended to be composed of low-level generalizations that lack conceptual sophistication, such as direct instruction, academic learning time, mastery learning.

The chapter concludes with a review of some of the specific difficulties with the four teacher effectiveness research strategies and a suggestion that these research strategies are based on questionable assumptions concerning the dynamics of teaching. The essential characteristics of these questionable assumptions are explored in Chapter 3.

THE LAWS OF LEARNING

From the very beginning, those who engaged in the scientific study of teaching thought it important not only to know which teaching technique or form of school organization is most effective but also to gain insight into why the observed effect actually occurs. Rice cogently made this point in 1902 as he discussed his finding that additional time devoted to a subject does not necessarily lead to added achievement:

> But when we know what results can be accomplished and the
> time in which reasonable results ought to be obtained, we have
> simply secured the needed foundation for the study of pedagogy
> on the inductive principle. It is not enough to know that some
> schools are very much more successful than others; we must also
> try to learn the reasons why some have succeeded and others have
> failed, and in this way endeavor to discover certain fundamental
> laws of teaching which may be applied by all. (1914, p. 12)

Charters, Thorndike, and other pioneers in the quest for an empirical science of education would have been pleased to endorse Rice's search for fundamental laws of teaching.

The search for laws of teaching placed the emerging field of the scientific study of teaching within the dominant research tradition of twentieth-century social science. Above all else, mainline social science research aims at formulating theory, especially the establishment of lawful relationships among variables. Nagel (1969) identifies the search for individual laws or generalizations as one of four possible approaches to theory development. Not only did pioneer teacher effectiveness researchers seek lawful relationships between student learning and such teacher characteristics as personality or classroom behavior, but in addition these researchers quickly adopted the disciplinary perspective of psychology, one of the most vigorous of the turn-of-the-century social sciences. Solidly based in the rapidly developing social sciences, the teacher effectiveness tradition seemed in the early years of the twentieth century to have a bright future.

Among the most prolific and influential of the early twentieth-century scholars in search of teaching-related laws was E.L. Thorndike. Thorndike believed that human as well as animal behavior could be explained in terms of what he called S→R bonds. Learning should be viewed, he believed, as specific responses (R) that were directly connected to specific stimuli (S) in certain situations. While a person enters this world with certain inborn connections between stimuli and responses, these original tendencies are modified from the moment of birth. However, the alteration of connections—that is, learning—is not a random process; several laws of learning govern the ebb and flow of stimulus-response connections. The Law of Exercise or Use suggests that repetition tends to perpetuate S→R bonds; failure to exercise tends to suppress these connections. A second major law, the Law of Effect, proposes that learning experiences accompanied or followed by feelings of satisfaction are strengthened, while the opposite is true of those not so favored. Through these two primary laws and a few subsidiary laws of learning, Thorndike felt he had provided the fundamental ideas that both explain why learning occurs and prescribe how the teacher can maximize learning: "The laws whereby...connections are made are significant for education and all branches of human engineering. Learning is connecting; and teaching is the arrangement of situations which will lead to desirable bonds and make them satisfying" (1923, p. 174).

The history of Thorndike's laws, however, is more a study of erosion than of triumph. W. J. McKeachie (1974) in his article "The Decline and Fall of the Laws of Learning" traces the fate of Thorndike's Law of Effect and his Law of Exercise, particularly as these laws were interpreted by B. F. Skinner. After reviewing recent research that necessitates qualifying the Law of Effect (now called reinforcement) and the Law of Exercise (in a state of decline even in Thorndike's own lifetime), McKeachie asserts that the classical laws of learning fail when carried into the classroom partly because man has greater conceptual ability than other animals and partly because of the "failure to take account of important variables controlled in laboratory situations but interacting with independent variables in natural educational settings" (p. 9). As an example of the interaction of setting variables with reinforcement theory he cites growing evidence that social class affects instructional achievement; middle-class youngsters seem to learn more effectively with informational feedback while lower-class children require more tangible rein-forcers for achievement to increase. McKeachie also cites research evidence that indicates that the well-known principle of immediacy of reinforcement is not true under certain conditions. Skinnerian learning principles, he concludes, "apply most clearly to the learning of animals in highly controlled artificial situations" while meaning-ful educational learning is too complex to yield to uniform instruc-tional prescriptions based on principles of learning (p. 10). "This complexity, so frustrating to those who wish to prescribe education methods, is a reminder of the fascinating uniqueness of the learner" (p. 11).

EFFECTIVE TEACHING BEHAVIORS

While few researchers on teaching now believe that the "laws of learning" are adequate explanations of complex human learning, these researchers continue to seek prescriptions for increasing the effectiveness of the teacher in everyday teaching situations. One research strategy seeking such prescriptions entails the search for effective teaching behaviors. Barr's 1929 study is an early example of an attempt to identify effective teaching behaviors, and Charters' use of activity analysis often involved him in specifying teaching behaviors thought to be effective in producing student learning. However, modern researchers in pursuit of effective teaching be-haviors tend to reject the work of Charters and Barr, largely because both men relied on expert judgment as a criterion of effectiveness rather than appealing to such direct measures of student outcomes as achievement tests.

Contemporary research emphasizing the identification of effec-tive teaching behaviors usually falls in a tradition called process-product research. In this tradition, effectiveness is defined in terms of relationships between observed teacher behaviors (processes) and student outcome measures (products). While Barr (1929) made gross counts of teaching behaviors characteristic of his "good" and "bad" teachers, most modern process-product studies are based on a correlation between a specific teacher behavior and a particular student outcome. However, such a process-product correlation does not permit one to claim that the process is the cause of the associated product. As a result there have been recent attempts to design experimental studies on process-product variables so that teacher behaviors can be identified that are causes of desired student outcomes (Gage & Giaconia 1981).

In 1971 Rosenshine and Furst conducted a comprehensive review of fifty correlational studies available at that time. While they acknowledged that "we know very little about the relationship between classroom behavior and student gains" (p. 37), they did present five teacher behavior variables for which there was "strong support" from the correlational studies and six variables for which there was "less strong" support from the same studies. These eleven variables are: clarity of teacher presentation; variety of instructional procedures and materials; teacher enthusiasm; task-oriented or businesslike teacher behavior; student opportunity to learn what is subsequently tested; teacher recognition and use of student ideas; criticism of students (negatively related to achievement); teacher use of structuring comments; varied types of questions; teacher probing of student responses; and student perception of the difficulty of instruction. However, doubt was cast on these findings when Heath and Nielson (1974) demonstrated that Rosenshine and Furst's (1971) review contained a variety of errors, including mismatches between variables in the correlational studies and the eleven derived variables as well as the tendency to accept studies with weak research designs. It is interesting that Rosenshine's (1979) analysis of the subsequent research on the eleven variables resulted in his continued endorsement of only two: task-oriented or businesslike teacher behavior and student opportunity to learn what is later tested. He also noted that "recent work has shifted from studying specific variables to looking at larger patterns" (p. 31).

Is it reasonable to find nothing more than weak associations between student achievement and such individual teacher behaviors as teacher clarity or teacher use of varied types of questions? Medley, for one, argues that process-product research is based on a "widely believed but almost certainly incorrect idea that there exists a single set of performance competencies—of skills and abilities—which all or nearly all effective teachers have, and which all or nearly all ineffective ones lack" (1973, p. 43). The assumption that some teaching behaviors are effective and others ineffective goes back at least to Barr's 1929 study, yet the research findings of the last fifty years are unimpressive. Perhaps Medley is correct when he counsels that we ought to entertain an alternative assumption, namely, "that teacher effectiveness is not a unidimensional trait but a very complex one" (1973, p. 43).

APTITUDE-TREATMENT INTERACTIONS (ATIs)

One research strategy that introduces a second dimension into teacher effectiveness research is the study of the interactions that occur between treatments (one dimension) and student aptitudes (a second dimension). In ATI research the term *treatment* refers to style of instruction or some other type of teacher behavior while the term *aptitude* is defined as *"any* characteristic of the person that affects his response to the treatment" (Cronbach 1975, p. 116). An ATI study tries to discover the relative effectiveness of treatments when combined with differing student aptitudes. In contrast to process-product research, which seeks to find out which teacher behavior is effective across a range of situations, ATI research attempts to discover what is the best method of instruction for learners having a particular characteristic.

An example of a typical two-group ATI study should clarify what it means to select the best method of instruction for a particular student characteristic. Domino (1971) hypothesized that an instructor who dominates a class would obtain poorer results from students who liked to set tasks for themselves than he would from students who liked to meet requirements set for them. He also hypothesized that an instructor who encourages independent activity by students would obtain the opposite results. Domino found that when the student's style of learning corresponded with the teaching style of the instructor, the outcomes were better for all but one of the dependent variables, that is, the treatment (teaching style) did interact with an aptitude (learning style).

Cronbach, who first called for ATI research more than twenty-five years ago, recently assessed the status of the study of ATIs. Cronbach and Snow conclude that while ATIs do exist, "no Aptitude X Treatment interactions are so well confirmed that they can be used directly as guides to instruction" (1977, p. 492). Other analysts of the ATI literature concur with this negative assessment; Tobias, for example, states that "there are few replicated interactions that permit prescriptions such as: 'Use method X with this kind of student, whereas this other student should be instructed by method Y.'" (1976, p. 63). At present there is consensus that ATI research cannot be used as a basis for instructional decisions (Snow 1977, 1980; Tobias 1981, 1982).

But what promise does ATI study hold for the future? Will this research yield verified aptitude-treatment interactions which can be used as a basis for both instructional decisions and teacher training activities, or is ATI investigation merely an elaborate blind alley? Those who have inquired into why ATI research has not been productive do not give a favorable prognosis. Cronbach (1975) notes that first-order interactions—between an aptitude variable and a treatment variable—are in turn moderated by further variables. Therefore, might not the inclusion of a second aptitude variable or a second treatment variable reveal a more refined truth than the first-order interaction of one treatment variable and one aptitude variable? For instance, in the ATI example concerning the interaction of teaching style and learning style, the inclusion of additional aptitudes—perhaps the student's social class or her educational philosophy—might have yielded a more sophisticated understanding of the type of individual better suited to "dominant" or to "independence-demanding" teaching styles. Similarly, an improved placement decision for a particular individual might result from the inclusion of additional treatments besides one dimension of teaching style. Moreover, other factors such as subject matter or type of learning outcome may interact with teaching and learning styles (Cronbach & Snow 1977, pp. 21–22, 517–18).

Cronbach hypothesizes that interactions beyond first-order ones are the basic reason that he and Snow found many "inconsistent findings coming from roughly similar inquiries" (1975, p. 119). For generalizations about instructional phenomena—that is, instructional theory—to reflect the true complexity of these phenomena, analysis must encompass interactions of the "third order or fifth order or any other order" (p. 119). "Once we attend to interactions," notes Cronbach, "we enter a hall of mirrors that extends to infinity" (p. 119). These interactions can be so complicated that even listing them becomes difficult. Further, these higher-order interactions are both time and place bound so that "enduring systematic theories about man in society are not likely to be achieved" (p. 126).

Instructional theory, therefore, must be composed of highly qualified generalizations. These generalizations cannot necessarily be restricted to a single dimension of teaching style and to a single dimension of student aptitude. For example, such varied student aptitudes as social class, age, and sex may need to be taken into consideration. Neither can instructional theory exclude subject matter, a point to which I will return in the next chapter. Taking these multiple dimensions into account, Snow concludes that "instructional theory may be possible...but it should concern itself only with narrowly circumscribed local instructional situations, relatively small chunks of curriculum for relatively small segments of the educational population" (1977, p. 12). A typical instructional theory, therefore, might apply to "the teaching of arithmetic in grades 1-2-3 in Washington and Lincoln schools in Little City, but perhaps not to the two other elementary schools in that town" (p. 12).

DIRECT INSTRUCTION

Since the kind of multidimensional theory envisioned by Snow entails literally thousands of separate theories, there is a real doubt whether the ATI paradigm is a feasible strategy for deriving instructional theory. On the other hand, though the process-product research strategy involves a limited number of studies focused on a limited number of teaching behaviors, this strategy is not likely to yield behaviors that are effective across all situations, a point argued several years ago by Medley (1973) and more recently by Doyle (1977, 1981), Good (1979), and others. Searching for individual teacher behaviors effective across varied situations seems simplistic, while trying to find a separate theory for each and every situation seems overly complicated.

Recently several attempts have been made to work at a level somewhat more sophisticated than the search for generic teaching behaviors but not so complex as the multidimensional approach advocated by Snow (1977). Prominent within this middle range of teacher effectiveness research is the development of the model of direct instruction. According to Rosenshine (1979), direct instruction refers to instruction with the following dimensions: an emphasis on academic goals, student awareness of these goals, strong teacher direction of classroom activity, a stress on large-group instruction, questions typically at a low cognitive level in order to maximize correct responses, extensive coverage of content, and a task-oriented but not authoritarian classroom environment. This definition includes the two teaching behaviors that Rosenshine (1979) believes may still have general applicability: task-oriented or businesslike teacher behavior and student opportunity to learn what is subsequently tested. However, these two behaviors are now integrated with other behaviors into a pattern or teaching model rather than being individually considered.

Many recent reviewers of research on direct instruction imply that it is the most effective approach to teaching (Peterson 1979,

p. 58). For example, while Good (1979) grants that "direct instruction . . . may be *inconsistent* with the goals of certain subjects (e.g. social studies, art)" (p. 62), he nevertheless claims that "in comparison to other available treatments (or at least those conventionally present in classrooms), direct instruction may have superior general effects for all types of students" (p. 60). In a similar way, Rosenshine (1979) reports that the direct instruction research he has reviewed is limited to the areas of reading and mathematics, but he also leaves the reader with the impression that this model is as good or better than other approaches for achieving a wide variety of cognitive and affective objectives.

Peterson (1979) argues that direct instruction is being oversold. She believes it may be effective for attaining some educational outcomes but not others. Using a variety of studies, Peterson compared the actual size, not the statistical significance, of the effects of "open" versus more direct or traditional approaches; she employed an "effect size" measure that gives an indication of the size of the difference in effect between the experimental and control groups in terms of the standard deviation.

The results of Peterson's analysis of cognitive and affective outcomes are mixed. Direct instruction did fare better than open instruction in the case of mathematics and reading achievement, but the effect sizes were small: only about one-eighth of a standard deviation. In the areas of creativity and seven affective outcomes, the differences all favored open instruction, with the effect size ranging from one-thirtieth to two-fifths of a standard deviation. Thus, while few of the effect sizes were large, the choice of a teaching approach appears to be connected to the type of educational objective being sought. Peterson also presents evidence relating student characteristics to outcomes when using "open" and "direct" approaches; there were some differences, especially in relation to students' locus of control (internal locus-of-control students achieved more in open approaches while students who felt controlled by outside forces achieved better in traditional approaches).

The lesson in Peterson's analysis is that we need to be cautious about embracing direct instruction. For certain purposes and types of students, direct instruction may be better than less direct approaches, but even in these cases the actual differences in effect size seem to be small. To claim that direct instruction is an important advance is to risk overestimating both its effect and its range of applicability. Nevertheless, prominent researchers are now suggesting that direct instruction, or "active teaching" as it is now sometimes called, merits widespread use in the elementary school (Good, Grouws, & Ebmeier 1983; Stevens & Rosenshine 1981) and deserves to be stressed in preservice teacher education (B.O. Smith 1980, chap. 10). Peterson describes such enthusiasm for direct instruction as "unidimensional" (p. 66), a characterization reminiscent of Medley's (1973) criticism of the search for teaching behaviors effective in all situations.

CAN THE TEACHER EFFECTIVENESS MODEL BE SAVED?

One way to visualize teacher effectiveness research is on a continuum whose underlying factor is range of applicability. At one end would be those research efforts whose thrust is generic, for instance, effective teacher behaviors or models of instruction intended to be applicable to a wide variety of situations. Examples of generic approaches include Thorndike's laws of learning, Rosenshine's eleven teaching behaviors, or, to a lesser extent, the model of direct instruction. At the other end of the continuum would be those research efforts that are context sensitive, for instance, aptitude-treatment interactions or models of teaching intended for use in specific situations. An example of a context-sensitive instructional theory would be the ATI research recommended by Snow (1977); in this case several types of context are built into the theory, for instance, curricular area (arithmetic), grade level (grades 1, 2, and 3), type of student (those at Washington and Lincoln schools). Such a context-sensitive theory as Snow's theory for teaching arithmetic in grades 1, 2, and 3 in Washington and Lincoln schools in Little City would be responsive to a large number of variables; however, we would need to develop as many theories as there are combinations of variables. On the other hand, the generic theory approach is a more feasible research strategy because it involves the creation of fewer theories, yet the history of teacher effectiveness research suggests that the potency of generic theories is limited, especially if these theories are conceived of as teaching behaviors or "laws" applicable to *all* situations.

In teacher effectiveness research there seems to be a trade-off between accuracy and generality, as well as accompanying issues of research-design feasibility. If we desire accurate and potent theories, we will want to build into our research designs such diverse contextual variables as social class, type of objective, age of student, type of subject matter, and so forth. But a systematic program of teacher effectiveness research that controls for the relevant contextual variables is of doubtful feasibility because it would be excessively expensive and impossible to complete. On the other hand, a more feasible research strategy is the development of a limited number of generic instructional theories, but these generic theories are likely to be weak. Should we shoot for accurate but forever incomplete context-specific theories or should we settle for widely applicable but impotent generic theories? The choice is not a nice one, but it is there, unless we decide to select a middle position between the context-specific and the generic ends of the continuum.

Selecting such a midpoint might provide the advantage of having each end point, accuracy and generality, without the problem of either developing a huge number of instructional theories or worrying about the potency of these theories. Once we settle at the midpoint, we are back to one of the options previously examined: direct instruction. I have already noted how the advocates of direct instruction tend to see this model as having wide applicability, thus emphasizing its generic potential (for example, Brophy 1979; Good 1979; Rosenshine 1979). But the direct instruction model has emerged out of research on a particular classroom context—mathematics and reading achievement, especially at the primary level—and there is neither a conceptual nor an empirical basis to support the generic potential of direct instruction. Instead of attempting to discover "whether direct instruction is more effective than more indirect or open ways of teaching," we would be better off, according to Peterson, if we asked a less generic question: "For what educational outcomes is direct instruction most effective and for what kinds of students?" (1979, p. 58). The answer to this question seeks a balance between generality and accuracy by focusing on the conditions under which direct instruction is most effective. At the same time, this research approach seems feasible because there is a limited number of instructional models besides direct instruction that are in need of examination.

In order for us to start matching instructional conditions with the direct instruction model, we must have insight into the reasons why direct instruction is, at times, effective. Without knowledge of the factors that contribute to, or inhibit, the success of direct instruction, we are literally unable to construct an informed research agenda for identifying the conditions under which it is appropriate to apply direct instruction. Unfortunately, the answer to the question "Why does direct instruction work?" is, according to Good, "largely unknown" (1979, p. 57).

While Good does speculate about the explanation for direct instruction's effectiveness, his three "general reasons" why teachers experience success with direct instruction are ambiguous and not particularly informative. First, he claims that direct instruction provides "a positive motivational source that encourages teachers to plan their days more fully, take their responsibilities more seriously, and thus fulfill their expectations" (p. 57). Second, Good believes direct instruction helps teachers decide to focus on a few of the "vast array of goals" facing the contemporary teacher, a process he labels "proactive stimulation" (pp. 57–58). Third, and somewhat more specifically, he suggests that "the model provides a plausible, practical system of instruction," by which he means that large-group instruction, a central characteristic of direct instruction, enables the teacher to focus on detailed planning, obtain feedback from a large number of students quickly, and spend less time organizing for instruction than in the case of individualized and small-group instruction. The third reason seems to boil down to a contention that large-group teaching has instructional and managerial advantages over small-group and individualized teaching.

To assert that direct instruction has the capacity to motivate teachers, focus their energies on a few goals, and help them use their time more efficiently is not to offer a comprehensive and conceptually precise analysis of the success of direct instruction. This low-level explanation, however, does reveal the conceptual simplicity of the direct instruction model, a condition that is understandable when one considers the origins of this model. Instead of deriving the direct instruction model from a conceptualization of causative factors in children's achievement (as recommended, for example, by Mitzel 1977), the developers of the direct instruction model generated the model by examining which processes (teacher behaviors) were correlated with certain products (student learning), primarily in the areas of mathematics and reading. The model, therefore, specifies a pattern of teacher behavior (large-group instruction, specific goals, etc.) often associated with student learning in mathematics and reading. Such behavioral correlations, of course, are below the level of conceptualization, thereby severely limiting the explanatory power of the direct instruction model.

Indeed, direct instruction is not so much a model as it is a factual claim that a cluster of teacher behaviors is associated with student learning. Even if experimental studies are conducted to discover whether a particular pattern of teacher behaviors "caused" student learning (Gage & Giaconia 1981), we are still left with a low-level empirical generalization. It is hard to imagine how our understanding of the dynamics of the teaching-learning process will be expanded by the accumulation of such factual correlations. Without a conceptual framework to guide our inquiry, these correlations become nothing more than isolated bits of information, identifying that something the teacher is doing may be having an impact on students but not helping us understand the nature of that impact. Borich (1979), after examining the difficulties involved in deriving implications for teacher training from process-product correlations, recommends that researchers give more attention to the neglected task of developing theoretical formulations that can account for the reported correlations and less attention to the search for immediately useful conclusions consistent with these correlations.

Conceptual poverty is a characteristic not restricted to the direct instruction model. Other approaches to process-product research also tend to look for behavioral regularities, without much attention to a guiding conceptual framework. Examples of raw empiricism within the process-product tradition include Rosenshine's eleven teacher behaviors, the PBTE movement, Barr's 1929 study, Charters' Commonwealth Study, and Rice's study of the relationship between instructional time and spelling achievement.

Recently a major research effort, the Beginning Teacher Evaluation Study (Denham & Lieberman 1980), returned to Rice's question concerning the relationship of instructional time and learning. The major conclusion from the study is that student achievement correlates positively with academic learning time, defining academic learning time as "the amount of time a student spends engaged in academic tasks of appropriate difficulty" (p. iii). This commonsense conclusion is the inverse of Rice's finding that increasing drill time (a task of inappropriate difficulty) does not necessarily lead to added proficiency in spelling. As in the case of direct instruction, the concept of academic learning time occupies a midpoint on a continuum between the generic pole (academic learning time is seen as relevant to a wide variety of teaching tasks) and the context-specific pole (each student is to experience a relatively high level of instructional success).

Considerable research money has been expended to document the mundane finding that students who attend to instruction learn more than those who do not. Moreover, as in the case of direct instruction, the concept of academic learning time provides little insight into the dynamics of the teaching-learning process (Denham & Lieberman 1980, chaps. 3 and 10). Because academic learning time's tie to achievement is both obvious and conceptually barren, the implications of this tie for practice are unclear. About all that researchers can do is suggest that teachers maximize student engagement in tasks of appropriate difficulty (Fisher, Marliave, & Filby 1979; Rosenshine 1979, pp. 34–36, 47; Stallings, 1980), neither a new idea nor a very sophisticated one. Moreover, by focusing attention on the relation between academic learning time and achievement test scores, researchers tend to endorse a simplistic view of subject matter (Confrey 1981).

Some may argue that I am too harsh in my criticism of such conceptually barren models as direct instruction and academic learning time, as well as the entire process-product research tradition. After all, the field of research on teaching, so the counter-argument runs, is in its infancy, and time is needed to "produce a data base that will allow truly prescriptive teacher education to emerge" (Brophy 1976, p. 34). According to this point of view, we must build up a large volume of "reliable and replicated data about classroom processes" before "explanatory concepts" are derived; indeed the purpose of the concepts is to tie together the data (Brophy 1979, p. 738). What is unclear, however, is how the concepts are to emerge from the spider web of alleged empirical relationships. Borich sees this process as involving "insight and judgment," and laments that more process-product researchers do not attend to the derivation of explanatory theories (1979, p. 78), but such theories are not so much created by research as they are tested by research (Popkewitz, Tabachnick, & Zeichner 1979).

So far no powerful concepts have emerged out of the data. All we have are some low-level empirical claims such as direct instruction or academic learning time, which are masquerading as conceptual models. The hope that the midpoint between the poles of accuracy and generality might yield the advantages of each end point has been dashed by the conceptual simplicity and the technical orientation of the existing models. The future of the teacher effectiveness research approach seems in doubt, though I must note that my attention has been restricted to behavioral research approaches rooted in psychological behaviorism. In Chapter 6 I will examine more cognitively oriented approaches to building an applied science of education.

CONCLUSION

The analysis in this chapter illustrates that teacher effectiveness research strategies have serious difficulties. The attempt to derive laws of learning appears to have failed because human beings have more conceptual ability than animals and because humans do not react to stimuli in a uniform way. The generic approach to teacher effectiveness implicit in the search for laws of learning was continued by researchers who focused on effective teaching behaviors. However, researchers have not been able to find individual teaching behaviors that are effective in all situations. Disenchantment with generic approaches led some researchers to study aptitude-treatment interactions, but the need to include higher-order interactions makes the search for ATIs a long and extremely expensive process. Equally discouraging have been the attempts to build instructional models that transcend the difficulties inherent in the study of either individual behaviors or multiple levels of interaction. In addition to being empirically inconclusive, these instructional models— examples of which include direct instruction, academic learning time, and mastery learning—are conceptually simplistic and, therefore, do not provide much insight into the dynamics of the teaching-learning process. Such models may even divert our attention from such important issues as the quality of subject matter to be learned by students.

The long trail of unfulfilled expectations suggests that the research strategies discussed in this chapter may be based on inaccurate assumptions about the teaching-learning process and that there may even be fundamental problems with the concept of teacher effectiveness. In the next chapter I will examine both of these possibilities.

·3·

FLAWS IN THE TEACHER EFFECTIVENESS APPROACH

The analysis in the last chapter of the various teacher effectiveness research strategies cannot help but leave the practitioner discouraged. The eagerness with which E. L. Thorndike (1912) awaited the impending development of a science of education seems quaint in light of our failure to find laws of teaching, effective teaching behaviors, well-confirmed aptitude-treatment interactions, or potent models of instruction. Surely with such a miserable track record, the teacher effectiveness research tradition ought to be on its last legs, particularly since researchers in this tradition have a strong commitment to "listen to the data" (Brophy 1979, p. 734). Even a cursory historical review of the meager research results from this tradition should cause teacher effectiveness researchers to consider abandoning their approach.

But teacher effectiveness researchers have tended not to question the viability of their enterprise. Rather, the inability to derive substantial findings has led most of them to argue for refinements in research technique so that the phenomenon of teaching and its impact on student learning can be analyzed in more sophisticated ways. Berliner (1976), for example, sees three areas where improvement is needed: instrumentation, methodology, and statistics. More recently Berliner (1980) argues that such serious problems exist with traditionally designed large-scale observational studies that clinical studies, using small samples and dense observation, may be a more profitable approach. On the other hand Peterson (1979) does not suggest abandoning large-scale studies, but wants to redirect effort away from asking whether one teaching model is more effective than another to asking for what educational outcomes and types of students a particular instructional model is best adapted. Brophy believes we already have considerable knowledge about the linkages Peterson wants to explore further; he sees the need for research in the 1980s to "analyze and explain why teacher behaviors have the effects that they do on students" (1980, p. 20). In order to achieve understanding of the impact of teacher variables on student learning, Brophy urges researchers to attend more to the impact of teacher behaviors on those student *behaviors* that in turn lead to student learning; such student behaviors include "attention and task engagement, success rates, response sets, and error patterns" (p. 21). Though Berliner, Peterson, and Brophy see the problem in different terms—the need for improved research design and more clinical studies, for matching instructional models with different types of students and educational outcomes, and for attending to intermediate student behaviors as well as to student outcomes—they all assume that knowledge of teacher effectiveness is possible if only certain improvements are made in the research techniques employed by teacher effectiveness scholars.

It is my contention, however, that inadequate research technique is less to blame for the failures of teacher effectiveness research than are certain faulty assumptions commonly made by teacher effectiveness researchers. The purpose of this chapter is to explore the validity of three assumptions central to the conduct of teacher effectiveness research. The first assumption is the belief that there is a direct tie between teaching behavior and student learning and that this link represents a one-way flow of influence: from teacher to student. Two subsidiary assumptions are also briefly introduced: the centrality of the teacher and the passivity of the student. A second assumption is the belief that teaching is a natural phenomenon whose stability makes possible the identification of enduring regularities and whose "givenness" justifies removing from educational inquiry the human purposes which underlie teaching behavior. A third doubtful assumption is the implicit belief that for the technical dimension of any instructional problem there exists a "one-best-solution." Further, in theory this solution is discoverable before the act of teaching through the application of behavioral and social scientific research strategies to teaching phenomena. Each of these three assumptions, as we shall see, is fundamentally flawed.

THE TEACHING-LEARNING LINK:
ITS STRENGTH AND DIRECTIONALITY

Underlying the tradition of teacher effectiveness research is the assumption that teaching directly produces learning. Review carefully two sample quotations by prominent researchers:

Since it may be assumed that whatever effect a teacher has on pupils must result from his behaviors, it is only necessary to identify the crucial behaviors, record them, and score them properly to measure effectiveness in process. (Medley & Mitzel 1963, p. 258)

If teachers do vary in their effectiveness, then it must be because they vary in the behaviors they exhibit in the classroom.... There seems to be no more obvious truth than that a teacher is effective to the extent that he causes pupils to learn what they are supposed to learn. (Dunkin & Biddle 1974, pp. 13–14)

These two quotes, and similar ones, make clear that many teacher effectiveness researchers believe that teacher behavior can cause student learning to occur.

This behavior-to-behavior link—that is, teacher behavior to student learning—is what I call the billiard ball hypothesis. The pool player (the teacher) aims the cue ball (his behavior) so that it will strike the target billiard ball (the student) at exactly the right angle to cause the billiard ball (the student) to go into a pocket (the achievement of what the student is supposed to learn). Not only does the billiard analogy visualize how many teacher effectiveness researchers view teacher behavior as directly leading to student learning, but in addition the analogy suggests two subsidiary assumptions: the centrality of the teacher and the passivity of the student.

Just as the pool player and the cue ball are the focal points of billiards so do teacher effectiveness researchers concentrate on the teacher and his behavior. The centrality of the teacher and his behavior is obvious in the case of research emphasizing the identification of either effective teaching behaviors or potent instructional models, but even in the case of ATI studies the emphasis is more on the teacher's behavior (the treatment) than on the student's characteristics (the aptitudes). Remember that aptitude is defined as *"any* characteristic of the person that affects his response to the treatment"* (Cronbach 1975, p. 116), thereby defining aptitude in terms of treatment and making it clear that the conceptual focus in ATI study is on the nature of treatments and on matching treatments to aptitudes. So strong is the "teacher" emphasis in the teacher effectiveness tradition that when it was popular several years ago to measure classroom interaction through observational systems, the best known system, Flanders Interaction Analysis, had seven categories of teacher behavior but only two categories of student behavior.

The billiard analogy also helps highlight the passive role attributed to the student by teacher effectiveness researchers. Just as pool players naturally think of how they can use the cue ball to move the other billiard balls to desired locations, so too do teacher effectiveness researchers think in terms of how teacher behavior can be manipulated in order to obtain the desired results, that is, student learning. Latent in teacher effectiveness research, especially in the dominant process-product approach, is the belief that teachers initiate behaviors and students respond either by learning or by not learning. Since the processes in the process-product paradigm refer entirely to teacher behavior and other teacher activities, the only role for the student in this paradigm is to be a receptacle.

The accuracy of the billiard ball and related assumptions—the hypothesized direct tie between teaching and learning and the subsidiary assumptions of teacher centrality and student passivity—are critical to the maintenance of the teacher effectiveness tradition, especially to the process-product paradigm which has become virtually synonymous with the concept of teacher effectiveness. For example, if there are significant factors which intervene between teacher behavior (process) and student learning (product), then the process-product paradigm must either be reconceptualized or abandoned; this paradigm currently cannot account for such intervening factors, a reason perhaps for its failure to yield substantial findings. Similarly, the process-product paradigm assumes influence flows from the teacher to the student so that any evidence that students affect teacher behavior tends to reduce the explanatory and predictive power of the process-product paradigm. Therefore, to the extent that the billiard analogy and related assumptions are inaccurate, doubt is cast upon the teacher effectiveness enterprise as it is currently conducted.

Analysis of the validity of the three interconnected assumptions is facilitated by their empirical nature. Their normative content—that is, assertions about what ought to be—is minimal. Rather than being statements about what is good or bad, they are statements about relationships that are thought to be true. To test their validity, I draw primarily on published research, but I also refer to personal experience and to commonsense knowledge relevant to these assumptions. After examining the validity of the assumed direct tie between teacher behavior and student learning—that is, the billiard ball hypothesis—I also evaluate the validity of focusing research on the teacher and his behavior and of construing the student as the passive recipient of teacher behavior. The discussion of these assumptions, while separated for the sake of conceptual clarity, in reality represents an interrelated set of issues. With that qualification in mind, I turn now to the assumed direct tie between teaching and learning.

Earlier I quoted Medley and Mitzel to the effect that "it may be *assumed* [emphasis added] that whatever effect a teacher has on pupils must result from his behaviors" (1963, p. 258). Few people state the so-called billiard ball hypothesis so baldly, but the assumed direct tie between teaching behavior and student learning has guided the thinking of teaching effectiveness researchers for a half century. Initially there were attempts to find a linear relationship between teacher behavior and student learning, but later researchers conceived this relationship as being either curvilinear or situational. In all three conceptualizations, however, teacher effectiveness researchers see the tie between teacher behavior and student learning as being direct.

The linear approach assumes that there is a correlation between how often an effective teacher behavior is exhibited and how much student learning occurs. Following in the footsteps of Barr's 1929 study, a researcher employing the linear approach counts the number of teacher behaviors that fall into categories thought to be related to effective teaching and then determines the actual correlations between the various categories and some criterion of effectiveness (pupil gain scores, supervisor ratings, or similar items) (Gage 1963, pp. 114–15; Medley 1973, p. 44). Clearly, a research approach built on the premise that the more often an effective teacher behavior occurs the higher will be student achievement is a research approach which presumes a direct tie between teacher behavior and student learning.

This style of research—that is, the search for teaching behaviors whose potency is proportional to the frequency of their use—has not been particularly fruitful, leading some researchers to posit a curvilinear relationship between effective teaching behaviors and learning outcomes (see, for example, Soar & Soar 1976). Under the curvilinear hypothesis, increasing an effective teaching behavior indefinitely does not necessarily lead to corresponding gains in student learning. Rather, for many teaching behaviors there is a point at which more of a potent teaching behavior leads to a flattening out of the learning curve and ultimately to a decrease in learning. The key question therefore becomes one of finding the optimal frequency of use for a particular behavior or teaching model, a balance that may need to take into account certain student aptitudes and/or the type of educational objective to be mastered. For example, when an indirect teaching style is being used to foster student creativity, the optimum level of indirectness may vary for low-anxiety as opposed to high-anxiety students (Soar 1968). Since the curvilinearity of teaching behavior is interrelated with student aptitudes and curricular outcomes, we are once again back to

aptitude-treatment interactions, including all the higher-level interactions needed to construct useful instructional theory.

An alternative to both the linear and the curvilinear assumptions
is the belief that *when* a teaching behavior is used is more important
than either *how often* it is used or how well it is *matched* with student
aptitudes or curricular outcomes. Berliner makes a strong case for
the situational appropriateness of effective teaching:

> In our classroom observations we have become acutely aware of
> the difference between a higher-cognitive question asked after a
> train of thought is running out, and the same type of question
> asked after a series of lower-cognitive questions has been used to
> establish a foundation from which to explore higher-order ideas.
> We have seen teachers ask inane questions, or direct questions to
> what we believe was the wrong child. We have seen positive
> verbal reinforcement used with a new child in the class, one who
> was trying to win peer-group acceptance, and whose behavior the
> teacher chose to use as a standard of excellence. We watched
> silently as the class rejected the intruder, while the teacher's
> count in the verbal praise category went up and up and up. (1976,
> p. 372)

These experiences with the appropriateness of teacher behavior,
similar to the concerns raised by A.S. Barr (1939, 1958, 1961a,
1961b), caused Berliner and his colleagues to "reassess our strong
behavioristic stance in the study of teaching. We still regard frequency counts as very useful information.... [But] we must [also]
address the appropriateness issue in order to study the information-
processing and decision-making skills of human teachers" (1976, pp.
372–73).

To pose the appropriateness question—that is, when a behavior
is used—takes us rather quickly beyond strictly behavioral considerations into the realm of thinking and perception. In the example
cited by Berliner, for instance, teacher praise was ineffective because
of the youngster's desire for peer-group acceptance; teacher praise
actually had the opposite effect intended by the teacher because the
praise set the youngster apart from the very group with whom he
wanted to be identified. The teacher's effectiveness, therefore, can be
greatly dependent on his insight into a youngster's motives.

The potency of this example is with its capacity to reveal the
simplemindedness of the billiard ball hypothesis. Instead of the cue
ball (teacher behavior) striking the target billiard ball (the student)
at the precise angle needed to deflect that ball into a pocket (a
learning goal), we now see that the target billiard ball is a cause of its
own movement in a particular direction. Student motives, for

example, can act as an irregularly shaped barrier located just in front of the target billiard ball; this barrier absorbs the impact of the cue ball but does not necessarily transmit the force of the cue ball exactly in the way this force was received. In fact, the billiard ball can completely override the intended effect of the cue ball, if, for instance, the student decides to drop out of school.

The phenomenon I have been describing is labelled *mediation* by some researchers (Anderson 1970; Doyle 1977; Glick 1968). In the most general sense, mediation refers to "certain processes that presumably intervene in the relationships between teacher variables and student learning outcomes" (Doyle 1977, p. 165). Student motives or student rejection of schooling are only two types of intervening processes; other examples of mediating processes include: the demands of the classroom environment (Cusick 1973, pp. 49–56; Doyle 1977); student attention to instructional tasks (Anderson 1970); student familiarity (or unfamilarity) with the intellectual operations employed by the teacher (Berliner 1976, p. 378); the classroom peer group (Schmuck & Schmuck 1983; Zeichner 1978); student perception of the fairness, considerateness, and other personal attributes of the teacher (L. M. Smith & Geoffrey 1968); teacher ability to interpret to the child the significance of objects, events, and ideas in the cultural environment (Feuerstein 1980); and the specialized structure of a subject matter (Bantock 1961; Resnick & Ford 1981; Shulman, 1974). Any or all of these factors can mediate the impact of teacher behavior on student learning.

To better understand how mediating variables can deflect (or enhance) the thrust of teacher behavior I will examine briefly two examples. These two categories of mediating variables, student perceptions of the teacher's personal characteristics and the structure of a subject matter, are selected not so much because they are more powerful than other mediating forces but rather because educational researchers have tended to ignore them.

In my own personal experience one of the clearest examples of mediation involves the varying reactions of my two sons to the same elementary teachers. In the case of a strong-willed and highly organized teacher, one son thrived while the other rebelled and literally refused to work. On the other hand, the "rebellious" son enjoyed the classroom of another teacher who behaviorally was very similar to the first teacher but who was also psychologically supportive; the other son found little difference between the experience with the first and second teachers. A third, low-key teacher who paid careful attention to the governing motivations of students became both sons' favorite teacher. In the end I came to believe that it was not so much what the teachers did that influenced how much effort was expended by my sons as it was how the teachers were perceived by my boys. The son who is at times rebellious, including running away from school on more than one occasion, has a strong internal drive for perfection and worries about whether a teacher might yell at him for making errors; he seems to need understanding and support from his teachers before he will risk an activity in which he might fail. The other boy appears to view teachers as people who set goals, often high goals, which he should strive to meet; he too has concern about failure, but this concern causes him to redouble his efforts when he perceives the teacher is dissatisfied with his work.

I can easily envision both of my sons being placed in the high-anxiety cell on an achievement-anxiety dimension in some ATI study. However, though both boys are anxious to succeed, their reactions to an anxiety-related situation may either be essentially the same or quite different, depending on the cues to which each attaches importance and on their personal constructions of the situation. Only after probing the perceptions they have of themselves, including their self-confidence, does one start to see the reasons why these two boys, outwardly similar in their desire to achieve and in their concern about failure, can react so differently in one behavioral setting and literally the same in another setting. To the boys, the behavioral settings are not necessarily the same, for it is their personal interpretations of the teacher's behavior to which they respond, not to the teacher behavior itself. While a few researchers, especially those coming out of an ethnographic tradition, are sensitive to the mediating impact of student perceptions, most teacher effectiveness researchers either are indifferent to these perceptions or are interested in them only in so far as they can be manipulated by the teacher (see, for example, Gage 1978, pp. 69–74).

While the covert nature of student perceptions may account for why they are largely ignored by researchers on teaching, a far more tangible mediating variable, the structure of a subject matter, is equally overlooked by these researchers. It is common for researchers to restrict their research and theorizing to the student and the teacher. Thus the ATI model examines the interaction between student aptitudes and teacher treatments, and the focus of those seeking "laws" of learning or effective teaching behaviors is obvious. Scholars who believe that the character of a subject matter must be central to any significant inquiry into effective teaching feel it necessary to argue this point (see, for example, Bantock 1961; Gowin 1970; Resnick & Ford 1981, chap. 1; Shulman 1974). That these arguments are indeed needed is well illustrated by the way researchers frequently portray subject matter as inert material, divisible into small blocks that are movable from one location to another (see, for example, Bloom 1971, pp. 32–36; Gage 1974; Gagné & Briggs 1974; Rosenshine 1979).

One need not be an advocate of teaching the structures of disciplines to realize that subject matter is something more than a building that can be torn down brick by brick and moved to a new location. While most subject areas do have some relatively discrete bits of information—for instance, historical facts or scientific terms—each field also has complex intellectual operations and conceptual structures that are not necessarily the sum of these bits of information and, indeed, cannot be well taught unless they are intimately understood by the teacher. Research that is insensitive to the intellectual operations and concepts a youngster must master in order to learn the core of a subject matter is not likely to have fruitful outcomes. It may well be no coincidence that whatever success teacher effectiveness researchers have had is largely limited to basic skill instruction, instruction which does not emphasize specialized intellectual perspectives.

Unfortunately, there is little hope in the near future that a significant number of educational researchers will attend to subject matter characteristics. Psychologists continue to dominate our notion of legitimate inquiry into teaching, and psychologists are predisposed to conduct generic research. "For the psychologist of learning," notes Gage, "a concept is a concept and a principle is a principle in very much a universal form regardless of accidents of subject matter. And concepts and principles are learned, and hence can best be taught, in much the same way, regardless of subject matter. . . . At least that is the assumption guiding the search for general principles of effective teaching or teaching competencies" (1974, pp. 176–77). Shulman (1974, p. 328) attributes the widespread support among researchers for a generic view of teaching effectiveness to the legacy of E.L. Thorndike, a scholar whose predisposition was to believe that general laws of learning would ultimately provide the best methods for teaching each specialized subject matter (see, for example, Thorndike 1922, chap. 4).

The view that a concept is a concept and a principle is a principle is true only if these items are divorced from the network of conceptual interrelationships at the core of most subject matters. There is evidence that educational researchers are starting to gain interest in the psychology of subject matters (Doyle 1977, 1982; Resnick 1981). Resnick and Ford, for example, have tried to illustrate how a psychology of mathematics can be useful to a teacher or to a curriculum developer. They argue that only when we start to address the question "How is it that people think about mathematics?" instead of the question "How do people's thought processes develop?" will we be able to help teachers improve their ability to deal with such real-life tasks as improving the teaching of particular subject areas. For any subject matter, however, there is more than one variant of its structure; mathematics, for example, can be viewed as a computational field, an interrelated set of concepts, rules, and procedures, or a way of problem solving and reasoning. Each conception of mathematics leads to a somewhat different set of research questions and research strategies. As a result, much remains to be done before we have a full-fledged psychology of mathematics, though Resnick and Ford confidently envisage "not only a well-developed psychology of mathematics but also a science of instruction based on that psychology" (1981, p. 6).

Such optimism has been echoed many times before, but it is refreshing to see a few psychologists acknowledge that the characteristics of a subject matter must be central to research on effective teaching. Perhaps if more researchers took seriously the character of subject matters and student perceptions, as well as other mediating factors, we could banish forever the naive idea that teaching is a direct cause of learning.

Recognizing that certain factors—for instance, student perceptions, the nature of subject matters, and student attention to instructional tasks—can mediate the impact of teacher behavior on student learning challenges the validity of the direct-tie assumption underlying the process-product paradigm. Yet the existence of mediating processes can apparently be accounted for by making the process-product paradigm more elaborate. Instead of a two-step paradigm (teacher processes produce student outcomes), Gage expands the paradigm into three steps: teacher processes are seen as influencing student processes (such mediating factors as attending, comprehending, persisting) that in turn influence student outcomes. Gage summarizes this paradigm as follows: *"teaching-process* ⟶ *student-process* ⟶ *student-product"* (1978, p. 71). The revised paradigm, therefore, does include mediating processes, though mediating processes external to the student are omitted, for example, curricular objectives or the characteristics of subject matters.

However, the use of one-way arrows suggests a problem with the revised paradigm. Gage assumes we ought to focus on the flow of influence from teacher to student. While he recognizes that influence on student learning comes "from sources other than the teacher," he argues that teacher effectiveness researchers need to focus their efforts on teachers, not on those other sources of influence: "The teacher," notes Gage, "is the one primarily responsible for determining what goes on in the classroom and for enhancing its educational value" (1978, p. 72). This claim is a clear statement of the assumed centrality of teacher behavior to student learning.

Though Gage may be technically correct that teachers are "primarily" responsible for "what goes on in the classroom," a growing literature suggests that student behavior is the cause, as well as the effect, of teacher behavior (see, for example, Bossert 1981; Fiedler 1975; Haller 1967; S. S. Klein 1971; Noble & Nolan 1976). In a particularly fascinating experiment, Gray, Graubard, and Rosenberg (1974) trained seven so-called incorrigible junior high students in behavior modification techniques so that these students could change the hostile attitude that many teachers held toward them. The techniques taught in a special class for the students included such things as smiling, establishing eye contact with teachers, asking for extra help with lessons, sitting up straight, nodding in agreement while teachers spoke. During the five weeks in which the incorrigible students used these techniques to reinforce teacher behaviors desired by the students, the number of positive comments from teachers increased fourfold, and the number of negative comments declined almost to zero. By the end of the experiment the teacher clients were enthusiastic about the project, though most teachers tended to believe that the changes were in the youngsters rather than in themselves. That teachers saw the changes occurring in youngsters may well suggest that teachers do not share the common researcher assumption that influence flows primarily from teacher to student. In an experiment with a similar design, Sherman and Cormier (1974) illustrated that reducing student disruptive behavior led to systematic changes in teacher behavior.

The recognition that student behavior can "cause" teacher behavior suggests that focusing research exclusively on *teacher* effectiveness is unwise. In reality, it is just as reasonable to call for research on pupil effectiveness to identify ways in which "students are able to help their teachers improve their teaching behavior" (S. S. Klein 1971, p. 403). A student effectiveness perspective suggests that differential teacher behavior toward students by sex, by socio-economic status, or by expected level of performance may not result so much from fixed teacher attitudes as it does from the impact of student behaviors on teacher behaviors (Noble & Nolan 1976). At least some recent research (see, for example Bossert 1981) does seriously consider how differential teacher behavior toward boys and girls can be in response to variations in the behaviors and interests of the pupils and not simply prompted by their gender. As a result, studying which student behaviors encourage sex equity practices by teachers can be a major contribution to teaching effectiveness research.

The tendency of traditional teacher effectiveness researchers to conceptualize the teacher as the center of classroom influence has led some scholars to call for a major reconceptualization of research on teaching (Doyle 1977; Glick 1968; Winne & Marx 1977). While it may be possible, as Gage (1978) argues, to expand the process-product paradigm to include mediating variables, this paradigm is incapable of accounting for influence which flows from the student to the teacher. Inherent in the process-product paradigm is the commitment to a research focus on how teaching behavior can more effectively bring about student learning (Popkewitz, Tabachnick, & Zeichner 1979). Rather than studying the bidirectional nature of influence, teacher effectiveness researchers "must be concerned with the ways in which teachers could be made to play a more 'central role' in defining [student] performance expectations" (Gage 1978, p. 73). Thus we arrive at the third questionable assumption of teacher effectiveness research: the passivity of the student.

The logical correlate of making the teacher's behavior central to research on teaching is to assume that the student's learning is an outcome to be maximized. In experimental language, student learning is a dependent variable, thereby suggesting that the student is an object to be acted upon. The student, therefore, becomes "a passive receptacle whose learning and performance are directly determined by input variables" (Anderson 1970, p. 349).

The student, however, is inevitably an active agent in his learning, an understanding long possessed by classroom teachers but only recently being discovered by many researchers. Witness the relatively recent acknowledgment by researchers of the critical role of student mediating processes in learning content. So grooved have educational researchers been on seeing the teacher as an initiator and the student as a recipient that any discovery of student impact on learning, and on classroom life more generally, is often received with surprise. For example, note Dunkin and Biddle's emphasis on the role of tradition and teachers in the formation of classroom culture and their reluctance to grant students any significant involvement in this process:

> Classrooms are also similar in their cultures—in the activities that take place in them.... Pupils must learn to take turns, since only one person can be heard at a time, and to enter the conversation one must raise one's hand and be called on by the teacher. Departure from the classroom is strictly regulated.... Individual teachers, too, have their foibles and tend to create elements of culture that are perpetuated from class to class. Thus, teacher A demands formality, teacher B can be diverted from the topic by questions about her vacation last summer.... *Even*

[emphasis added] pupils can *sometimes* [emphasis added] create
elements of classroom culture, for we have all experienced one or
more pupils who were classroom clowns or dunces and who set
the tone of interaction for an entire year. (1974, pp. 34–35)

If we have all witnessed the impact of such students on classroom
culture—and who has not—why must Dunkin and Biddle use the
words *even* and *sometimes*? Why is there a note of disbelief when
they find students exerting impact on the nature and direction of
classroom culture?

Such disbelief and skepticism come, I believe, from the implicit
belief of many researchers that teachers act upon and change
students, without there being a high degree of reciprocity. Even after
Dunkin and Biddle cite the clown and dunce example and further
state that "teachers not only induce but also react to pupil behavior"
(p. 44), these two researchers proceed to conclude that "it is possible
to assume that observable changes in pupil behavior are a function of
teaching and hence evidence of the success or failure of the teacher's
efforts" (p. 45). Despite reservations, Dunkin and Biddle operate with
the working assumption that students are passive recipients of
teacher influence.

Interestingly, Dunkin and Biddle claim that "most teachers"
believe that changes in pupil behavior are a function of teacher
activity (p. 45). On the contrary, I find most teachers believe students
have considerable responsibility for how much learning occurs, both
because individual students decide whether to attend to instruction
and because successful instruction depends on a variety of factors
rooted in the social system of the classroom, for example, the desire
of individuals for peer-group acceptance, the dynamics of a particular group, and so forth. If I am correct that teachers assume learning
is the responsibility of students as well as teachers, then their
assumption is more in line with recent research evidence than is the
"teaching is the fundamental cause of learning" assumption adhered
to by many teacher effectiveness researchers.

When we add together the evidence on the billiard ball assumption, including the evidence relevant to the centrality of the teacher
and the passivity of the student, I believe it is clear that this cluster of
assumptions is seriously flawed. Teacher influence on students is
mediated by a variety of factors, and this influence is bidirectional
(Glick 1968). As a result, the process-product paradigm that underlies
teacher effectiveness research, and the concept of teacher effectiveness itself, are brought into question.

But the problems with the process-product paradigm and with
the concept of teacher effectiveness extend beyond the nature and

flow of teacher-student influence. An equally fundamental problem concerns two other assumptions researchers typically make about teaching: that teaching is a natural phenomenon and that teaching is a technical activity in which each teaching problem has a one-best-solution. In the next two sections, the nature, importance, and validity of these two assumptions are examined.

TEACHING PHENOMENA: NATURAL OR SOCIALLY CONSTRUCTED?

No assumption is more important to educational researchers interested in the establishment of stable regularities than the belief that teaching phenomena are natural. This assumption is so fundamental that it is often stated as a primary truth. Dunkin and Biddle, for example, declare that "the activities of teaching are reasonable, natural, rational events" without feeling the need for extensive defense of this assertion (1974, p. 12). Kerlinger is equally certain that educational researchers must use social scientific methods for "the controlled pursuit of relations among natural phenomena" (1968, p. 480). Most educational researchers do not even bother to make explicit their assumption that teaching phenomena are natural.

Viewing educational phenomena as natural is a critical assumption because the study of natural phenomena may lead to formulating relations among variables—ideally lawlike relationships—that extend over time and space. The key to this potential generalizability is the stability of natural phenomena. Natural phenomena, basically independent of man, are fundamentally the same from one generation of scholars to another. Whatever change occurs in our knowledge of natural phenomena is largely traceable to researchers—their new questions, new techniques, new instruments—rather than to the evolution of these phenomena. In this way the stability of natural phenomena makes possible the development of cumulative, cross-cultural knowledge (Weisskopf 1979). The knowledge base developed in the natural sciences is an outstanding example of what can happen when relatively stable, natural phenomena are intensively studied.

The stability of educational phenomena, however, is open to question. As early as the 1930s Monroe asked: "Is the educational situation sufficiently stable to make inferences concerning what may be expected that are dependable enough to be worthy of designation as contributions to a science of education?" (1937, p. 46). While he foresaw relatively little change in the pupil population, Monroe did predict that other educational variables would change rather substantially over the years. He suggested that research findings be divided into two classes: "Those whose applicability appears to be relatively permanent and those whose applicability is limited by the changing educational situation" (p. 47). From today's perspective, we are hard pressed to cite research findings that have proved to be relatively permanent. Even such a venerable generalization as the tendency for teachers to talk two-thirds of the time, a regularity that has been documented over decades, does not hold true for certain forms of individualized instruction or for open education. Open education itself, of course, is rapidly disappearing along with alternative schools, new math, open-space schools, minicourses, and so forth, to be replaced by minimal competency tests, gifted programs, mainstreaming, mastery learning, and so forth.

Instability, moreover, occurs not only in curricular and administrative organization but also in the specific content of the instructional program. We may emphasize basic skills and play down the arts, or we may stress some new conception of moral education. We also expect the schools to serve the purposes of social reform when we go to the courts to press for districtwide or interdistrict busing of students. Whether it is because of the impact of social purpose on schools, the honest desire of school leaders to respond to educational "needs," or outright faddism, the instructional situation is anything but stable (Glass 1972, p. 15).

The instability of educational phenomena is directly traceable to the man-made nature of these phenomena. Education, to use the words of Ebel is "a human invention, a construction, a cultural institution designed and built by men" (1967, p. 83). Formal education is a social institution, a means by which a society attempts to perpetuate the knowledge, skills, and attitudes deemed important. Educational phenomena, therefore, will tend to change as a society redefines its central purposes and as educational leaders initiate new programs and new teaching approaches in order to achieve these redefined purposes. In brief, the instability of educational phenomena is a reflection of the instability of the human purposes underlying these phenomena.

The pursuit of laws or generalizations about teaching without regard to underlying human purposes has caused researchers to ask truncated and therefore trivial questions. For example, the moral dimension of teaching in which one person temporarily controls the functioning of another (Hawkins 1973) becomes reduced to the study of teacher effectiveness, that is, how more content can be taught faster. Similarly, rather than focus on the central curriculum issue— the need to make choices among the vast array of content and to justify these choices (Kliebard 1977)—researchers on teaching strive to discover instructional theory, which turns out to be nothing more than an attempt to maximize learning without regard to the quality of that learning. However, the maximization perspective, so potent when phenomena are indeed natural, makes little sense if educational phenomena are not so much an instance of fundamental natural regularities as they are the creative attempt of man to determine what succeeding generations are to know and to believe.

The recognition that educational phenomena are man-made rather than natural does not reduce our need to study education (Ebel 1982). What this acknowledgment does do is to help us realize that we should not be trying to comprehend one of the "givens in our universe" so much as we should be trying to redesign and reconstruct education to "serve our human purposes better" (Ebel 1967, p. 83). Since formal education is a social institution, it can be understood only if its observable features—those focused on by conventional educational research—are directly related to the purposes education is designed to serve. This link between activity and purpose is critical, and it is exactly this link that traditional research on teaching ignores, or perhaps more accurately, that traditional research on teaching attempts to break so that educational phenomena can be studied independent of underlying human purposes.

That educational phenomena can be construed as socially constructed is consistent with arguments made by a variety of contemporary social scientists (for example, Berger & Luckmann 1966; Blumer 1962; Simon 1981). But education differs from other categories of socially constructed phenomena in that it is a second-order social construction, that is, our educational system is constructed in order to orient the young to such other social constructions as human institutions and the humanities, as well as to the natural world. Even the so-called natural world is increasingly a social construction as mankind either deliberately manipulates natural processes (genetic engineering) or unavoidably intervenes in nature (as when attempts to recreate a wilderness environment in Yellowstone Park result in driving the grizzly bears out of the park; Chase 1983). As a second-order social construction, teaching is doubly contingent on human motives and purposes.

TEACHING: IS THERE REALLY A ONE-BEST-WAY?

In the previous section I have implicitly argued that it is not wise to view teaching as a purely technical activity. That is, teaching has a normative as well as a technical dimension, and inquiry into teaching must attend simultaneously to both of these dimensions. I shall now argue that inquiry into the technical aspect of teaching should not be restricted to the conventional social and behavioral science disciplines because such discipline-based inquiry is grounded on the false assumption that there is a one-best-way to resolve any particular teaching problem. Stated differently, the concept of teaching effectiveness employed by behavioral science researchers is a meaningful concept only if some teaching behaviors or models are consistently more potent than others, either in general or, more likely, in specific situations.

The search for such a hypothesized one-best-way of teaching is the driving force behind teacher effectiveness research. As an introduction to evaluating the reasonableness of this assumption, some exploration of the meaning of the one-best-way assumption is useful. This exploration is done in terms of the aptitude-treatment interaction perspective, though the overall argument applies by analogy to such other approaches as direct instruction, effective teaching behaviors, and so forth.

Applied to the aptitude-treatment interaction orientation, the one-best-way assumption posits that for any particular student in a specified learning situation there is a teaching approach that will maximize his learning. Typically the one-best-way assumption is implicit, but occasionally an educational researcher spells out his reasons for making this assumption. Peck, for example, begins an article on needed research and development in teaching by asserting the obvious: that "different students react differently to different kinds of teachings" (1976, p. 18). With this fundamental reality in mind, he notes that a number of educators have developed individualized systems of instruction, for example, Individually Guided Education, Individually Prescribed Instruction, Personalized Teacher Education, and so forth. So far, so good. However, at this point he jumps directly from asserting the truism that individuals tend to respond differentially to instruction to concluding that a best technique exists for each learning problem, though he does concede that "there is very little research-based evidence, so far, about what works best for different kinds of students" (p. 18).

So pervasive is the belief in the existence of best answers to instructional problems that thoughtful researchers often view this belief as self-evidently true: "It is *inconceivable* [emphasis added] to us," note Cronbach and Snow, "that humans, differing in as many ways as they do, do not differ with respect to the educational treatment that fits each one best" (1969, p. 193). This passionate language should neither obscure the weak empirical basis for the one-best-way assumption nor obscure the logical gaps in the reasoning of those who assert that looking for the one-best-way is a reasonable search.

The lack of empirical support—that is, the failure to date of teacher effectiveness research, including ATI—has already been explored, but I want to go further and challenge the logic of those who believe that the search for the one-best-way is a reasonable endeavor. From the perfectly sound premise that students tend to react differently to different kinds of teaching, they move to the conclusion that for each student there is a one-best-teaching-solution to each learning problem. Is it not possible, as Jackson has suggested, to reach a different conclusion:

> Suppose that we begin by imagining two ways of teaching . . .
> that work equally well in the case of a particular student. . . .
> Must there always be a discriminable difference in the quality of
> outcome between alternative methods? . . . Surely skinning
> cats is not the only activity for which there is more than one
> equally effective strategy. And once we have conceded that there
> may be two methods of equivalent "goodness" why not three, or
> ten, or seventy-eight, or four thousand and six? That isn't so hard
> to imagine, is it? (1970, p. 19)

No, it is not difficult to imagine multiple solutions that are of equivalent effectiveness in solving a particular teaching problem. The reason we in education are so fixated on searching for the one-best-solution is partly linguistic, for example, Cronbach and Snow use the word *fit*, which implies degrees of precision. In addition, many researchers are inclined to believe that teaching is directly tied to learning, an overly simplified notion of causality that implies there is a one-best-way of teaching for each type of learning. And we have considerable faith in the power of science to discover fundamental regularities (Popper 1979), regularities which in our field surely demarcate better, if not best, solutions to teaching problems. In short, many educators are oriented toward searching for the one-best-way not because there is any compelling reason for this search but because of the influence of language and the impact of certain belief systems on our view of the teaching-learning process.

Some may argue, however, that even though "there is not [now] *necessarily* a best way of proceeding in the individual case surely the *possibility* of there being such a condition is sufficient to justify our continued search for it" (Jackson 1970, p. 21). This argument does seem plausible, particularly since many scientific discoveries would never have occurred if scientists had failed to pursue possible but not compelling alternatives. However, there is reason to believe that even if a one-best-way were knowable, it would be knowable only after the fact, that is, after one had completed the act of teaching. The critical variables of the teaching-learning process—teaching objectives, subject matter, student aptitudes, and so forth—often are not capable of being specified prior to the teaching act. The teacher may change objectives from month to month or from week to week; unforeseen events—a hot day or one student's open cruelty toward another— may necessitate revising plans; the demands people place on the schools can change from year to year, from community to community; a student's self-confidence may grow or his regard for his teacher may drop; a district may adopt a new math curriculum or may eliminate the arts in favor of more emphasis on the "basics." All of these variables ebb and flow so that the teacher cannot necessarily construct his battle plan in 1984 for 1985, in September for May, on Monday for Friday, or during second hour for third hour. Neither, of course, can we necessarily predict the specific character of mediating processes nor can we anticipate the ways in which these processes will affect the impact of teaching behavior.

Even ATI research, which purportedly is more sensitive to specific situations than are other forms of teacher effectiveness research, is a static approach based on the assumed permanence of objectives, student aptitudes, and teaching conditions. It is through this assumption of permanence that the researcher is able to conduct conventional social science research in education; the researcher needs durable phenomena in order to construct a scientific regularity—that is, before-the-teaching-act knowledge—that becomes needs durable phenomena in order to construct a scientific regularity—that is, before-the-teaching-act knowledge—that becomes

Acknowledging that teaching phenomena do vary over time has at long last forced some educational researchers to postulate that the effective teachers are those teachers whose behavior is "inherently unstable." "Such teachers," notes Berliner, "are expected to change methods, techniques, and styles to suit particular students, curriculum areas, time of day or year, etc." (1976, p. 374). Hunt believes that "teachers' adaptation to students is the heart of the teaching-learning process" and that successful adaptation involves "reading" the student's misunderstanding and "flexing" or adjusting teacher communication in accordance with what was read (1976, p. 268). In a sense Berliner and Hunt, as well as some other contemporary educational researchers (see, for example, Brophy 1980, pp. 13, 23–24) have rediscovered the ancient maxim that the effective teacher is flexible, that is, adapts his behavior to the teaching situation.

The plasticity inherent in this flexibility, plus the changeableness of the teaching situation and the unpredictability of mediating processes, suggest that the before-the-act teaching knowledge desired by teacher effectiveness researchers is not likely to be developed. The dynamic nature of teacher adaptability, mediating processes, and the teaching situation itself means that we can recognize teaching effectiveness, if at all, only after the fact. The attempt to find before-the-act teaching knowledge on the best procedures for enhancing learning is also of dubious value because there are neither compelling logical reasons nor empirical evidence for believing that a one-best-solution exists for each teaching problem or even for believing that some solutions are consistently better than others. (For a counterargument on the last point, see Gage 1980.)

CONCLUSION

Once teaching phenomena are recognized as being man-made and teaching problems are viewed as having multiple potential solutions whose effectiveness is largely unknown prior to the act of teaching, then the potential of teaching effectiveness knowledge is dramatically reduced. The man-made character of educational phenomena means that any regularities identified through the study of the teaching-learning process are limited in generality and likely to shift over time. Even the search for a regularity of limited generality is likely to be unsuccessful because the typical teaching problem may well have multiple appropriate solutions and because teacher-student influence is both bidirectional and mediated by a variety of factors. Lastly, teaching effectiveness knowledge—should we ever find any—will be inherently trivial, since it is generated by applying a purely technical perspective to phenomena intimately connected to underlying human purposes.

The effective teacher, therefore, is not necessarily the one who has been programmed with research-based prescriptions for various teaching problems. Instead the effective teacher may be the one who is able to conceive of his teaching in purposeful terms, analyze a particular teaching problem, choose a teaching approach that seems appropriate to the problem, attempt the approach, judge the results in relation to the original purpose, and reconsider either the teaching approach or the original purpose. This and similar conceptions of teacher effectiveness are strongly normative and situational, a feature well captured by Dewey's analysis of the essence of practical activity: "Judgment and belief regarding actions to be performed can never attain more than a precarious probability.... Practical activity deals with individualized and unique situations which are never exactly duplicable and about which, accordingly, no complete assurance is possible" (1929a, p. 6).

Yet it is exactly a striving for certainty that propels those who want to develop general laws of learning and other types of knowledge concerning teaching effectiveness. Researchers on teaching have fixated on certainty, even though teaching-learning phenomena are not capable of being predicted with any degree of assurance. Fortunately, even if teacher effectiveness researchers do not discover significant and enduring regularities, their work may be of use to practitioners. Instead of being a source of rules for guiding practice, research results might serve either as evidence for testing the beliefs of practitioners or as schemata for helping practitioners see classroom events in new ways (Fenstermacher 1982). A few teacher effectiveness researchers seem interested in having teachers use research findings for evidential purposes (for example, Berliner 1982; Good & Power 1976), but few teacher effectiveness researchers envision their work as a source of schemata—one reason, perhaps, why teacher effectiveness inquiry is so conceptually barren.

In focusing on why certainty—or even substantial generalizations—cannot be achieved through the teacher effectiveness model, I have largely ignored an important weakness of this approach. Defining teaching success in terms of raising achievement test scores leads researchers to equate learning with the relatively simplistic content commonly included in these tests. While I believe this overly narrow conception of subject matter to be a disastrous error, I wanted to emphasize the empirical shortcomings of the teacher effectiveness model to illustrate that this model *fails in its own terms*. Research on effective teaching does not enlighten us about the technical secrets of teaching, let alone about which subject matter is worthy of being taught.

·PART II·

TEACHING AS A MORAL CRAFT

The problems with the applied science metaphor are legion, not the least of which is a century-long failure to identify empirical regularities that underlie successful teaching. Early attempts by Rice, Charters, Barr, Thorndike, and others have been superseded by equally unsuccessful contemporary efforts to discover the secrets of effective teaching: performance-based teacher education, aptitude-treatment interactions, effective teaching behaviors, and such models as direct instruction.

The failure of these varied approaches, I have argued, is traceable not so much to shortcomings in research technique as it is to three questionable assumptions commonly made by those who conduct teacher effectiveness research. The complexity of the interrelationships among variables, the need to attend to purpose as well as to teaching technique, and the instability of teaching situations all suggest that researchers are not likely to be able to establish "teaching as an applied science" in which teachers are provided with "specific, data based information that will enable them to diagnose particular situations accurately and follow through with 'treatment' established as effective or at least probably effective in such situations" (Brophy & Evertson 1976, pp. vii, ix). Faced with a real instructional problem, the teacher is likely to find such data-based information simplistic, incapable of addressing the normative dimension of teaching, and/or out-of-date.

The natural question, therefore, is whether the applied science metaphor can be replaced with a metaphoric representation that is more consistent with the socially constructed and interactive nature of teaching, an orientation toward teaching that does not presume there is a one-best-solution to each teaching problem. If we can identify a more apt metaphor for teaching than the inadequate applied science view, then we may be able to rethink a variety of areas of educational practice, ranging from teacher education to teacher evaluation, and even to redirect research on teaching in more productive directions.

The purpose of Part II is to identify and discuss an alternative metaphor: teaching as a moral craft. In Chapter 4 I argue that teaching is a moral endeavor in at least two senses. On the one hand the unequal power relationship between teacher and student makes this an inherently moral relationship, while on the other hand teaching presupposes that something worthwhile is to be taught. In contrast to the desirable ends at issue in the moral dimension of teaching, Chapter 5 examines the craft basis of teaching, partly through an extended comparison between fishing and teaching and partly through a detailed discussion of Kohl's (1976) interpretation of the craft of teaching. I attempt to illustrate that craft as applied to teaching need not be restricted to trial-and-error learning and ought not be viewed solely in empirical terms. Chapter 6 brings together the analysis of craft and moral and leads to the formulation of the moral craft metaphor. I also discuss how well teaching is represented by other commonly used metaphors, namely, teaching as an art, teaching as an applied science, and teaching as a craft.

·4·

THE MORAL
BASIS OF
TEACHING

It is commonplace today to point out that the public is demanding that schools become increasingly involved in moral education. Such a demand apparently exists for a variety of reasons, including popular support revealed through the Gallup polls for a school role in moral education; our society's need to come to terms with racism and sexism; the necessity for citizens to adopt intelligent positions on such moral issues as abortion, drug use, and the rights of handicapped people. All of these considerations, and others, suggest to many educators that "the public seems to be asking schools to prepare future generations to provide more adequate answers" to these "moral questions" (Hersh, Miller, & Fielding 1980, p. vii). Educators have already prepared a variety of elementary and secondary curricula to help youngsters address moral questions. These curricula are based on such varied approaches as inculcation of fundamental societal values; promotion of higher levels of moral reasoning; clarification of values; analysis of public issues; and community-action projects (Superka et al. 1976).

Viewed from the perspective of moral education, teaching is a moral activity when a particular class of content is addressed. For example, when I taught high school social studies classes using the public issues materials originally developed by the Harvard Social Studies Project (Oliver & Shaver 1966), I was acting in a moral way because I was helping adolescents learn how to analyze and develop positions on public issues. All of these public issues had a moral component that I had to address by teaching my students to make value judgments by reacting to the adequacy of their reasoning for their preferences, or by revealing my own value commitments. Even if I had been using a values-clarification approach in which the teacher is supposed to pass no judgment on the value preferences of the students (Raths, Harmin, & Simon 1966), inevitably I would have been teaching a preferred moral stance to my students: the stance of moral relativism. There is no doubt, therefore, that to engage in the moral instruction of the young is to make teaching into a moral activity.

However, when I contend that teaching is a moral activity, I am referring to more than the instruction of the young in the nature of right conduct. The argument made in this chapter for the moral basis of teaching goes beyond those teaching activities involved in moral instruction. In brief, I will argue not only that all teaching is moral but in addition that it is moral in two distinct ways. First, teaching involves a moral relationship between teacher and student that is grounded in the dominant power position of the teacher. Second, teaching is moral in the sense that a curriculum plan selects certain objectives or pieces of content instead of others; this selective process either explicitly or implicitly reflects a conception of desirable ends.

Before initiating the discussion of the two ways in which teaching can be considered to be moral, I want to be as specific as I can about what I mean by *moral*.

A WORKING DEFINITION OF MORAL

It should be clear from the introduction to this chapter that I do not want to restrict *moral* to questions of right and wrong actions or behaviors. In addition to right conduct—a conception of moral that frequently involves measuring behavior against a personal or social code of ethics—I am using *moral* to refer to more general questions of valuation: What really matters during one's life? During one's career? During the next day or two? To what end does one pursue a particular activity? However, not all instances of valuation are moral. Take, for instance, questions of taste such as preferring chocolate ice cream to vanilla, or preferring Camus' writing style to Sartre's. To decide that Camus' literature is stylistically superior to Sartre's has no more moral import than a decision to have a vanilla instead of a chocolate ice cream cone.

The key that distinguishes valuational concerns that are moral from those that are not is the implicit or explicit introduction of desirable ends. Such desirable ends may involve explicit criteria by which behavior is judged to be right or wrong, or may be implicit in the choice of one position or course of action instead of another. Each of us comes to terms with countless moral situations in a lifetime, though we frequently choose to leave unexplored the desirable ends latent in these situations. Since the moral issues I have mentioned so far are personal, the case for requiring that desirable ends be made explicit is not necessarily compelling. Whether a person chooses to live an examined life—as Socrates advocated—is an individual decision.

But when we move to moral situations involved in teaching, the case for carefully analyzing and reflecting on desirable ends is considerably more persuasive. Teaching, after all, is a social act involving at least two people and usually carrying the sanction of a public institution. While much is in dispute concerning what it means to act in a moral way, there is widespread agreement that we need to take great care when our actions affect other people.

It can be argued that all situations involving humans are at least potentially moral (P. G. Smith 1976). But moral valuations are not the only possible valuations in a social setting. For instance, besides a moral point of view focusing on desirable ends, a person in a social setting may adopt a legal, an aesthetic, or an economic point of view. While nonmoral perspectives may be somewhat related to certain desirable ends—as when the legal perspective implies the importance of obeying the law—our awareness of these varied social valuational perspectives helps demarcate moral from nonmoral valuations.

To summarize, by *moral* I mean both a concern for the rightness of conduct and a broader concern for what is deemed important or valuable, provided that these valuational situations clearly entail desirable ends. While the desirable ends related to personal moral situations may justifiably remain latent, the ends related to social moral situations—for example, teaching—are legitimately subject to public scrutiny, especially when these situations occur in officially recognized institutions.

THE MORAL DIMENSION OF
THE STUDENT-TEACHER RELATIONSHIP

That the student-teacher relationship is an inherently moral one is the major theme of this section. This theme is developed by describing and analyzing the student-teacher relationship in terms of several characteristics that make it, at least in part, a moral relationship. Then I examine the views of three educators on what the proper relationship between teacher and student ought to be. I use specific examples in part to illustrate the range of views that can be taken on the nature of the proper relationship and in part to show how educators who deal seriously with this topic seem to include in their analyses certain key concepts, for example, authority, responsibility, autonomy, subject matter, equality.

The moral basis of the teacher-student relationship is grounded, I believe, in the inherent inequality of this relationship. The dominant position of the teacher is succinctly captured by Hawkins:

> The [teacher-learner] relationship, by its very nature, involves an offer of control by one individual over the functioning of another, who in accepting this offer, is tacitly assured that control will not be exploitative but will be used to enhance the competence and extend the independence of the one controlled, and in due course will be seen to do so. (1973, pp. 8–9)

In other words, the teaching relationship entails giving the teacher control over developing the student in desirable directions, that is, in enhancing competence and extending independence. By accepting this obligation to foster these desirable outcomes the teacher assumes moral responsibility for the student.

Since assuming moral responsibility for the development of another person is a grave obligation, we are well advised to make sure that the condition on which this moral responsibility is based— the natural dominance of the teacher over the student—is a sound assumption. After all, history is strewn with examples of how the assumed inferiority of a particular group or role has helped the dominant group or role justify morally objectionable practices, for example, slavery, sexism, and ethnic discrimination. Indeed, we have all known teachers who seem so to enjoy having power over others that they prolong unnecessarily the period of student dependence. Even the teacher who is not using his students to satisfy his own psychological needs may neglect to consider whether there is sound justification for the knowledge and skills he offers them. As a result, we ought to grant the teacher moral responsibility for students' intellectual and social development only to the extent that we can justify teacher authority over students.

When we examine the basis for a teacher's power over students, we find that the case for this necessity is strong. In the first place, the teacher acts not so much as a student's personal leader as he does an institutional leader (Waller 1932). By this I mean that the teacher typically works in a social situation—the school—where there exist, independent of his personal dispositions, certain expectations for his classroom conduct. These socially defined expectations include a wide variety of curricular responsibilities and behavioral norms, some sanctioned by state law or regulations, some by local regulations, and still others by school and community custom. While the teacher has latitude in how he will interpret these curricular and behavioral expectations, Waller concludes that "the teacher-pupil relationship is a form of institutionalized dominance and subordination" (p. 195).

Even considering teaching independent from its institutional context, there is at least one other characteristic of teaching, its goal-directed nature, that suggests the teacher inevitably has power over the student. Before examining this link, we need to explore briefly the goal-directed nature of teaching.

Teaching is an intentional activity designed to bring about student learning, a view held by educators of widely differing persuasions (see, for example, Hirst & Peters 1971, chap. 5; Phillips 1981; Scheffler 1960, pp. 60–63; Stephens 1967, pp. 67–69). The intentionality of teaching is sometimes denied, as when we resort to the oft-used slogan, "We teach children, not subjects." But if after observing an instance of teaching I asked the teacher, "What have you been trying to get the students to learn?" and the teacher replied, "Nothing, I'm just teaching," I would be perplexed. While a negative answer was possible if I had asked whether the youngsters were learning what the teacher was teaching, Scheffler surely is right in his claim that "no one can be engaged in teaching anyone without being engaged in teaching him something" (1960, p. 39). To teach, therefore, is to engage in an intentional or goal-directed activity with the hope that the student ultimately develops in certain desirable directions.

Acknowledging that teaching is at heart an intentional activity leads us to see that the teacher inevitably has power over the student. In an attempt to cause the student to master certain worthwhile content, the teacher engages in a variety of directive activities, for example, correcting errors, identifying exceptions to a generalization, specifying the next task, stimulating student interest in a new topic, and so forth. These and other directive activities are natural teacher activities involved with structuring the learning situation (Dearden 1976, pp. 66–67). Even Dewey, despite all his talk of shared activity, explicitly acknowledged the obligation of the teacher to structure the teaching environment to foster certain learnings:

> There is no such thing as sheer self-activity possible—because all
> activity takes place in a medium, in a situation. . . . The value
> of the formulated wealth of knowledge that makes up the course
> of study is that it may enable the educator *to determine the*
> *environment of the child*, and thus by indirection to direct. . . . It
> [the course of study] says to the teacher: Such and such are the

capacities, the fulfilments, in truth and beauty and behavior, open to these children. Now see to it that day by day the conditions are such that *their own activities* move inevitably in this direction. (1956, pp. 30–31)

Clearly the teacher has power over the student when the teacher through the course of study "determines the environment of the child" for the purposes of encouraging the student to learn worthwhile content.

Many educational reformers have found the power inherent in the teaching situation to be potentially coercive. These reformers have tended to identify teacher power or authority with authoritarianism and have, therefore, wanted to reduce or eliminate the importance accorded to teacher intentions (Hirst & Peters 1971, pp. 28–32). Believing that the teacher's task is to draw out the latent personality of the child, these reformers see the child as an autonomous being in need of a friend and helper rather than a temporarily dependent being in need of the guidance and direction provided by teacher intentions. Teacher and students, so the argument goes, ought to be a community of learners. In order to establish a more "democratic" relationship between teacher and students, the teacher must surrender some authority to students. The end result is a cluster of individuals—teacher and students—all of whom have approximately equal authority for establishing the goals toward which teaching is directed.

Ignoring for the moment the validity of the argument for equalizing authority in the teaching situation, we should recognize that such equalization does not necessarily eliminate the inequality of the teacher-student relationship. The ultimate test of authority is who decides what the distribution of authority will be, and this decision is the teacher's province. There are, of course, constraints on the teacher's decision-making power, especially when teaching is carried out in the context of elementary and secondary schooling. But these institutional constraints, though undoubtedly real, should not blind us to the central role of the teacher in distributing instructional authority. The teacher who delegates authority to students in order to establish a democratic classroom is exercising authority just as much as the teacher who creates an authoritarian classroom. Note also that in both cases the teacher is developing the student in a desirable direction: toward autonomy or toward dependence on the teacher's competence.

Upon examination, we find that Hawkins' assertion of the inherent inequality of the student-teacher relationship is a valid claim. In a general sense the teacher assumes responsibility for enhancing student competence and for extending student autonomy; in a more specific sense the teacher naturally engages in a variety of directive activities designed to bring about student learning of worthwhile content. Any attempt by the teacher to equalize the student-teacher relationship only serves to accent the teacher's dominant power position. Lastly, the institutionalization of teaching both provides legal and community support for teacher authority and concurrently sets limits on how an individual teacher can exercise this authority.

Even with the institutionalization of teaching—the predominant context for teaching in modern industrial society—there are a variety of ways to define the proper student-teacher relationship. I want to examine briefly three conceptualizations of this relationship conceptualizations proposed by Hannah Arendt, Herbert Kohl, and Paulo Freire. While these conceptualizations do not necessarily represent extreme positions, they nevertheless illustrate varying ways in which the teacher can assume moral responsibility for the development of the student. At the same time, these conceptualizations contain a common core of vocabulary needed to address systematically the question of the proper relationship between teacher and student.

Arendt believes that education in America is in a state of crisis. The crisis results partly from widespread implementation of progressive education and partly from our commitment to the idea of equality. She finds the concept of equality particularly troublesome because it encourages us to erase in so far as possible the differences between young and old, gifted and ungifted students, and students and teachers. Such equalization can be "accomplished only at the cost of the teacher's authority" (1968, p. 180). At the same time, Arendt worries that we place too much emphasis on "a child's world and a society formed among children that are autonomous" (p. 181), while in reality "childhood is a temporary stage" for a human being who is in "preparation for adulthood" (p. 184).

On the way to adulthood the child must learn about our society and its traditions, a task Arendt allocates to the school. The teacher is the representative of this world and must assume responsibility for it, even though she did not make it and may wish that it were different. Assuming responsibility for the world and for introducing the child to it is an expression of the teacher's authority, which the child cannot throw off as if he were part of an oppressed minority. Unfortunately, "authority has been discarded by the adults, and this can mean only one thing: that the adults refuse to assume responsibility for the world into which they have brought the children" (p. 190).

Arendt believes, therefore, that the proper student-teacher relationship occurs when the teacher accepts responsibility for instructing the young about our society and its past. The authority involved in the teacher's acceptance of this responsibility must be honored by the student. "To avoid misunderstanding," notes Arendt, "it seems to me that conservatism, in the sense of conservation, is of the essence of the educational activity" (p. 192). In short, the teacher's task is to interpret our society's past traditions and current realities to the young; the student's task is to master these learnings. The relationship between teacher and student ought to be one-sided, with full responsibility residing in the teacher, at least until the student achieves adult status.

Kohl concurs with Arendt that the teacher is deeply involved in taking responsibility for the development of the student, but Kohl focuses on building a progressive future rather than instilling respect for the past. "Teaching," he notes, "has to do with the future, with whom we encourage our young people to be, and ultimately, of course, with who we will be as a nation and as people sharing the earth" (1976, p. 12). The teacher is not neutral about the desired characteristics of our future culture but rather ought to be involved in "remaking this culture and society in a humane and just way" (p. 100).

While Kohl's definition of the teacher's job involves the teacher's attempting to influence the students toward certain values, he believes that the students are the moral equals of the adult teachers:

> Moral equality can be threatening to adults, for it implies that the same rules apply to you as to your students. You cannot hurt or bully them, destroy their work, interfere with them when they are working. If you give them the opportunity, your students will let you know when you are making their lives intolerable or uncomfortable. You have to learn how to listen to these criticisms and, if they are well-founded, change your own behavior. (1976, p. 84).

Arendt might well object that Kohl is refusing to take full responsibility for teaching the world to students, while Kohl would probably counter that Arendt's conception of the teacher-student relationship does not recognize the moral rights of students.

Unlike Arendt, Kohl sees clear limits to the teacher's authority over students. For example, even though openness, love, closeness, and intimacy are interpersonal virtues which facilitate a productive relationship between teacher and student, there are ways in which these virtues can be abused, for example, love of some students more than others can lead to favoritism, or excessive intimacy can lead the teacher to make herself the curriculum. Similarly, the teacher who attempts to politicize her students, a natural tendency while committing students to humane and just values, may become overly dogmatic and be ignored by students. Kohl concludes that teachers must temper their authority over students: "We have to become tough with ourselves and realize that teaching in an open setting does not give us license to play out our fantasies or fulfill all our needs through the lives of young people. Our job as teachers should be to turn our students on to themselves, to each other, and to all things there are to learn about in the world" (p. 105). To a certain extent, therefore, Kohl accepts responsibility for the world as it is—in much the same way advocated by Arendt.

Freire places the student-teacher relationship in another perspective by declaring that during "real" teaching—what he terms problem-posing teaching—the entire question of teacher authority becomes irrelevant and even the separation between teacher and student tends to dissolve. But before Freire's concept of problem-posing education and its implications for the student-teacher relationship can be meaningfully explored, we must look at his reasons for rejecting the traditional student-teacher relationship. The typical relationship in which the teacher tells and the student listens is grounded in the "banking" concept of education in which "knowledge is a gift bestowed by those who consider themselves knowledgeable upon those whom they consider to know nothing" (1970, p. 58). The student's role is nothing more than to receive, file, and store the "deposits" from the teacher-banker.

As long as we operate from a banking concept of education, the world—its established social and political relationships, including its inequities—is considered to be a given. The more the student works at passively depositing ideas provided by the teacher the more the student adapts to the world as it is. But the teacher who desires to liberate students from their naive acceptance of oppression cannot do so by telling them about the nature of their oppression. To employ revolutionary slogans is to continue to use the banking concept of education, which is inconsistent with true liberation because one set of "givens" is replaced with another. Revolutionary banking is no better than status quo banking.

The teacher committed to authentic liberation attempts through question posing to encourage students to see their apparently natural cultural context as problematic. The dialogue initiated by this problem posing redefines the teacher-student relationship:

> The teacher-of-the-students and the students-of-the-teacher cease
> to exist and a new term emerges: teacher-student with students-

teachers. The teacher is no longer merely the-one-who-teaches,
but one who is himself taught in dialogue with the students, who
in turn while being taught also teach. They become jointly
responsible for a process in which all grow. In this process,
arguments based on "authority" are no longer valid. (Freire 1970,
p. 67)

This joint attempt to analyze the problematic basis of the cultural
context would be seen by Arendt as the teacher's failure to accept
responsibility for the world but would be viewed by Kohl as consistent with his commitment to the moral equality of teacher and
student.

The factor that brings together teacher and student and comes
close to eliminating the distinction between these two roles is their
common concern for subject matter. Rather than viewing subject
matter as his "private property," the teacher according to Freire
should see it as "the object of reflection by himself and the students."
No longer passive listeners, the students are now "critical co-inves-
tigators in dialogue with the teacher," and the teacher both "presents
the material to the students for their consideration, and re-considers
his earlier considerations as the students express their own" (p. 68).
To symbolize the growing identity of teacher and student when
a particular subject matter is explored through problem-posing
teaching, Freire uses the terms *teacher-student* and *student-teacher*. As
a result, Freire comes very close to rejecting the inequality of the
teacher-student relationship, though we must remember that Freire
is concerned with the teaching of adults.

It is fascinating to observe how Arendt, Kohl, and Freire appeal
so frequently to a common core of concepts as each of them argues for
a particular ideal version of the student-teacher relationship. Since I
have focused on the degree to which the student-teacher relationship
is, and ought to be, dominated by the teacher, it is not surprising that
the concepts of equality, authority, and autonomy are continually
employed. The concepts of responsibility and subject matter are
somewhat less obviously related to the question of dominance, but
these concepts figure prominently in discussions by Arendt, Kohl,
and Freire of the proper student-teacher relationship, thereby
suggesting these concepts may be of use to others who want to
develop their ideas on this topic.

One consideration that may account for some of the variation in
the views of Arendt, Kohl, and Freire is the different-aged student on
which each author focuses. Freire's ideas, growing out of work with
adult illiterates, seems to assume that the student is an adult, while
Kohl, who has taught students from kindergarten through twelfth

grade, and Arendt appear to assume the student is in elementary and secondary school. Only Arendt explicitly addresses how the changing age of a student would alter her conception of the teacher's authority; she states that the authority of teachers over young pupils must not be applied by analogy to adults whose subjugation would be a violation of human dignity (Arendt 1968, p. 192).

That achieving adult status alters Arendt's conception of a person's autonomy brings to mind our tendency to defend paternalistic treatment of youngsters but to abhor such treatment of adults. But the basis for this child-adult distinction is rarely explored, receiving even less attention than the question of the proper student-teacher relationship (for example, see Hendley 1978). In an attempt to address the child-adult distinction, Schrag (1977) convincingly demonstrates that the paternalistic treatment of youngsters cannot be based on their incomplete development of such capacities as linguistic competence, physical strength, rational decision making, or self-sufficiency. Since there appears to be no defensible criterion for distinguishing our treatment of youngsters and adults, we are left with a stark choice: either deny that freedom is an unqualified good or reject paternalism for children.

Claiming that making children the legal equals of adults would result in an unthinkable cruelty to the young, Schrag develops two positions that would allow us to maintain paternalism for children. One position, following our modern philosophical tradition, posits a sharp distinction between child and adult, while the second position, a utilitarian one, assumes a more gradual shift of power based on the child's increasing ability as he gains more experience to judge what will make him happy. The first position seems consistent with Arendt's insistence that the power of the teacher over the student is clear-cut, as long as the student is being introduced to the world as a whole (perhaps until graduation from college). The second position envisages a student-teacher relationship that lets power gradually flow toward the student as the student expands his experience and understanding and thereby becomes a better judge of what will make him happy. Though none of the three earlier explications of the ideal student-teacher relationship is grounded in such a gradualist perspective, a reasonable basis for slowly transferring power from teacher to student could well be the increasing maturity and understanding of the student.

However, Schrag notes that making the exercise of freedom contingent on student maturity and understanding could justify the withholding of freedom from adults because some adults may well be incapable of judging what will make them happy over the long run. Twenty years from now, for example, we may deeply regret our current decisions concerning resource conservation or our diet. To the extent that maximizing our future happiness becomes the criterion, then farsighted individuals might be justified in "restraining us in our own interest" (1977, p. 175). In the end, therefore, Schrag opts for the first view—that of clearly distinguishing childhood from adulthood—because he does not want to risk having paternalism creep into our adult lives and because he is willing to gamble that "in seeking their own good in their own way, most adults will fare better than most children would" (p. 177). The choice Schrag makes for establishing a firm boundary between childhood and adulthood is, as he notes, a "moral choice" in that this choice can have "an impact on how human beings perceive and hence act towards each other" (p. 177).

Clearly the reasoning we use to justify some degree of paternalism in our treatment of the young student is a complex process. We need to consider the student's age—and possibly his capacity for understanding—as we attempt to justify the proper relationship between student and teacher. I have given this topic special consideration because typically so little attention is devoted to the interrelationship of age and the student-teacher relationship.

THE MORAL BASIS OF THE CURRICULUM

As I examined the moral basis of the student-teacher relationship, I sometimes went beyond the confines of the relationship itself to explore more broadly the concept and context of teaching. For example, I examined the tendency for teaching to occur within an institutional setting called the school, the necessary tie between teaching and intentionality, the frequent confusion in teaching between authority and authoritarianism, the link between teacher power and the fostering of desired outcomes. That these contextual and conceptual issues were relevant to the topic of the student-teacher relationship is evidence that this relationship can be examined profitably not only in its own terms but also in relation to the broad range of activity involved in teaching. To raise the issue of the proper student-teacher relationship is, therefore, to prompt one to confront deeper questions about the nature and context of teaching.

Within the field of education, the term *teaching* (or instruction) is commonly distinguished from the term *curriculum*, with teaching considered a process and curriculum considered a plan to help the teacher prepare for that process. Typical of those who differentiate teaching from curriculum in this way is Macdonald who defines instruction as "the activity which takes place primarily in the classroom or some other suitable place under the guidance of someone called a teacher" (1971, p. 126). One of the major determinants of what will occur in the instructional situation as the pupil and teacher interact is the "curriculum plan" (p. 126). Conceiving of curriculum as a plan for teaching or instruction is the way I will use the term in this book. It is important to note, however, that curriculum often is used in a much broader sense, for example, an enterprise in guided living, all experiences that students have under the auspices of the school, or a vital and complex interaction of people and things in a free-wheeling setting (Tanner and Tanner 1975, pp. 21–25). Not only do such definitions mix together teaching (or instruction) and curriculum but also in some cases they fail to distinguish the activities of the school from those of other social or institutional entities.

Restricting the term *curriculum* to whatever is involved in creating a plan for teaching gives some reasonable boundaries to the term, thereby making the question of the moral basis of curriculum a more concrete and comprehensible question than if a broader definition were to be employed. The answer to this question, however, is by no means obvious, because there is a long tradition within the curriculum literature of deemphasizing the moral basis of curriculum. (For an exception to this generalization, see Hayes 1977.) Before directly examining the moral basis of the curriculum, I want to review the dominant tradition within the field of curriculum so we can see why the moral basis of curriculum only recently has been widely recognized.

The clearest and most persuasive statement of contemporary curriculum theory and practice is Ralph Tyler's *Basic Principles of Curriculum and Instruction*, written over thirty years ago as a syllabus for a curriculum course. Tyler's formulation has been so influential that it has come to be known as the Tyler rationale. This rationale begins by identifying four fundamental questions that must be answered in developing any plan for instruction. These are:

1. What educational purposes should the school seek to attain?
2. What educational experiences can be provided that are likely to attain these purposes?
3. How can these educational experiences be effectively organized?
4. How can we determine whether these purposes are being attained? (Tyler 1950, pp. 1–2)

These four questions are easily convertible into a four-step curriculum development process: selecting and stating objectives, selecting learning experiences to achieve these objectives, organizing these experiences effectively, and evaluating outcomes against the stated objectives. The Tyler rationale is an examination and elaboration of these four steps.

The starting point and the core of the Tyler rationale is the statement of objectives, for it is around this first step that the other three are organized. Without objectives the Tyler rationale loses its anchor, though many teachers in their daily practice do not give the stating of objectives the pivotal position accorded this process by the Tyler rationale (Koeller & Thompson 1980; Zahorik 1975). Thus the need for starting curriculum planning by developing objectives—the key step of the Tyler rationale and the central dogma of contemporary curriculum theory—is by no means central to the practice of teachers. Later I will return to this apparent conflict between classroom practice and the Tyler rationale, but first I want to explore how Tyler's focus on objectives has influenced how we view the field of curriculum.

Working from the premise that "all aspects of the educational program are really means to accomplish basic educational purposes," Tyler poses the problem: What educational purposes should the school seek to attain (1950, p. 3)? He then identifies three sources of educational objectives: studies of learners, studies of contemporary life, and suggestions from subject matter specialists. Once potential objectives are obtained from each of the three sources, these objectives need to be filtered through the "screens" of philosophy and psychology of learning in order to select a small number of "important" and "feasible" objectives (pp. 22, 25). By including the essentialist's concern for subject matter, the progressive's focus on the child, and the reformer's concern with contemporary social problems, Tyler attempted to weave together these diverse and often warring educational orientations into a coherent approach to curriculum planning.

But Tyler's eclectic approach to selecting educational objectives has several weaknesses. Kliebard demonstrates that one source, subject matter, is really not a separate source of objectives so much as it is "a means of achieving objectives drawn from the other two [sources]" (1970, p. 269). More importantly, in discussing the remaining two sources of objectives, Tyler does not adequately relate the issue of desirable ends to the selection of objectives, a contention that can be demonstrated by examining his discussion of learner needs as a source of objectives.

After defining education as "a process of changing behavior patterns of people," Tyler proceeds to argue that studies of the learner can identify "needs" to serve as targets for behavioral changes (1950, p. 4). However, he recognizes that the concept of need does not identify a target for change unless a norm is also specified. Indeed, Tyler defines a need as a "gap" representing "the difference between the present condition of the learner and the acceptable norm" (p. 5). The typical study of student needs, therefore, has two steps: "First, finding the present status of the students, and second, comparing this status to acceptable norms in order to identify the gaps or needs" (p. 6). The key question, of course, is how these acceptable norms are to be established.

On the complex issue of establishing such desirable norms, Tyler is remarkably silent. His examples suggest these norms are not merely statistical, that is, we are not to accept a norm just because it is widely adhered to. For example, a hypothetical finding that most ninth-grade boys in a school read nothing outside school except comic strips does not necessarily mean that "the school needs to teach these boys how to read comic strips more rapidly or with greater satisfaction" (p. 10). In fact, Tyler contends such reasoning is the response to be expected from an "unimaginative teacher" (p. 10). A better response, Tyler implies, would be to see that the tendency to read comic books reflects the narrowness of the boys' reading interests and suggests the need to broaden these reading interests. But Tyler does not explain the reasoning the teacher might use in establishing the norm of broadened reading interests or in establishing any of the other norms mentioned in his examples. All he does is to talk vaguely about the desirability of appealing to the norms "in the field [of study]" and of using caution "because the same items of data permit several possible interpretations" (p. 10). We are left with the uneasy feeling that the key factor in determining an acceptable norm is "the nature and strength of the teacher's conviction" (Kliebard 1970, p. 264).

The closest Tyler comes to discussing how acceptable norms are established is when he examines the role of the school's educational and social philosophy in screening out unimportant and inconsistent objectives. According to Tyler, every school should have a statement of philosophy that defines "the nature of a good life and a good society" and outlines "the values that are deemed essential to a satisfying and effective life" (1950, p. 22). The basic values that underlie the vision of the good life and the good society become the basis for selecting objectives: "Objectives that are consistent with these values will be included and suggested objectives which are inconsistent with these values will not be included in the school's educational program" (p. 23). In brief, Tyler believes that the values on which a school's philosophy is based are the best criteria for selecting educational objectives.

Unfortunately, Tyler never really gets down to specifics to

explain precisely how the philosophic screen helps us to identify the "small number" of "highly consistent" objectives he believes is essential to effective curriculum development (p. 22). What, for example, do we do when the values underlying the philosophy are in tension or even in conflict? Such a social value structure—a likely outcome if minority perspectives and civil liberties are taken seriously—can easily lead to selecting objectives that are internally inconsistent. Further, since numerous objectives might be consistent with any particular social or educational value, we may find that using a philosophic screen fails to produce the small number of objectives on which effective curricula are to be built. As if these complications were not serious enough, we who have participated in regional accreditation visits to high schools know that a school philosophy is rarely the "clear and analytical statement" Tyler argues is the most helpful screen for selecting objectives (p. 24). On the contrary, school philosophies tend to be vague and broad, largely to paper over philosophic differences within a faculty and a particular community.

In a similar way, Tyler may be said to paper over the difficulties involved in using an educational philosophy to identify a small number of consistent objectives. He asserts that this "screening" can and ought to be done, but he neither discusses how to accomplish this goal nor anticipates some of the problems likely to arise as objectives are measured against an educational philosophy. It is not surprising, therefore, that contemporary curriculum theorists who identify with the Tyler rationale tend to ignore Tyler's discussion of the central role of a philosophic screen. Objectives retain their central position in mainline curricular thinking, but the emphasis is on stating them clearly and behaviorally, not on selecting the objectives consistent with the desirable ends underlying a particular school philosophy.

In other words, Tyler's initial question, "What educational purposes should the school seek to attain?", has become reduced to the technical operation of stating precise behavioral objectives. The classic statement of how to specify objectives is *Preparing Instructional Objectives* by Robert Mager. Mager (1962) ignores the question of selecting important objectives and concentrates his attention on the mechanics of stating behavioral objectives. While there is no doubt that Tyler endorses the idea of behavioral objectives, he does attempt to address, however incompletely, the complex philosophic issues underlying the selection of objectives (1950, pp. 28–40). As a result, Tyler's conception of curriculum development is more sophisticated than that of his mentor, W. W. Charters, who believed that objectives could be set without making any normative judgments.

Having closely examined Tyler's ideas on identifying objectives, we can start to understand why teachers and curriculum workers have been so slow to see the moral basis of the curriculum. The reason is not so much that Tyler ignored the moral basis of curriculum. Indeed Tyler is explicit that objectives are "desired educational results" selected because of their link to certain values (p. 40), a definition similar to my earlier definition of the term *moral*. Rather, Tyler does not cultivate our awareness of the moral perspective because his analysis of the moral basis of curriculum is poorly done. In addition to Tyler's inadequate analysis, other factors that have inhibited our awareness of the moral dimension include both our historical propensity to study curriculum and teaching in a "scientific" or value-neutral way and the appearance of such persuasive technical approaches to objectives as the one by Mager. Counteracting these inhibiting factors is the recent development of a literature on ways the school encourages learning outcomes not part of the official curriculum, namely, the "hidden curriculum" of unintended cognitive and affective learnings (Gordon 1980; J. R. Martin 1976), and the critical theorists' analyses of how schooling reproduces class-based social and economic inequalities (see, for example, Apple 1979, 1982a, 1982b; Willis 1977, 1981). Though these analyses are controversial—especially those done by the critical theorists (Hurn 1978; Westbury 1980)—the literature on the hidden curriculum and on cultural and economic reproduction has sensitized us to the moral dimension of the curriculum.

Aside from all of this speculation about why we have been so slow to see any moral basis for the curriculum, we are left with the question of the size of the curriculum's moral component. In part, the moral basis of the curriculum is rooted in the need to create a plan for teaching by selecting some content instead of other content. Even if a teacher does not begin her planning by stating content in terms of objectives (Koeller & Thompson 1980; Zahorik 1975), this teacher still needs to select among the available content. Selection cannot be arbitrary, or we would not see the subsequent teaching activity as being educational. Peters convincingly argues that education necessarily involves the identification and preservation of worthwhile content:

> [The concept] "education" relates to some sorts of processes in which a desirable state of mind develops. It would be as much of a logical contradiction to say that a person had been educated and yet the change was in no way desirable as it would be to say that he had been reformed and yet had made no change for the better.... To call something "educational" is to intimate that

the processes and activities themselves contribute to or involve
something that is worthwhile. (1965, pp. 90–92)

That is, educational processes are moral, according to our earlier
definition, in that such processes are expected to involve the pursuit
of desirable ends.

Some may object that this reasoning rules out contrary evidence
by defining as noneducational any curricular planning (and subsequent teaching) that reflects random selection of content. Is it fair
to have a proposition that cannot be falsified because a key term,
education, is defined in a restrictive way? Fair or not, Peters is correct
in his contention that education is associated in the popular mind, as
well as in professional discourse, with the pursuit of the worthwhile.
A curriculum based on random content selection—or on any other
arbitrary criterion—is seen as being educationally irresponsible.
Fundamental to the curriculum worker's responsibility is the identification of a worthwhile direction for learning, regardless of whether
objectives are used to specify and organize content or whether
content is selected without reference to objectives. Curriculum development involves choosing certain content (or objectives) over other
content (or objectives) with the intention that worthwhile learning
will result for the student (see, for example, Belkin 1974; Berson
1975; Kliebard 1977; L. M. Smith 1977; Tyler 1950).

Ultimately the estimate of what is worthwhile learning is
grounded in a conception of desirable ends, a connection that causes
many curriculum developers to be ill at ease. How do we know
conclusively which way to proceed since the relative desirability of
ends is debatable? Among the strategies used by curriculum workers
to avoid such troublesome judgments are the techniques of needs
analysis and activity or job analysis. Both of these techniques seem to
promise that curricular priorities can be objectively set, either by
studying the student and/or the society to identify learning "needed"
by students or by studying a task or job to see what "activities" are
central to this task or job.

The analysis of Tyler's rationale has already illustrated how
a need cannot be established unless an acceptable norm is also
proposed, thereby illustrating that needs analysis cannot escape
questions of desirability. Similarly, activity or job analysis, especially as implemented by W. W. Charters, was criticized by Bode who
argued that delineating the components of a job or an activity can
never furnish us with objectives or ideals for the performance of this
operation (1924; 1927a, chap. 5). Activity analysis "tells us what is,
but not what ought to be" (1927a, p. 112). That is, activity analysis,
just as in the case of needs analysis, cannot become the basis for

educational action unless some norm of desirable performance is established.

To summarize, it should be evident by now that curriculum planning has a sizable moral component. Key to this moral component is the fact that planning a curriculum inevitably entails selecting some objectives (or content) instead of other objectives (or content). Even if this selection process does not involve the use of a philosophic screen as recommended by Tyler, some nonrandom approach to selection must be used if the subsequent teaching is to be educational. A curriculum plan, therefore, must contain a conception of desirable ends, though the care with which the case for these desirable ends is made may vary considerably from one plan to another. Attempts to make curriculum planning less controversial and more scientific generally fail; such technical approaches as needs analysis or activity analysis do not really bypass the complex priority decisions underlying every curriculum plan.

CONCLUSION

Far too often the term *moral* is used to isolate a category of behavior—that behavior relating to right conduct—from other forms of human behavior. While such a division may be productive in some areas of human conduct, this restrictive conception of moral seems inappropriate to the field of teaching. In a sense, almost every aspect of teaching involves a moral component, partly because teaching is by definition a social encounter and partly because the social encounter involved in teaching entails an intervention by one person in another person's intellectual and personal development. The comprehensive nature of the moral basis of teaching is well-summarized by a reaction to my initial discussion of this issue (Tom 1980c):

> I conceive of the classroom as having a moral order which permeates nearly every aspect of student life and activity. The status differential between teachers and students is one aspect of this moral order, but there are many more; establishment of behavioral norms and academic expectations, reward and punishment strategies, distribution of teacher help and attention, grouping decisions. I think the overarching concept of a moral order is broad enough to encompass most of what we do as teachers, but I think the definition of *moral* needs to be spelled out quite carefully. It is a word which invites misinterpretation. (Mergendoller 1981)

I hope that misinterpretations have been minimized by defining moral in terms of social valuational situations in which desirable ends are at issue.

The discussion in this chapter of the moral basis of teaching is reminiscent of the earlier analysis of teaching as a socially constructed phenomenon. When I examined the flaws of the teacher effectiveness approach, I noted that the problems with the process-product paradigm—and with the concept of teacher effectiveness on which this paradigm rests—go beyond false assumptions about the nature and flow of teacher-student influence. An even more fundamental flaw is the failure of teacher effectiveness researchers to acknowledge the socially constructed nature of teaching. To view teaching as a social construction is to see teaching as a cultural artifact that evolves as people refine and redefine which knowledge, skills, and attitudes are important for future generations. At the root of the socially constructed conception of teaching, therefore, is the question of desirable ends, an endpoint that brings us back to the moral basis of teaching.

In the discussion of the socially constructed basis of teaching, my analysis did not go further than to claim that teaching is guided by human purposes, that these purposes evolve over time, and that the study of teaching cannot ignore these purposes. In the present chapter, however, this rudimentary analysis of the role of human purposes in teaching has been extended by illustrating that the human purposes—that is, the desirable ends—involved in teaching can be examined from at least two perspectives. Both of these perspectives—the character of the student-teacher relationship and the curricular selection process, in the hidden as well as the official curriculum—sensitize us to concrete ways we can think about the educational encounters we collectively want to create. Taking personal responsibility for our work as educators is easier once we go beyond the global realization that educational phenomena are created and see that certain issues are key elements of this social creation.

To say that educational endeavors are socially constructed and that certain issues seem central to this building process is not to say that each of us can create any type of educational effort she wants to devise. Unless we are speaking of an individual teacher interacting with an individual student outside an institutional context, there are a variety of constraints on any potential educational construction. Not the least of these constraints is the social nature of an educational construction; some community of people must coalesce around a position on such key issues as the proper student-teacher relationship and the basis for selecting curricular content. Without some consensus on these issues, various components of the educational endeavor may well be working at cross purposes with one another, a not infrequent outcome. Other constraints upon an individual teacher include statutes, state administrative regulations, community customs, the bureaucratic structure of schools, and academic traditions. As a result, identification of education as a socially constructed phenomenon does not mean that an individual can build any desired construction; there is an already existing educational construction with a complex set of legal and historical roots.

What the recognition of teaching as both moral and socially constructed means is that education is not one of the givens of the universe. Human beings—not some supernatural being or set of underlying natural regularities—cause education to be the way it is. The extent to which the individual educator can affect the direction of any particular educational endeavor may well be open to question, but educators must accept responsibility for the educational constructions we find around us. In Part III, I will discuss in some detail the nature of the responsibility each educator—or "moral craftsman" as I choose to call us—has for thinking about the moral dimension of the socially constructed phenomena of education.

· 5 ·

THE CRAFT
BASIS OF
TEACHING

The craft conception of teaching has not had a "good press" among educators. A commonly made criticism is that conceiving of teaching as a craft makes it impossible to develop the occupation of teaching into a profession. According to this argument, a profession is based on a body of theoretical knowledge while a craft is based on bits and pieces of information accumulated through trial and error. Therefore, so the argument goes, if we really want professional status for the occupation of teaching, we must vigorously pursue the development and codification of educational theory and concurrently attempt to discredit the craft conception of teaching (Broudy 1956; Schaefer 1970). Howsam et al. forcefully summarize this point of view when they claim: "Professionals cannot exist without an undergirding science. *To fail to develop principles, concepts, and theories, and to validate practice is to restrict the occupation to the level of a craft"* (1976, p. 11).

In recent years, however, a few educators have once again become interested in the craft conception of teaching. The bases for this reconsideration are varied, including the contention that teachers think and behave as if they were craftsmen (Lortie 1975); the belief that a craft conception of teaching and administration will increase our ability to understand and reform educational practice (Cohen 1977); the contention that schools as now structured inhibit the natural craftsmanship learning style of children (R. J. Martin 1978); and the argument that accountability will have a negligible impact until it is based on a conception of education consistent with the craft orientation of the typical teacher (Wise 1978). Apparently, educators are on the verge of taking a serious look at the craft conception of teaching, which, with minor exceptions (see, for example, Bagley 1930; Highet 1950; Stephens 1960), has had few proponents since the end of the normal school era of teacher preparation.

To illuminate what it means to claim that teaching has a craft basis, I am going to compare teaching with the widely known craft of fishing. Fishing, I argue, has three components: mechanical skill (e.g., accurate casting of lures), analytic knowledge (on how to find and tempt fish), and the ability to apply analytic knowledge to specific situations (e.g., the locating of spawning bluegills on lake 38 at Busch Wildlife Preserve on May 16, 1982). Similarly, teaching has elements of mechanical skill and analytic knowledge and involves the application of analytic knowledge to specific situations. However, the purpose of this comparison is not so much to argue that teaching and fishing are conceptually identical as it is to derive new perspectives for viewing the activity of teaching.

The craft similarities of fishing and teaching lead one to believe that analytic craft knowledge would be valued by teachers as well as by fishermen. Certainly there is a strong tradition of oral and written fishing lore, but teachers have remarkably little interest in craft knowledge, either in oral or written form. In this chapter I briefly explore several possible reasons for the denigration of analytic knowledge about teaching, including the lack of time teachers have to write about their craft, the low status of craft knowledge in the college and university settings that house our teacher preparation programs, the tendency for teachers to believe that one must develop a highly personal style of teaching.

But underlying these "reasons" why craft knowledge about teaching is deemphasized is an even more fundamental consideration: teaching is a more complex craft than fishing. In contrast to fishing, teaching's criterion of success is more debatable, teaching involves a triadic relationship (including subject matter) rather than a dyadic one, and teaching has a larger and more central moral component than does fishing. The very complexity of teaching, which makes craft knowledge even more critical for success in teaching than for success in fishing, also makes the conceptualization and codification of craft knowledge on teaching an extraordinarily difficult task.

TEACHING AND FISHING

When I consider the craft of fishing, I think not so much of mechanical skills—for instance, playing a fish or casting an artifical lure to the correct location—as I do of the analytical task of finding fish. The technicalities involved in these mechanical skills long ago became second nature. However, even for lakes well-known to me, I must analyze a wide variety of factors that influence where fish might be located on a particular day: water temperature, time of year, wind direction, time of day, cloud condition, weed cover, and so forth. Past experience with similar conditions is carefully processed, and estimates are made of probable locations of fish. Using live bait or artificial lures that have worked under similar conditions in the past, I try various locations in the hope that my analysis is accurate. Unfamiliar lakes are challenging because everything beneath the surface is initially a mystery; the locations of such critical variables as drop-off points, sand or rock bars, weed beds, or old river channels are unknown. Nothing is more satisfying than determining the probable location of a school of fish and then catching a fish on the first cast. One's expertise as a skilled fisherman is thereby confirmed.

In addition to estimating the location of fish and selecting appropriate bait or lures, there are a variety of mechanical skills involved in fishing. Setting the hook, keeping a tight line on a hooked fish, and dozens of other technicalities must be mastered and then integrated into various routinized sequences. It is these mechanical skills that the master typically teaches the novice fisherman first. These operations must be executed correctly and in sequence, lest the bite be missed or the hooked fish lost.

While these rudimentary mechanical skills are being learned through demonstration and explanation, the more experienced fisherman naturally, and almost unconsciously, passes on to the novice a large amount of fishing lore on locating and enticing fish. Gradually all the analytic knowledge that the master has assembled through a lifetime of fishing is conveyed to the beginner, though the beginner's judgment in employing this knowledge may not equal that of his more experienced colleague until years later if at all. Mechanical skill, therefore, is a necessary but insufficient condition of becoming a good fisherman; a good fisherman not only masters the technique of cranking fish into the boat but also analyzes where to find and how to tempt fish. Moreover, the analytic knowledge related to finding and tempting fish must be adapted to a specific situation. As a result of the foregoing discussion, success in fishing might be said to be composed of three components: mechanical skill, lore or knowledge on the analytic task of finding and tempting fish, and the ability to apply fishing lore to a particular fishing spot.

But the fisherman's expertise does not guarantee success. On a given day, a beginner may catch considerably more fish than a master fisherman, and on other days neither of them may be successful. Blaisdell notes:

> Far too often we fishermen make the common mistake of
> underestimating the strength of the opposition. With misplaced
> faith in what we regard as our skills, we believe that when we
> take no fish this is conclusive evidence that no fish are present....
> It would probably be completely demoralizing if we ever knew
> exactly how many trout refuse our offerings in any given mile of
> stream. (1969, pp. 20–22)

Failure does indeed come to all fishermen, even to those whose skill and knowledge earn them the distinction of having what Blaisdell calls the "touch." Uncontrollable factors—weather, overfishing, time of year, and so forth—can combine to neutralize the abilities of the best of fishermen. In short, there is no certainty in fishing lore, though there is a school of fishing effectiveness research which aspires to make fish behavior predictable (Mueller 1976).

The teacher also frequently experiences failure. Rules for complex teaching tasks are, in Scheffler's terms "inexhaustive," that is, no matter how closely we follow such rules, we may fail because of factors beyond our immediate control (1960, pp. 67–71). For example, at the critical learning moment, the student's attention may wander, or the teacher's explanation may employ an unfamiliar concept, or any number of unforeseen factors may intervene. Success in such cases may well depend on "factors outside of one's trying: the universe must co-operate" (p. 68). Only in the simplest of situations can teaching principles be said to "exhaustively rule out failure" (p. 71).

When the universe does not cooperate, the craftsman teacher observes the failure and analyzes its cause—no easy task when the teacher is immersed in the act of instruction—and brings to bear on the situation a revised strategy that pedagogical knowledge and past experience with varied situations suggest may work. The ability to analyze teaching situations and the possession of a broad repertoire of teaching strategies seem to distinguish the craftsman teacher from the novice. In a similar vein, Hunt (1976) argues that at the heart of the teaching-learning process are two teaching skills: the "reading" of student cues and the "flexing" of teacher behavior to adapt to the perceived cues. Hunt's two teaching skills are parallel to two components of fishing mentioned earlier. Reading student cues is similar to the task of finding and tempting fish, while flexing or adapting one's teaching behavior to perceived cues is analogous to applying fishing lore to a particular fishing spot.

But what aspect of teaching is parallel to the mechanical technicalities of fishing, that is, to those aspects of fishing whose skillful execution is essential, but not central, to catching fish? Another way to pose this question is to ask what, if anything, about teaching is a necessary precondition to reading student cues and flexing one's teaching behavior? Certainly the mastery of a subject matter is a precondition to the act of teaching, yet such mastery is clearly not mechanical. A more reasonable parallel to the mechanics of fishing is the topic of classroom management, an aspect of classroom life that is both mechanical and a precondition to successful teaching. There is wisdom in the age-old teacher concern about the negative implications for teaching of losing classroom control. However, we are probably well-advised to distinguish classroom management from classroom teaching, a distinction that recognizes management and teaching as coordinate but separate aspects of instruction (Hudgins 1971). Having control does not necessarily cause teaching to occur, but successful teaching is hard to envisage—at least in group-based elementary and secondary instruction—unless classroom control exists.

Teaching and fishing, therefore, may be seen as having considerable similarities. Both activities require mechanical expertise—the skills of casting or playing fish in one case and of classroom management in the other—but this expertise is not at the core of either activity. Both activities entail considerable analytic ability, largely because their rule structures are inexhaustive, and both activities involve the ability to adapt one's behavior to the unique characteristics of a specific situation. Teaching and fishing seem to involve a mixture of mechanical expertise, analytic ability, and adaptability to situational factors.

These craft similarities lead one to believe that analytic craft knowledge would be highly valued by both teachers and fishermen. In the case of fishing there is both an oral tradition for conveying fishing lore and an enormous number of magazines and books on the craft of fishing. But teachers have remarkably little interest in teaching lore, in either oral or written form. Few practicing teachers write about their craft, an outcome that is understandable in light of teaching's physical intensity and its emphasis on talking. Also understandable is the lack of emphasis in teacher education programs on craft knowledge, especially if these programs are lodged in research-oriented universities where scientifically based studies and programs are prized. What is puzzling is the tendency of experienced teachers to deny that their mechanical and analytic skills can be of value to other teachers. For instance, it is not unusual for a cooperating teacher to turn the class over to a student teacher near the beginning of the latter's assignment, to make few evaluative comments about the student teacher's performance, and to start leaving the room as soon as the teacher feels the beginner has control of the class. In other words, there is a widely held belief that each teacher must develop his own style by discovering what works for him, a combination of matching strategies and ideas to one's personality and to one's unique classroom of youngsters. The result of receiving minimal craft culture in preservice training and of believing that each teacher must develop his own teaching style is a conception of teaching as an individualistic enterprise to be learned by trial and error.

On the other hand, the idea that fishing craft is related to personality seems ludicrous. While styles of fishing differ from person to person, my decision to adopt a new fishing idea has little to do with my personality. As long as the idea helps me catch fish and is legal, I will make it part of my fishing style. Neither would I consider suspending my son's fishing instruction merely because he had mastered the rudiments of the craft and could conceivably catch a fish or two on his own. In fishing, unlike teaching, apprenticeship usually continues until the skill of the novice equals that of the master. Even at the point of equal competence, the ardent fisherman can continue to learn through exposing herself to fishing lore in codified form: articles, books, television programs.

Is it possible that while both fishing and teaching can be viewed as crafts, the more complex of the two crafts is fishing, and that this higher level of sophistication is the reason that fishermen rely more on craft instruction and codified knowledge than do teachers? But this claim that fishing is more intricate than teaching seems rather odd. After all, there are several ways in which teaching is a more complex activity than is fishing. First, the criterion for successful fishing is far less debatable than is that for successful teaching. That is, there is little argument that a fish either has or has not been caught, while what constitutes evidence of good teaching is both nebulous and controversial. There is a centuries-old controversy concerning what kind of learning is an indicator of good teaching, and there is not even agreement on whether the accomplishment of learning is a necessary condition of successful teaching. Second, teaching involves a triadic relationship among teacher, learner, and subject matter in which subject matter is a mediating element between teacher variables and student learning. Fishing on the other hand is a simple dyadic relationship between fisherman and fish. Third, the moral component of fishing is moderate and less central to the activity of fishing than is true in the case of teaching; a comparison of the moral basis of fishing and teaching is made later in this chapter.

Comparing the complexity of fishing and teaching leads us to see that there are at least three ways in which fishing is a less sophisticated activity than teaching. In contrast to teaching, fishing has a clearer criterion of success, involves only a dyadic relationship, and has a less direct moral basis. Yet we are left with the reality that fishermen place more emphasis on craft instruction and codified craft knowledge than do teachers. Perhaps our original supposition—that the more complex a craft is, the more craft knowledge and instruction are likely to be stressed—is wrong.

The relationship may well be just the opposite: the simpler the craft, the more likely we are to be able to provide useful craft instruction and to codify meaningful craft knowledge. The very complexity of teaching—for example, its moral nucleus, the mediating impact of subject matter, and the uncertainty of what entails success—may make the master teacher wary of imposing his teaching style on the student teacher or of devoting time to writing about his craft. If all the teacher had to cope with was the inexhaustive rule structure of teaching, then craft instruction and codification might well be as intensive for teaching as it is for fishing. But an inexhaustive rule structure compounded with ambiguous criteria for success, mediating effects of varied subject matters, and difficult moral issues seems to reduce both the possibility of coherent craft instruction and the possibility of codifying craft knowledge about teaching.

CRAFT: TOWARD A DEFINITION

Stressing all the complications involved in developing craft knowledge about teaching makes it possible to see why teachers are reluctant to instruct one another. In part they worry that the rules of teaching practice are inexhaustive, that is, there appear to be no teaching principles that invariably lead to success. They also know that different subject matters entail different teaching strategies, different teachers emphasize different goals, communities vary in what they expect of teachers, and many of the agreed-upon goals of teaching are foggy at best. Therefore, rather than offer prescriptions to colleagues, teachers are inclined to qualify advice they give with such statements as, "This idea works for me, but you'll have to see if it works for you."

On the surface, such advice appears simplistic and seems to justify our defining the term *craft* as work in which "experience improves performance" with the implication that learning is by trial and error (Lortie 1975, p. 266). Other evidence that appears to support a trial-and-error definition of teaching craft is the oft-made observation that teaching lacks a technical culture (see, for example, Lortie 1975, pp. 68–70, 80); the claim that teachers behave intuitively and are conceptually simpleminded (Jackson 1968, pp. 143–50); the assertion that teachers' concrete and practical orientation makes theory-based research appear irrelevant to them (Doyle & Ponder 1977–78; Richek 1979). Added together, these claims lead us to conclude that there is no craft culture because teachers are random searchers for specific solutions to practical problems, that is, teachers are trial-and-error craftsmen. The contention that trial-and-error learning is the essence of craft activity is so crucial to attempts to discredit the craft approach to teaching that I want to examine this claim in detail.

There is no doubt that teachers can and do approach teaching as a trial-and-error activity, just as fishermen, potters, actors, and other craftsmen can rely upon random ways of learning their crafts. But as the discussion in the prior section illustrates, it is possible to view teaching as a craft without assuming that craftsmanship means trial-and-error behavior. Teaching can be seen as involving a combination of mechanical skills, often organized in routinized sequences; analytic knowledge; and the ability to adapt analytic knowledge to specific situations. But if teaching can conceivably be viewed as having elements of analytic knowledge as well as routinized sequences of skills, why is it that craft—as used in reference to teaching—continues to lead so many people to think of trial-and-error behavior? Why do Lortie (1975), Jackson (1968), Broudy (1956), and other eminent educational scholars persist in equating craft with trial-and-error learning?

I suspect that the major reason that educators continue to see teaching craftsmanship as a trial-and-error effort is because craft knowledge in teaching is rarely codified. Further, when it is codified, its presentation lacks conceptual precision and its organization makes it hard to apply this craft culture to real teaching situations. Descriptions of teaching craft tend to be rambling accounts of the specifics of teaching (see, for example, Lillard 1980), thereby providing us with neither the analytic knowledge needed to examine specific teaching situations nor any model analyses of such situations. To the extent that craft accounts of teaching are highly personalized descriptions of teaching activity, it is not surprising that educators tend to equate craft with trial-and-error learning.

An interesting exception to this pessimistic assessment of the utility of craft accounts of teaching is Herbert Kohl's *On Teaching*. In part, Kohl's book is useful because he divides up the world of teaching in ways that mirror recurring problems of practice, that is, gathering resources, developing a curriculum theme, setting limits, making transitions, losing control, avoiding fatigue, and so forth. These topics fall under a cluster of activities he labels the "craft of teaching"; the other major division in his book is the "politics of teaching," under which he includes such topics as knowing the school hierarchy, planning change, knowing the community, understanding the goals and strategies of teacher organizations. Kohl's division of teaching activity into recurring problems of practice is consistent with Cohen's observation that "in any craft, *knowledge accumulates around certain critical areas of judgment*" (1977, p. 17).

A second advantage of Kohl's analysis of teaching craft is his tendency to identify and explore issues of practice rather than to prescribe specific resolutions to these issues. This characteristic, which I shall call issue stating, can be illustrated through an example from his discussion of setting limits. In that section, Kohl states his belief that certain classroom rules must be enforced for the sake of group survival, for example, no person (student or teacher) can bully or injure another, and no one can be allowed to prevent others from working. He then deals with a variety of issues involved in implementing limit-setting rules, including when these rules should be introduced to the students, who should assume responsibility for enforcing rules, what alternatives are open to the teacher when students deliberately break rules, and techniques of anticipating and defusing fights and other disruptive acts. What starts out by being the straightforward statement of several rules, therefore, ends up being a relatively complex analysis of the timing for rule introduction, the responsibility for rule enforcement, the sanctions and other possible responses to rule infractions, and the prevention of serious violations of classroom rules.

As Kohl explores the various aspects of setting limits, he follows a general pattern of identifying the issue succinctly and explaining an alternative or two he has used to resolve this issue. However, he generally does not recommend to the reader his particular way(s) of coping with the issue. Indeed, he frequently explains why his approach proved unworkable, as when he once tried to introduce the rules *before* he had explained to his students both how his classroom and his curriculum were to be organized and why certain rules were necessary preconditions to this organizational plan. In the absence of such a rationale for classroom rules "some students became hostile the first day, almost by reflex. I said 'you can't'—their bodies responded 'I will.' These rules became challenges to battle, rather than accepted conditions for mutual survival" (1976, p. 82). For the future, Kohl resolved to provide the explanation about his classroom and curriculum first, then introduce the rules that establish needed limits on classroom behavior.

But Kohl does not go to the next step and prescribe his successful approach for establishing a rationale for classroom rules. Neither does Kohl recommend that the reader adopt the specific rules he believes to be appropriate. Instead, Kohl explains his view of the overall problem of classroom rules, gives his position on which rules he feels are sound, and summarizes his experience with introducing these rules to students. Then he drops the topic and moves on to another aspect of setting limits, thereby implying that the reader will have to think through not only how to introduce the rules to students but also how the problem of rule setting is to be conceptualized. To summarize, issue stating, as I have applied this idea to Kohl's work, involves the identification and exploration of a curricular or teaching issue, including related subissues; the examination of one or more possible ways of resolving this issue; and an invitation for the reader to use Kohl's ideas as a point of orientation, but to realize that she ought to define and resolve the issue herself.

A third characteristic of Kohl's interpretation of teaching involves the synthetic nature of his analysis. On the surface this claim may seem odd because Kohl emphasizes the nuts and bolts of teaching. But these detailed observations are clustered around problems of teaching practice, a characteristic which was noted earlier, and the resultant clusterings are frequently related to a variety of broader considerations. Kohl is explicit about the need to integrate craft and context:

> Survival, the ability to acquire and use political power for humane purposes, and the development of the craft of teaching are themes of this book. It is possible to close the door of one's classroom and concentrate exclusively on work with one's students. It is also possible to become obsessed with politics and forget that teaching well involves more than having decent ideas and struggling for justice. The tension between politics and good practice as a teacher has to be accepted and integrated into one's life. Teaching is serious, difficult work. It has to do with the future, with whom we encourage our young people to be, and ultimately, of course, with who we will be as a nation and as people sharing the earth. It is not simply a job, especially if you question the system you work and live in and set out to change it. (1976, pp. 11–12)

This call in the book's introduction for interrelating craft and context is not just rhetoric; throughout the book Kohl attempts to draw interconnections between the details of teaching craft and broader educational and political goals.

This attempt at integration can be clarified by an example. In Kohl's discussion of the way his feelings and attitudes affect his work with students, he starts by examining some of the specific dynamics of this process. For instance, he looks at such empirical questions as the impact of his moods on his effectiveness with youngsters and the tendency of teachers to praise students who conform to teacher expectations. But he goes beyond these analyses of the connection of teacher affect and student learning to argue for the importance of "openness, naturalness, and closeness" for any teacher who is "serious about remaking this culture and society in a humane and just way" (p. 100). These virtues, however, are hard to achieve, so Kohl tries to help the teacher anticipate some of the problems that are likely to occur as the teacher pursues the attitudes of openness and closeness, for example, the tension between "loving" students and being fair to everyone; the danger of a teacher wanting her students to ˙understand her personal life; and the inappropriateness and ineffectiveness of trying to politicize one's students. In a narrow sense, therefore, Kohl attempts to give the reader some insight into the impact on students of teacher feelings, but he also tries to identify the proper affective relationship a teacher should attempt to establish with students, especially if the teacher values social reform. We must be careful, Kohl concludes, not to bring all of our hang-ups into the classroom because "our job as teachers should be to turn our students on to themselves, to each other, and to all things there are to learn about in the world" (p. 105).

In brief, the synthetic way Kohl portrays teaching entails concurrent attention to the details of craft knowledge and to the interconnection of this knowledge with broader contexts, particularly with political and social goals but also with reform-minded educational stances. After finishing the book, the reader realizes that Kohl is attempting to model his belief that "the tension between politics and good practice as a teacher has to be accepted and integrated into one's life" (pp. 11–12). There are, of course, others who have stayed close to the realities of classroom life but who have also anchored these realities in broader contexts, for example, Dennison (1969), Kozol (1981), McPherson (1972). But Kohl manages—better than most—to move back and forth easily between the details of classroom life and contextual considerations. Kohl's approach is consistent with Cohen (1977) who argues that understanding phenomena in synthetic terms is characteristic of the craft orientation, though Cohen focuses on synthesizing the elements of practice and largely ignores interconnections between practice and the broader social context.

The three characteristics I have abstracted from Kohl's discussion of teaching provide a good case that craft need not be defined as trial-and-error activity. Kohl, for example, organizes his craft knowledge around recurring problems of practice, a clear statement that he does not think that learning to teach from a craft perspective is a random process. Yet Kohl neither prescribes how issues are to be conceptualized nor recommends how they are to be resolved; instead he emphasizes an issue-stating approach that ultimately involves the teacher in determining how issues ought to be construed and resolved. Such an issue-stating approach is not consistent with a trial-and-error conception, unless the teacher were to be given no guidance in the issue-stating process. But Kohl, obviously, does try to provide guidance in the overall process without insisting that his specific ways of dealing with issues be adopted. Lastly, Kohl stresses the synthetic nature of craft activity, including the link between craft and educational and political context. Of course, Kohl's underlying premise that teaching entails extensive interconnections is an implicit argument against picking and choosing one's teaching activities at random.

Keeping in mind Kohl's orientation toward teaching and the earlier comparison of teaching and fishing, I want to return to the question of defining craft. Up to this point I have emphasized the ways in which the craft orientation is not adequately represented by the image of trial and error. It is equally true that craft is not reducible to experiental learning.

Nothing, of course, is learned directly from experience in that "knowledge is always mediated or specified through some form of human activity" (Olson & Bruner 1974, pp. 128–29). However, there is frequently the supposition that craft learning is closely associated with having appropriate experiences and modeling certain aspects of those experiences. For example, student teaching commonly is seen as involving an "apprentice" teacher observing a master teacher so that the novice can imitate competent teaching. If the master teacher goes beyond being a model for the practice teacher and starts to explain and analyze his teaching effort, then many educators contend that we have gone beyond a craft conception of teaching. Explanation, analysis, theoretical evaluations, and other abstract considerations are seen as beyond the scope of craft activity, which is usually assumed to be restricted to the observation and imitation of successful teaching behavior (see, for example, Arnstine 1975; Broudy 1979).

The earlier comparison of fishing and teaching, as well as the subsequent discussion of Kohl's interpretation of teaching craft, suggest that any definition that identifies craft as the observation and modeling of successful teaching behavior is overly restrictive. Craft activity in teaching can involve the ability to conceptualize issues, the application of knowledge to specific situations, and the ability to think synthetically, both internal to craft considerations and between craft and context. Craft activity, therefore, clearly can go beyond observing and imitating skilled practice.

In addition to viewing craft as nothing more than trial-and-error learning based on experience, many people associate craft with manual expertise:

> I guess I am not taken with craft as the best descriptor of teaching. The definition of craft is, of course, crucial and one can make it what one wishes, but when one puts down your paper [Tom 1980c] he will drift toward the street meaning of craft. And that emphasizes manipulative skill, manual expertise. The craft of violin making is hardly nonintellectual, but craft is more often now associated with skilled factory work or hobbies. (Palmer 1980)

I hope that when the reader puts this book aside, she remembers that even the mechanical aspect of craft is not limited to manual expertise. Moreover, the craft of teaching centrally involves intellectually based activities, including the mastery of craft knowledge, the ability to apply craft knowledge to specific situations, and the ability to relate craft considerations to context.

One last concern many educators have about the craft conception of teaching is that this approach encourages thinking that may be both vague and rigid:

> I am a bit concerned. . . about the craft metaphor because I'm wary of the romanticism and obscurantism which often comes to the fore, when people. . . argue against scientism. In fact, I fear this rather more because this attitude tends to make people impervious to evidence which goes against their belief. (Buchmann 1981)

This concern about the obscurantism and rigidity alleged to frequently accompany the craft orientation is by no means restricted to teaching. In alcoholism treatment, Kalb and Propper believe that there is a fundamental difference between the scientific or professional orientation and the craft or nonprofessional orientation. In contrast to the commitment of the scientist/professional to "engage in unique, independent thinking and to critically evaluate the work of one's teachers and peers" (1976, p. 641), the craftsmen/clinicians in alcoholism treatment supposedly validate their theories ideologically; resist the integration of research findings into their clinical treatment ideas; and refuse to question their own premises in light of conflicting evidence. Underlying this resistance to new data and to reconsideration of established ideas is a cognitive style characterized by Kalb and Propper as "intuitive-subjective-deductive" (p. 644).

Respondents to the article by Kalb and Propper note that alcoholism counselors are often flexible and that some of these counselors can carefully and thoughtfully analyze individual cases, choosing the treatment that seems most appropriate to a particular case. One respondent also observes that folk science is not limited to the craft group. He then cites the case of an alcoholic whose analyst felt that if the patient stopped drinking, the real nature of his problems could not be discovered. Subsequently, under the care of a different professional, the patient started taking medication and made good progress in therapy; the patient reported that "psychoanalysis would never have worked for me." This incident, moreover, is neither an isolated one nor is it restricted to alcoholism treatment. Drawing upon a wide variety of evidence, Mahoney (1976a, 1976b) argues that the storybook image of the dispassionate and flexible scientist is largely myth. Rather, the typical scientist may be no better at logical reasoning than other people, may have considerable difficulty in maintaining objectivity, and may have problems altering her views in light of new evidence.

That scientists have difficulty living up to some of the philosophical tenets of modern science is not an earthshaking finding; more interesting is the knowledge that craftsmen are the origin of many of these tenets. Historical evidence presented by Clegg indicates that it was European craftsmen, not academics, who were responsible for several developments key to the evolution of modern science (1979). In particular, these medieval craftsmen originated "the habit of careful observation of isolated problems [and the habit] of experimental testing of both devices and theories" (1979, p. 187). While documenting that medieval craftsmen believed knowledge should be based on observation and experiment (as opposed to the academic conception that knowledge is derived from authorities), Clegg also notes that craft apprenticeship emphasized observation of skillful practice but was not limited to copying such practice and that this careful observation did not end with the apprenticeship.

Not only did craftsmen travel around Europe to learn from one another, but in addition craftsmen prepared journals and other written materials for the instruction of fellow craftsmen, for instance, the notebooks of the French master mason Villard d'Honnecourt and the booklet on kitchen and herb gardening by John Gardener. In the craft manuals, observation was focused on a specific problem of practice such as the structure of a certain type of arch or the cultivation of a particular herb. Moreover, the stress was not on making the craftsman a passive observer of skillful practice so much as it was on preparing him for his own active attempts to solve problems of practice, thereby showing that the craftsman's "activity closely resembled experimental testing" (Clegg 1979, p. 191). Some craftsmen pursued experimentation with a vigor that led to significant inventions in such varied fields as glass making, farming, clock making, and oil-painting technique.

The major theoretical contribution of the European craftsmen involved the use of observation and experiment—referred to as *experience* by the craftsmen—"not only for invention and [technical] improvement, but also in the study of nature" (p. 198). The craftsmen's conception of experience even included the idea of the repeatable controlled experiment. Leonardo da Vinci was among the first to see that the craftsmen's observational and experimental science would ultimately clash with academics' appeal to scholastic books:

> Many will think that they can blame me, alleging that my proofs
> are contrary to the authority of certain men held in great
> reverence by their inexperienced judgements, not considering
> that my works are the issue of simple and plain experience, which
> is the true mistress. (Cited in Clegg 1979, p. 199)

Craftsmen and scientists who committed themselves to the mistress of experience were not only controversial; they were often persecuted. Ironically the central role of craftsmen in the origin of modern science is today "either forgotten or denied, or at best only partially admitted" (p. 200). Bernal, for example, notes that "science...started as a hardly distinguishable aspect of the mystery of the craftsman and the lore of the priest" (1956, p. ix). Hall concedes a somewhat larger role to craftsmen in bringing about the scientific revolution, though he argues that the trial-and-error activities of craftsmen were the "raw material" for the conceptual and theoretical accomplishments of scholars (1959).

That historians of science should pay so little attention to the role of craft in the origin of science is perhaps attributable to the general bias of academics against the craft orientation. Certainly, academics have made few positive comments about craft and craftsmen, especially within the context of teaching. Many scholars have oversimplified craft activity by claiming it is nothing more than trial-and-error learning in which the learner imitates skillful practice. I have tried to illustrate how these two characteristics represent only one aspect of craft activity, whether it be fishing or teaching. Other crafts are also more sophisticated than the trial-and-error and modeling images suggest, for example, basketball (Russell 1979, chap. 2), pottery (Needleman 1979), gardening (Wallace 1980), and hunting (Strung 1982).

By now, I believe I have established that it will not do to define craft as trial-and-error learning nor is it accurate to consider craft as nothing more than modeling. Kohl's discussion of teaching illustrates that craft knowledge can be clustered around problems of practice, can focus on issue stating, and can be synthetic. I have also tried to show that legitimate apprehension about connotations of manual expertise need not prevent us from viewing craft as an intellectual as well as a manipulative activity. Moreover, even though obscurantism and intellectual rigidity may well accompany the craft perspective, this fear is often overdrawn, particularly if we keep in mind the intricacies of craft activity and the central role of craftsmen in the origin of modern science. At the same time, we frequently forget that scientists have trouble living up to the image of the dispassionate and flexible inquirer. Scientists and craftsmen may not be so different after all.

One definition of craft that takes into account the comparison of fishing and teaching, as well as Kohl's analysis, is presented by Popkewitz and Wehlage: "Teaching should be viewed as a craft that includes a reflective approach toward problems, a cultivation of imagination, and a playfulness toward words, relationships, and experiences" (1973, p. 52). Though suggesting a bit of frivolity, this definition does seem to capture the analytic and the synthetic bases of craft. This definition, however, does not explicitly develop the moral basis of teaching, thereby indicating a major shortcoming in the definition. Since the moral foundation of teaching was developed in the prior chapter, I can now relate this foundation to my comparison of the crafts of teaching and fishing.

TEACHING AND FISHING REVISITED

Earlier I claimed that the moral component of fishing is both moderate in size and less central to the activity of fishing than in the case of the moral component of teaching. Now is an appropriate time to return to my assertion that the moral basis of fishing is considerably different from that of teaching.

In a paper several years ago, I stated the differences in the moral bases of teaching and fishing in strong terms:

> But the most dramatic difference between the two crafts is the amoral nature of fishing. Only if one is opposed to the killing of animals is it possible to consider fishing an immoral act. In any case, there is no sense in which the relationship between fisherman and fish may be said to be moral; issues of exploitation and autonomy are meaningless to the master fisherman. Indeed, the

fisherman rarely sees the object of his craft until the fish is
caught. Similarly, fishing entails no necessary movement toward
some more desirable state of affairs. The ultimate purpose of
fishing is to catch fish, an outcome that is both agreed upon and
value-free. There is no grand philosophy of fishing, only
technique. (Tom 1980c, p. 319)

One person criticized my claim that fishing is amoral:

I disagree that there are no philosophies of fishing, only
technique. I think commercial fishermen, for example, have a
different philosophy. There are some constraints built into sport
fishing that are not so unlike those built into teaching and these
involve values which the commercial fisherman doesn't share.
There may even be differences as to which fish are most worthy of
catching, and whether quantity may make up for lack of size, etc.
I think the analogy stretches a good deal further than you realize.
(Schrag 1980)

While Schrag stresses the differing values associated with sport
and commercial fishing, Linzey argues that a direct moral relationship exists between sportsman and animal, not because of the values
which accompany the catching of an animal but because of the rights
of animals:

Man's violation of animal life in this country also extends, with
little legal control and prohibition, to the hunting, coursing,
beagling and shooting of wild animals as well as popular angling
for sport.... I think that it follows clearly from our principle of
the rights of sentient life that needlessly to destroy animals is
immoral. In fact probably the best ethical defense that can be
given to these activities is the fact that they cause some human
beings enjoyment—a disturbing statement in itself. (1976, p. 39)

Certainly Linzey would not agree with my claim that the "issues
of exploitation and autonomy are meaningless to the master
fisherman." Or he might well agree that many fishermen are indeed
insensitive to these issues, contending that this insensitivity is
symptomatic of the moral adolescence of fishermen.

The key phrase in Linzey's analysis is the "rights of sentient life."
The logical extension of the principle that life capable of sensation
has rights is Albert Schweitzer's concept of "reverence for life." For
Schweitzer "ethics...consists in...that I experience the necessity of
practising the same reverence for life toward all will-to-live, as
toward my own. Therein I have already the needed fundamental

principle of morality. It is *good* to maintain and cherish life; it is *evil* to destroy and check life" (1923, p. 254).

The term *responsibility* appears frequently in Schweitzer's thought, especially when he discusses man's treatment of other forms of life, vegetable as well as animal. He urges each person not to unnecessarily violate another's will to live, but rather to make "distinctions only...under the pressure of necessity, as, for example, when it falls to him to decide which of two lives he must sacrifice in order to preserve the other. But all through this series of decisions he...knows that he bears the responsibility for the life which is sacrificed" (Schweitzer 1949, p. 233).

Schweitzer, therefore, cannot be dismissed as a dreamer whose ideas define literally every human action as immoral and thereby make living a moral life impossible. On the contrary, his ethic of reverence for life is tempered by a belief that "one existence survives at the expense of another" (1923, p. 257). More recently Aldo Leopold (1949), the ecologist, has written eloquently of the need to develop an "ethic dealing with man's relation to land and to the animals and plants which grow upon it" (1949, p. 203), while concurrently pursuing a career in conservation which daily forced him to weigh the competing demands of land, plants, game, and man. To extend the moral realm to all of man's environment does not necessarily force man into a continuous string of immoral actions; rather man must behave with great sensitivity toward all of creation.

But Leopold's and Schweitzer's extension of morality beyond mankind to animals, plants, and even the land is today viewed with skepticism by many philosophers. While such philosophers may well sympathize with those thinkers who express concern for all of creation, they usually want to draw the moral boundary at the edge of sentience. "I believe," notes Singer, "that the boundary of sentience—by which I mean the ability to feel, to suffer from anything or to enjoy anything—is not a morally arbitrary boundary.... There is a genuine difficulty in understanding how chopping down a tree can matter *to the tree* if the tree can feel nothing" (1981, p. 123).

According to Rollin, the key role of consciousness or awareness in defining the boundaries of moral concern explains why morality does not extend to all of creation:

> Although plants, bacteria, viruses, and cells in culture are alive and may be said to have needs, there is no reason to believe that they have interests. That is, there is not a shred of evidence that these things have any awareness or consciousness, and consequently, we cannot say that the fulfillment and thwarting of

these needs "matters" to them anymore than getting oil matters
to a car. (1981, p. 42)

Rollin's overall reasoning is similar to Singer's claim that the ability
to feel pain or experience enjoyment determines the border of the
moral arena.

Through Rollin's argument for extending the moral realm to
all entities who have consciousness and Schweitzer's concept of
reverence for all life we can better appreciate why sport fishing can be
viewed as a moral concern. Even if we adopt Rollin's more restrictive
idea that moral concern extends only as far as the limits of consciousness, fish may fall within the realm of the moral. Few fishermen
would deny that a hooked fish behaves as if it feels pain, and there is
research evidence that certain fish can communicate with one another (Bullock 1973; Hopkins 1974). In a more general sense Griffin
argues that there is no qualitative difference in human and animal
communication, though available evidence suggests "a large quantitative difference in complexity of signals and range of intentions"
(1981, p. 169). On the key question of whether animals are aware of
what they are doing, Griffin again opts for a position stressing the
continuity of human and animal life; he believes that it is reasonable to hypothesize a continuum of awareness across humans and
animals. While we do not have conclusive evidence in support of this
hypothesized continuum for human and animal mental experience,
"the available, negative evidence supports at most an agnostic
position" (p. 105). Whether animals are self-conscious, therefore, is
an open question. Since fish do communicate and may have some
level of awareness, it seems reasonable to include fish in the moral
realm—assuming consciousness marks the boundary of the moral.
For Leopold and Schweitzer, of course, the presence of consciousness
in animals is not a precondition for including animals in the moral
realm.

After thinking further about the moral status of animals, I now
consider as simplistic my original assertion that sport fishing is
inherently a technical activity (Tom 1980c, p. 319). While Schrag's
distinction between sport and commercial fishing philosophies does
not seem particularly useful to me, I do believe that a variety of
people have made compelling cases for including animals under the
umbrella of the moral domain. In the end, the human-animal
relationship may be said to be moral primarily for the same reasons
that the teacher-student relationship is moral: both relationships
bring together beings of unequal power yet beings who share the key
characteristic of consciousness. Even more interesting is the similarity of the vocabulary commonly used to analyze the two sets of

relationships: such terms as *autonomy*, *authority*, *responsibility*, and *subject matter* for the teacher-student relationship and such terms as *rights*, *responsibility*, *reverence*, and *consciousness* for the human-animal relationship.

But one term, *subject matter*, is really out of place among the others because this term does not refer to some attribute of a being. The other commonly used terms—for example, responsibility, autonomy, reverence, rights—all suggest some characteristic of a teacher, student, human, or animal. Subject matter, however, introduces an external factor into the teacher-student equation and demonstrates that teaching, unlike fishing, is a triadic relationship. To engage in fishing, all that need be present is a fisherman and hopefully a fish, along with some means (fishing equipment) for bringing these two factors together. Teaching, however, involves more than bringing together a teacher and a student, even if teaching techniques are present to link these two factors. To teach, as I have argued earlier, is to teach certain subject matter, not merely to teach students. The plan for the subject matter to be taught is conventionally called the curriculum, and the first step in curriculum construction—at least in the Tyler tradition—is the selection of objectives.

The selection of objectives is at root a normative process—remember the key role of Tyler's philosophic screen—but this normative process has no equivalent in fishing. The fisherman has no objectives for fish, and he certainly does not consider fishing to be a "process of changing behavior patterns of fish," to paraphrase the definition of education that underlies Tyler's curricular ideas (Tyler 1950, p. 4). Even if we abandon the Tyler rationale and fall back on a less behavioristic conception of education, we still cannot find any similarity between our aspirations for fish and those for students. Adapting Peters' concept of education as "some sorts of processes in which a desirable state of mind develops" (1965, p. 90) to fishing suggests an absurdity not in need of elaborate analysis. No fisherman sees himself as the modifier of fish behavior or the developer of worthwhile learning in fish. In short, there is no analogue in fishing to the moral basis of curriculum in teaching.

To acknowledge the naiveté of my earlier claim that fishing is nothing more than technique is *not* to conclude that the moral bases of fishing and teaching are equal in size. The moral component of teaching includes the attempt to alter the student's state of being in some worthwhile direction as well as the student-teacher relationship; fishing, on the other hand, is moral only in the sense that the fisherman-fish relationship requires the fisherman to decide if he wants to fish for sport.

Not only is the moral component of teaching larger than that of fishing but in addition I believe the moral component of teaching is more central to the activity of teaching than the moral component of fishing is to the activity of fishing. Essentially this contention boils down to the claim that the moral basis of curriculum is more central to teaching than is the fisherman-fish relationship to fishing. At the very root of teaching, as Peters (1965) so clearly points out, is the idea that education involves developing a desirable state of mind. That is, teaching's fundamental purpose entails moral activity. On the other hand, the essence of fishing is potentially broader than the moral relationship between fisherman and fish; the pleasure humans obtain from fishing is also at the heart of the idea of fishing. However, I recognize that some people, including Rollin (1981) and Linzey (1976), would argue that I cannot take pleasure in fishing without concurrently considering the impact of my activity on fish, a perspective that is inherently moral. As a result, a reasonable argument can be made that a moral dimension is at the taproot of both fishing and teaching, though it seems clear to me that the spread of the moral "root system" of teaching is broader than that of fishing.

I conclude, therefore, that the moral basis of fishing does differ from that of teaching, but that the difference is less than I imagined when I contended that "there is no grand philosophy of fishing, only technique" (Tom 1980c, p. 319). As a result of the comparison of the moral aspects of fishing and teaching, I hope I have illustrated that crafts involving a relationship between sentient beings are potentially moral, that the moral component of a craft assumes added complexity when an attempt is made to alter the state of mind of a sentient being, and that it is especially important that any definition of the craft of teaching directly confront the moral component.

CONCLUSION

Earlier I quoted a definition of craft from Popkewitz and Wehlage: "Teaching should be viewed as a craft that includes a reflective approach toward problems, a cultivation of imagination, and a playfulness toward words, relationships, and experiences" (1973, p. 52). This definition seems to highlight the analytic and synthetic bases of such crafts as teaching and fishing, but the definition may not alert the teacher to the moral dimension of her work. While a "reflective approach" might prompt the teacher to be aware of moral concerns based in the teacher-student relationship and in the curriculum, it is possible for reflection to occur in strictly empirical terms. That is, reflection on teaching can focus entirely on technical skill, for example, Hunt's (1976) "reading" of student cues and "flexing" of teaching behavior in response to the perceived cues. One can reflect on teaching from Hunt's perspective without ever raising any normative concerns; indeed, psychologists such as Hunt are prone to avoid such concerns, though there is no doubt that viewing teaching as a problem of "reading" and "flexing" involves the adoption of an analytic attitude toward teaching. Another instance of a reflective teaching perspective that appears to ignore normative issues is "reflective teaching" (Cruickshank & Applegate 1981; Cruickshank et al. 1981). My use of the term *reflection*, however, will stress its normative as well as its empirical orientation, a definition consistent with the work of van Manen (1977).

Any adequate conception of teaching craft must go beyond the empirical element of teaching, yet this conception must not neglect the empirical dimension of the craft. Nor is it wise to imply that craft is nothing more than trial-and-error learning. Other potential oversimplifications of the concept of craft equate it with modeling, manual activity, or rigid and ideological thinking. In contrast to these simplistic attributes, an examination of Kohl's approach to the craft of teaching illustrates that craft knowledge can be clustered around problems of practice, craft orientation can entail issue stating, and craft thinking can involve drawing interconnections between the details of teaching and broader contextual considerations.

The definition to be proposed in the next chapter is rooted in the idea that teaching both is moral and is a craft, i.e., is a moral craft. In addition to defining the moral craft metaphor, I will explore other common metaphors for teaching and briefly compare them to the moral craft metaphor. The teacher image derived from the moral craft metaphor is referred to as the "moral craftsman."

·6·

THE MORAL CRAFT AND OTHER IMAGES OF TEACHING

In the previous two chapters, I have argued that some elements of teaching are moral while other aspects of teaching are craftlike, though not nearly so simplistic as the conventional conception of craft would lead us to believe. It is time now to weld the craft and moral dimensions of teaching together, both to derive a new image of teaching and to compare the adequacy of the moral craft image to other representations of teaching, for example, teaching as an art, teaching as an applied science, and teaching as a craft.

However, before the comparisons among the various conceptions of teaching are made, I examine the concept *metaphor*—roughly defined as suggestive comparisons—and give some examples of commonly used metaphors for teaching and curriculum. In addition, I discuss some potential benefits of employing metaphors to think about teaching and some possible problems of using metaphors for this purpose.

In the discussion of the moral craft metaphor I give considerable attention to why the moral and craft dimensions of this metaphor can be seen as compatible and to the ways that the moral and craft dimensions can reveal aspects of teaching that are potentially in conflict. The moral craft metaphor is defined as "a reflective, diligent, and skillful approach toward the pursuit of desirable ends."

In the section on teaching as an art I examine why teaching is not analogous to a fine art. Foremost among the differences between the fine arts and teaching is the commitment to judging the fine arts by means of aesthetic criteria while teaching ought to be judged through practical and normative criteria. Nevertheless, an effective teacher often employs ideas and techniques derived from the fine arts. As a

120

result, the best role for the fine arts in teaching is not so much to serve as a metaphor for teaching as to be a source of teaching ideas and techniques.

In the section on teaching as an applied science, I examine whether teaching might be considered to be a scientifically based practical art. Most of the discussion focuses on a relatively new approach called information-processing psychology. This cognitively based psychology escapes some of the objections previously raised about behavioral approaches to research on teaching, but significant barriers seem to limit our ability to use information-processing psychology to build an applied science of teaching.

In the last section on teaching as a craft I move from looking at a scientifically based practical art to examining a practical art based on folklore and the accumulated experience of teachers. In such a craft-based practical art, emphasis is given to having the beginning teacher imitate or copy expert practice, often by apprenticing with a master practitioner. This image of craft as imitation is radically different from the conception of craft I developed in the prior two chapters.

To make sure that the analytic-based craft I favor does not become restricted to imitation, I argue that we need to add a moral dimension to the craft perspective. In this way I defend the adequacy of the moral craft metaphor. As a first step toward this conclusion we need to examine the role of metaphors, especially as they are used in education.

A WORD ABOUT METAPHORS IN EDUCATION

To think metaphorically is an alternative to literal thinking. That is, "instead of talking about the thing directly, in its own terms, we talk about one thing 'as if' it were another" (Pratte 1981, p. 310). In the process of talking about one thing as if it were another, we attempt to transfer the meaning associated with the first thing to the other, in order to provide new understanding or perspective on the second thing. This comparative function of metaphor for the purpose of providing insight is perhaps the closest we can come to a widely accepted theory of metaphor (Ortony 1975).

Metaphors abound in the educational literature. In the field of curriculum, for example, Kliebard (1972) suggests there are at least three metaphors: production, growth, and travel. When the curriculum is viewed as a means of production, the student is seen as raw material to be transformed into a useful product under the direction of a skilled technician, the teacher. The teacher carefully specifies the characteristics of the product, and attempts to discover the best means for manufacturing the desired product. Above all, the teacher eliminates waste and maximizes efficiency. In contrast to the industrial perspective of the production metaphor, the growth metaphor employs a gardening perspective. The curriculum is a greenhouse in which each student grows to realize her inherent potential. As a patient gardener, the teacher fosters the development of each student along the lines of her unique needs and is careful not to impose too much external direction on the educational process. The third curriculum metaphor, the travel metaphor, suggests that the curriculum is a path over which the student will travel under the guidance of an experienced and sensitive companion. Each traveler is affected differently by the unfolding adventure, an outcome that is not only inevitable but even desirable. Rather than try to plan how the traveler ought to be changed by the trip, the teacher-guide's task is to plot a journey that will be as rich and meaningful as possible. All three metaphors transfer a rich set of meanings to the field of curriculum.

Although comparing the curriculum with production, growth, or travel does imply new ways of thinking about curricular issues, we must remember that the comparisons developed through these metaphors are suggestive, not conclusively established relationships. The inconclusive state of metaphoric claims occurs because metaphors are typically very compact, leaving much about these claims to our imagination, our past experiences, and our personal ways of using language (Green 1971, p. 59; Ortony 1975, pp. 47–48). For example, some people are content to assert that "teaching is an art" without specifying either what characteristics of art are comparable to teaching or even whether art refers to a fine or practical art (Kazamias 1961). Clearly such a compact metaphor as teaching as an art merits more careful examination if we are to know whether the commonalities implied by this metaphor are defensible, or even just what commonalities are implied.

As a result, we can see that the major virtue of metaphors, their ability to suggest new relations among apparently dissimilar phenomena, can concurrently be their major strength and weakness when applied to education. Metaphors can indeed suggest new perspectives for viewing an established or familiar phenomenon yet may also confuse and obscure our thinking if they are left unexplored. Demonstration of the reasonableness of a metaphor—at least of a metaphor intended as a tool for thought (Sticht 1979)—requires considerably more than stating that metaphor. Hence I am stressing the ways in which the moral craft metaphor is inappropriate as well as the ways in which it provides insight into teaching.

Gowin (1960) believes that when we pursue the analysis of any particular metaphor, ultimately the metaphor will break down. The growth metaphor, for instance, provides a way of viewing the development of the biological organism of the child, but does not help us decide toward what ends the successive stages of the child's growth are to be directed. Should he be encouraged to be an artist? A social worker? A businessman? Remember that it is not possible to develop concurrently all of a child's potentialities and that choices to focus in certain areas are likely to delay if not eliminate the development in others. To teach the child is to make choices about how she should be encouraged to develop, but the growth metaphor envisions a largely passive role for the teacher as the child develops according to her own internal predispositions (see also Black 1944). Besides outlining the shortcomings of the growth metaphor, Gowin (1960) gives other examples of how metaphors break down upon careful examination.

In addition to the tendency for metaphors to break down, Green notes another problem; some well-established metaphors are viewed as though they are literally true. Such metaphors as "hierarchies of needs" or "levels of meaning" no longer seem to us to be problematic, that is, they no longer strike us as metaphorical. The comparisons implied by these metaphors have become so shrouded in custom and habit that either we assume they represent a fundamental truth or they are not even noticed. In any case such taken-for-granted metaphors—Green labels them "dead" metaphors—are "dangerous" because "they frequently obscure useful philosophical questions" by forcing us "to frame our investigations within unnecessary limits" (1971, p. 62). To challenge the constraints imposed on our thinking by a dead metaphor, we need a new metaphor to lead us to re-examine the relationships and assumptions associated with the dead metaphor. If it is true that "we cannot think without the use of metaphor, it is also true that we cannot think well without thinking *about* the metaphors we use" (p. 63).

I believe that the applied science metaphor is a dead metaphor, especially within the community of scholars interested in research on teaching. Many researchers seem to have forgotten that their work is grounded in a metaphor; those who do recall the applied science metaphor rarely bother to defend its appropriateness. I hope that the creation of the moral craft metaphor both stimulates us to reassess the applied science metaphor and enriches our perspective on teaching.

The moral craft metaphor, however, is not necessarily going to be more comprehensive than the applied science metaphor; neither is the reverse likely to be true. The phenomena of education are so rich and diverse that every metaphor is likely to omit much more territory than it highlights. Each metaphor provides a perspective on teaching that may not even overlap the perspectives associated with other metaphors. The key to establishing the adequacy of a teaching metaphor, therefore, is not necessarily the degree of a metaphor's comprehensiveness.

Yet adequacy is not an idle question, for choice must be made from among the many metaphors for teaching. Not only are some metaphors in conflict with one another—as is the case with the craft and applied science metaphors—but, in addition, the researcher and classroom practitioner ought not be guided in their work by so many perspectives that their work becomes excessively fragmented. To determine the relative adequacy of teaching metaphors we might address such questions as: Which metaphors alert the classroom teacher to the perspectives he ought to attend to? Which metaphors lead researchers to conduct significant inquiry? These and similar questions—all of them complex, including a considerable normative component and numerous terms in need of clarification—are at the core of this book.

The nature and function of metaphor in thinking and communication is a much more complex topic than I have hinted at in this brief discussion of educational metaphor (see, for example, Black 1979; Kliebard 1982a). On the one hand I have ignored metaphor's function as a communication tool for interchanging ideas among speakers and listeners and have instead stressed the function of metaphor as a tool for thought, that is, "with the discovery of relationships between seemingly disparate domains and an exploration of the extent to which they can be related" (Sticht 1979, p. 479). However, such an emphasis on the discovery of relationships rather than on their effective communication seems reasonable when we are probing the adequacy of root metaphors in a field of practice. Similarly, the complete omission of literary metaphors is reasonable in light of my purposes.

Perhaps less understandable is my failure to distinguish among such related terms as *metaphor, simile,* and *analogy.* However, in the case of simile and metaphor I find convincing the claim made by Ortony that there is no important cognitive difference between these two forms of comparisons (1975, p. 52). Neither does it appear necessary for my purposes to distinguish between metaphor and analogy, though I concur with Green that metaphors, because of their compactness, are more likely to mislead our thinking than analogies, whose similarities tend to be more explicitly developed (1971, pp. 57–59). The capacity of compact metaphors to mislead our thinking is the basic reason why I have stressed the need to examine in detail the commonalities suggested by a metaphor.

Rather than try to draw fine distinctions between metaphor, simile, and analogy or to ramble over the numerous functions of metaphor, I focus on metaphor's power to propose novel comparisons and to bring to life taken-for-granted comparisons. In addition, I caution that unexamined metaphors have the capacity to confuse as well as to enrich and clarify our understanding and that judgment of the adequacy of metaphors is a complex process. With these potentialities and dangers of metaphors clearly in mind let us proceed with an overview of the moral craft metaphor. One liberty I have taken is to use the terms *image*, *concept*, and *conception* as synonyms for the term *metaphor*, largely to avoid the repetition involved in relying totally on a single word.

TEACHING AS A MORAL CRAFT

To say that teaching ought to be conceived as a moral craft is easy, but it is difficult to accept as a meaningful conjunction of ideas. In part, combining these two ideas seems strange, I suspect, because we tend to associate craft with practical behavior, often resulting in tangible products, while moral brings to mind more grandiose endeavors, usually involving the welfare of other people. How can ceramics, fishing, or carpentry be sensibly connected to religious practice or to other forms of activity commonly associated with the term moral?

Remember, though, that the use of moral is not restricted to judgments concerning right conduct; moral is being viewed in a broader context. Within the term *moral* I am including those social valuational situations in which desirable ends are at issue, both through judgments about what is worthwhile and through evaluations of right conduct. The concept of *moral*, therefore, is not confined to the area of moral education; education itself, I have argued, is fundamentally moral. In essence I have expanded the small domain of the teaching enterprise usually identified as moral to embrace many of the day-to-day activities of teaching, especially those activities involving the student-teacher relationship and the development of the curriculum.

It is precisely these curricular and interpersonal activities that are often associated with the term *craft* when we speak of the craft of teaching, though craft for many people suggests a more arbitrary and random image than that engendered by identifying an activity as moral. Again, however, remember that I have argued that the concept of *craft* need not be restricted to such characteristics as trial-and-error behavior, rigid thinking, modeling behavior, or manual skill. On the contrary, the craft perspective can involve intellectual analysis, experimentation, and systematic thinking, all characteristics reasonably associated with moral, especially when a teacher is concerned with deciding what relationship he ought to establish with his students or determining what subject matter is worthwhile.

The juxtaposition of two apparently dissimilar terms in the moral craft image may not be as strange as first appears. Both terms can refer to a broad set of activities, entail intellectual analysis, and involve uncertainty or debatable conclusions. The major difference concerns the distinctive perspective each term brings to any context to which it is applied. A normative perspective dominates, of course, when the term *moral* is employed, since moral was defined as focusing on desirable ends. On the other hand the term *craft* engenders an empirical perspective, since craft generally involves a question of how to do something. Perhaps the only part of my analysis of teaching craft that transcends empirical concerns is Kohl's (1976) attempt to link the "nuts and bolts" of teaching with political and social goals as well as with reform-minded educational goals. Kohl is concerned not just with how to make this link but also with the importance of the link. Nevertheless, it is fair to conclude that craft is strongly associated with an empirical perspective and moral with a normative perspective.

If the two components of the moral craft metaphor are not incompatible but nevertheless possess differing emphases, then their combination can lead us to see subtleties in a teaching situation not revealed by either a craft or moral perspective by itself. For example, from a strictly craft perspective a teacher might choose a behavior modification approach to classroom management, because this approach tends to reduce the number and severity of classroom discipline problems. However, the moral portion of the moral craft metaphor may cause reconsideration of this choice, especially if the relationship between teacher and students entailed by the use of behavior modification comes into conflict with the type of student-teacher relationship desired by the teacher.

In such a case the teacher would have to weigh carefully the advantages of a workable classroom management system against the importance he attaches to a certain type of student-teacher relationship. Several possibilities might occur to him. Perhaps the behavior modification approach should be abandoned. Or maybe this approach can be altered in order to reduce the disparity between the desired student-teacher relationship and the relationship entailed by the current behavior modification approach. Perhaps the problem with discipline is so serious that for the time being the teacher will tolerate a student-teacher relationship not to his liking. In the end the teacher must either decide to live with the tension underlying this situation or take action to reduce it. This hypothetical example is but one instance of what might happen when a teacher considers the moral craft metaphor in his work.

In addition to illustrating how the moral craft metaphor can reveal some of the subtleties of teaching, the behavior modification example also prompts us to return to the question of defining the combined term *moral craft*. Prior definitions have stressed either the moral or the craft dimension but have not brought the two components together. In Chapter 5 I noted that the Popkewitz and Wehlage definition of craft was promising because it captured the analytic and synthetic bases of craft but that their definition did not necessarily alert the teacher to the moral dimension of her work, even though they stressed a reflective approach to craft. Reflection, I noted, can occur within a strictly technical or empirical perspective, though I personally use the term to refer to a normative as well as an empirical orientation.

Popkewitz and Wehlage conclude that "teaching should be viewed as a craft that includes a reflective approach toward problems, a cultivation of imagination, and a playfulness toward words, relationships, and experiences" (1973, p. 52). To this definition we need to add an explicit concern for the pursuit of desirable ends. Condensing the definition and concurrently adding the moral dimension might lead us to define moral craft as "a reflective approach toward the pursuit of desirable ends." Such a definition seems an improvement of the one proposed by Popkewitz and Wehlage, yet I doubt that most craftsmen would be satisfied with a definition of moral craft that restricted us to being reflective about the pursuit of desirable ends. It is not enough to be able to decide which goals are worthy of pursuit; we also expect a craftsman to persevere in pursuing these goals.

I am not arguing that no teaching occurs unless there is learning. The term *teaching* can indeed be used both in a task and an achievement sense (see, for example, Scheffler 1960, pp. 41–44). For instance, teaching that attempts to achieve student learning (the task sense) but is unsuccessful is no less an instance of teaching than is teaching that successfully reaches its goals (the achievement sense). While the task and achievement uses of teaching do differ about whether teaching can be conceptually distinguished from learning, both uses are based on a common concern: the attempt to get the student to learn something. That is, an intentional conception of teaching underlies both the task and achievement uses of teaching. As I noted in Chapter 4, there is widespread agreement among educators of varied persuasions that teaching is an intentional activity (see, for example, Hirst & Peters 1971, chap. 5; Phillips 1981; Scheffler 1960, pp. 60–63; Stephens 1967, pp. 67–69).

The perseverance inherent in an intentional view of teaching—in either the task or the achievement sense—means that we ought to expect the moral craftsman teacher to skillfully and persistently pursue desirable teaching goals. That is, reflection on what teaching goals ought to be pursued does not really become teaching until these intentions are acted upon in a teaching situation. Our definition of moral craft, therefore, must go beyond specifying a reflective approach toward desirable ends and capture the effort and skill associated with our practical expectations for craftsmen. For that reason, I choose to define moral craft as *a reflective, diligent, and skillful approach toward the pursuit of desirable ends.* Since this metaphor is being applied to teaching, the desirable ends are being pursued within a social environment.

This definition is compatible with either a task or an achievement sense of teaching. Obviously, both senses of teaching should involve reflection on desirable ends if we are to stress the moral dimension of teaching. Whether diligence and skill in the pursuit of these desirable ends entails a task or achievement sense of teaching depends upon the teaching context. If the teaching problem is clear-cut and within the student's intellectual competence, then the achievement sense of teaching is appropriate, assuming the student wants to learn the content involved. On the other hand, if the teaching problem is diffuse, beyond the student's competence, and/or outside the student's interest, then a diligent and skillful approach to teaching may not necessarily result in learning. As the teaching context changes so does our expectation about whether teaching ought to be considered in its task or its achievement sense.

The role of teaching context in helping us determine whether teaching ought to be seen in its task or achievement sense leads us to a more general insight about the interrelation of metaphor and context. "The analogy indicated by a given metaphor," notes Scheffler, "may...be important in one context but not in another" (1960, p. 52). Thus, the growth metaphor, as I noted earlier, breaks down when applied to education because this metaphor suggests no direction for growth other than predispositions internal to the child. Similarly the moral craft metaphor, apparently productive for examining the moral dimension of teaching, is not as useful when applied to fishing because fishing's moral dimension is less pronounced, that is, in fishing there is no equivalent to the curricular basis of morality in teaching. These and other examples indicate that great care must be taken when a metaphor is moved from one context to another. "The transplantation of metaphors may, indeed, be misleading inasmuch as it may blur distinctions vital in the new context though unimportant in the old" (Scheffler 1960, pp. 52–53).

It is because metaphor and context are so intimately related that I earlier proposed two context-related questions to help us judge the adequacy of metaphors. The first of these questions posed the context-metaphor connection directly: Which metaphors help to alert the classroom teacher to the perspectives he ought to attend to? This question is the focal point for much of the discussion in this book.

In this particular section on the moral craft metaphor I have tried to defend the idea that combining the *moral* and *craft* terms into a single metaphor is a reasonable idea, to illustrate how this metaphor can lead the teacher to identify subtle tensions within his own teaching (the behavior modification example), and to propose a specific definition of the moral craft metaphor. This definition identifies the moral craft of teaching as a reflective, diligent, and skillful approach (conducted in a social setting) toward the pursuit of desirable ends. With this elaboration of the moral craft metaphor completed, I want now to turn to several other metaphors to see how adequately these metaphors illuminate the teaching situation.

TEACHING AS AN ART

In contrast to the low regard accorded to craft-oriented metaphors, the "teaching as an art" metaphor has often been held in high esteem. Not only have academics frequently endorsed the teaching-as-art metaphor but in addition educational theorists have made a variety of attempts to apply aesthetic theory to educational phenomena. Among the specific applications proposed by educators are: conceiving of educational evaluation as connoisseurship (Eisner 1977, 1979); experimenting with ways of heightening the artistry of teachers (Rubin 1981); and training teachers to be better performing artists (Rives 1979; Travers 1979). Even a prominent researcher who has devoted his career to applying behavioral science research techniques to the study of educational phenomena believes that scientific findings must be related to an underlying art of teaching (Gage 1978).

While much of the enthusiasm within the educational community for the artistic metaphor is of recent origin, it is possible to find similar interest in the teacher-artist image at least a half century ago. Bagley, for example, argues that teaching can never become an applied science in the strict sense of the term; teaching's closest analogies are not with such technological arts as medicine or engineering but instead with such fine arts as music, painting, and acting. While the teacher-artist might make use of findings from the scientific study of teaching, this application is likely to focus on "the extra-teaching activities, as caring for the health of the learners and measuring their progress" rather than on the techniques of teaching (1930, p. 460). As a result, any technology of teaching is "supplementary rather than central in his [the teacher's] equipment, while quite the opposite is true of the physician and the engineer" (p. 457). Unfortunately, Bagley's penetrating critique of the technological view of teaching is not accompanied by an incisive analysis of the artistic basis of teaching. The artistic essence of teaching is, Bagley notes, "not easy to define," and the best that Bagley can do is to identify certain qualities central to the "sensitive soul" of the artist-teacher (pp. 456, 460). Appreciation, sympathy, and devotion are foremost among these qualities, and they come not so much from pedagogical instruction or from apprenticeship training as from "the forces, no less real but far more subtle, that we refer to as insights and intuitions and inspirations" (p. 460).

Recent discussions of the art of teaching are occasionally more precise than Bagley's description of the sensitive soul's qualities and the origins of these qualities. Eisner suggests that there are at least four senses in which teaching can be considered an art. Teaching can be performed with such "skill and grace that...the experience can be justifiably characterized as aesthetic" (1979, p. 153). Second, teachers, like fine artists, make "judgments based largely on qualities that unfold during the course of action" (p. 154). Third, teaching is an art in the sense that "the teacher's activity is not dominated by prescriptions or routines but is influenced by qualities and contingencies that are unpredicted" (p. 154). And last, teaching is artistic in that "the ends it achieves are often created in process" (p. 154). The themes of aesthetics, improvisation, and creativity explicitly developed by Eisner and hinted at by Bagley are also central to the thinking of other contemporary educational theorists interested in the artistic basis of teaching (see, for example, Arnstine 1970; Dennison 1969; Grumet 1983; Rubin 1981).

There is no doubt, therefore, that similarities exist between the fine arts and teaching; the issue is not whether it is possible to construct an artist-teacher metaphor but rather how productive this metaphor is. To approach the issue of adequacy I will return to one of the questions posed earlier: Which metaphors alert the classroom teacher to the perspectives he ought to attend to?

While a number of significant differences exist between the fine arts and teaching, the most telling difference concerns the distinctive criteria used for judging quality in the fine arts as compared to those employed for evaluating the quality of teaching:

> The serious artist proceeds by making judgments of aesthetic fittingness: how well or interesting things look, sound, and feel, or whether new elements contribute to or detract from what already exists. The art critic proceeds along similar lines; aesthetic standards are preeminent and what a work of art says doesn't count if it isn't aesthetically well presented. (R. A. Smith 1971, p. 567)

In the case of teaching, however, aesthetic judgments and criteria are of secondary importance. The focus in teaching is on the message to be communicated, not on the beauty of the communication effort. If after an instructional episode the student has learned the content, we generally take this mastery as evidence of competent teaching regardless of the aesthetics involved. If, on the other hand, the student did not master the content, then we question whether the teacher's skill and persistence are adequate to the task. No matter how aesthetically pleasing a lecture or a role play might be, we always consider the achievement of learning outcomes or the skill and diligence of the teacher before making a judgment of teaching competence.

Besides the use of differing criteria to judge the quality of teaching and art, there are other important flaws in the teacher-artist metaphor. Ralph Smith (1971) notes that the artist is much less concerned with an audience than is the teacher, an interpretation shared by one painter who states that "the true work of art is an expression of the artist's personal way of looking at the world and at life" (Adler 1972, p. 6). Similarly an actor may give a sensitive performance without being primarily interested in affecting his audience; he plays a role whose fulfillment is the creation of a character's image. In contrast, the teacher is not so much playing a role as performing a function, and this function intertwines him with his audience because he is attempting to alter certain dispositions or ideas held by the audience (Broudy 1974).

This interconnection between teacher and audience leads us to see yet another major distinction between art and teaching; artists enjoy considerably more freedom than teachers. For a teacher to give free reign to creative impulses in expressing a personal way of looking at the world and at life would gloss over ethical issues, not only those involved in the student-teacher relationship but also those concerned with the selection of content. The responsibility of the teacher goes considerably beyond fidelity to an artistic vision; teachers ought not "compose with the special characteristics of their pupils in the way that a painter composes with the qualities of his pigments and canvas" (R. A. Smith 1971, p. 567). The emphasis in the artistic metaphor on personal creativity means that this metaphor is not very useful for alerting us to the moral dimension of teaching.

One last major difference between art and teaching concerns the way the agent and the final product are causally related. "What happens to a canvas or piece of stone can be observed to be the direct outcome of the artist's actions. What happens to a student does not depend on the teacher alone" (R. A. Smith 1971, p. 567). By quoting this assertion I do not mean to claim that an artist's task is merely to impress upon her material an a priori internal vision. Eisner, as well as many other scholars (for example, Black 1944; Collingwood 1950), points out that artistic creativity is an unfolding and not necessarily predictable process in which a creative tension exists between the artist and the medium. Nevertheless, even though artistic material is not wholly passive, it still is reasonable to attribute the artistic product to the artist in a much stronger sense than we can ever attribute student learning to the teacher. For better or worse, people are less tractable than artistic media.

There are several other ways in which the artistic metaphor for teaching might be criticized. Since I consider these minor criticisms, I shall only list the additional differences. First, we expect each aesthetic experience to satisfy us as a whole in itself, while we expect an educational experience to connect to prior as well as to subsequent experiences (Beardsley 1970). Another contrast concerns the fantasy in artistic activity, especially acting, as compared with the "real" nature of teaching in which there are identifiable consequences for the participants; for example, changes in knowledge, character, and attitudes (Broudy 1974). A third difference is that we expect the artist to make an original, creative contribution, while we hold no similar expectation for the teacher, even the master teacher (Black 1944). While these three limitations to the artistic metaphor have merit they are not, in my view, so critical as the four differences analyzed earlier: varying criteria for judging the quality of art and teaching; the artist's lesser concern for the audience than the teacher's; considerable freedom for the artist to express creativity without regard for moral consequences; and the artist's stronger causal link between activity and product.

There are those educators who recognize the power of the objections to the artist-teacher metaphor but still believe that teaching is an art. Some no doubt use teaching as an art as a slogan to justify eliminating pedagogical training, except perhaps during student teaching. According to this view, an artistic teacher's creative powers are God-given and require only time and teaching experience to be drawn out and developed. A prospective teacher who has a knack for teaching and is well-prepared in her subject matter will know what to teach and have imaginative ideas for conveying a subject to students. To believe that teaching is simple if you have subject matter mastery and a talent for teaching underestimates the discipline and effort that goes into becoming an artist. It underplays the difficulties involved in elementary and secondary school teaching and concurrently ignores teaching's moral dimension (Shaplin 1961). In a similar way, Costin and Hewett (1971) argue that to view university-level teaching as an art not amenable to some form of systematic analysis and training is to attribute magical underpinnings to college teaching.

But even if we ignore the sloganeering sense of teaching as an art, and also recognize that there are fundamental flaws in the analogy between the creative arts and teaching, we are still left with another way in which teaching can be considered an art. Teaching, it can be argued, is a *practical* art in that "it is (speaking broadly) an activity, aimed at a goal that defines success, and improvable by rules that do not, however, guarantee success" (Scheffler 1960, p. 71). Viewing teaching as a practical art places teaching with a strange set of bedfellows, for example, cooking, medicine, weather forecasting, gardening, journalism, engineering, coaching, and law.

All of these practical arts activities have fairly clear-cut goals, but obtain their rules for improving practice from dramatically different sources. For such practical arts as medicine and engineering there is an underlying science(s) that helps guide the efforts of practitioners; these practical arts, therefore, are often considered to be applied sciences. Further, these science-based practical arts are accorded professional status, apparently because the underlying scientific knowledge, although it does not guarantee practical success, is seen as empowering the practitioner to understand and explain what she is doing.

At the same time, there are other practical arts that employ factual knowledge not necessarily obtained from systematic scientific inquiry. For example, rules for such practical arts as cooking and coaching come largely from "the heritage of common sense, or folklore, or the accumulated experience of practitioners. Such rules are, often, quite reliable but they are isolated in the sense that they are not clearly related to some theoretical structure of scientific statements" (Scheffler 1960, p. 73). Though helpful to the practitioner, folklore-based rules do not enable her to understand in a general sense what she is doing or to explain why her procedures work. As a result, professional status is not given to such practical arts as cooking and coaching; rather they are often labeled as crafts. The reasoning summarized in this paragraph is the case commonly made to argue that we ought to develop the scientific foundation of the practical art of teaching (see especially Scheffler, 1960, pp. 71–75, but also Gage, 1978, pp. 15–16, though Gage mixes together the fine and the practical arts metaphors).

At this point all I want to note is that conceiving of teaching as a practical art—with either an underlying scientific or craft basis—is so fundamentally different from the fine arts metaphor that objections to the latter cannot be said to apply to the practical arts conception of teaching. The fact that practical arts have a practical goal—ranging from tasty meals to a healthy patient—orients these arts toward the achievement of ends of interest to a particular audience. Unlike a fine artist, a practical artist does not accord preeminence to aesthetic criteria, is concerned about her audience, is not totally free to follow creative inspiration, and is somewhat less able to cause the outcome of her artistic effort.

By now, many will no doubt wonder how I can ignore the creativity and imagination that frequently accompany excellent teaching. Is not Eisner correct when he claims that "teaching can be performed with such skill and grace that, for the student as well as for the teacher, the experience can be justifiably characterized as aesthetic" (1979, p. 153). Of course; but what he does not acknowledge is that such an aesthetic experience becomes teaching only when skill and grace help the teacher pursue certain intentions. Aesthetic experience, at least in teaching, is an instrumental goal, not an end point.

The proper role of the fine arts in teaching, therefore, is not to serve as a metaphor but rather to be a source of ideas that can facilitate the work of the teacher. Among the fine arts, drama seems to be the most promising repository of teaching techniques. Informal experimentation by Rubin (1981) suggests that viewing the lesson as a dramatic vehicle increases student attention and helps illustrate the lesson's relevance. Moreover, he found that the related ability to stage absorbing assignments was useful to teachers, as was the ability to control classroom atmosphere through making teachers more aware of "presence." Also of value to teachers were such creative sensitivities as "reading class mood," anticipating student "turn off," or "injecting stimuli" such as humor or mock competition. Travers (1979) sees promise in developing the classroom personalities of teachers through the study and practice of Stanislavski's ideas. Yet another drama-based approach is demonstrated by a television series developed at the University of South Carolina on "Teaching as a Performing Art" (Rives 1979).

As long as the performing arts and related techniques are used in pursuit of educational goals, I believe it is appropriate to stress the contribution of the fine arts to teaching excellence. What we need to avoid is the suggestion that the fine arts is a reasonable metaphor for teaching or that the arguments used against the fine arts metaphor are also applicable to the practical arts metaphor. A logical next step is to turn to the science-based aspect of the practical arts metaphor, that is, teaching as an applied science.

TEACHING AS AN APPLIED SCIENCE

Earlier I noted that Brophy and Evertson define applied science in teaching as being "specific, data based information that will enable them [administrators and teachers] to diagnose particular situations accurately and follow through with 'treatment' established as effective or at least probably effective in such situations." The data base which will be "applied" to the work of practitioners is to be composed of "dependable relationships between particular situations, particular teacher behavior, and particular student outcomes" (1976, p. ix). As we have seen, educators' commitment to think of teaching as the application of research findings to teaching problems is both strong and long standing. Perhaps the major difference among twentieth-century proponents of the applied science metaphor is that early in the century the enthusiasm for finding laws of teaching was considerable (see, for example, Thorndike 1912), while by the 1930s there was movement toward our current stress on hypotheses that identify "dependable relationships" among variables (see, for example, Freeman 1930). Modern proponents of the applied science metaphor tend to separate the empirical study of teaching from normative issues involved in teaching (see, for example, Brophy 1980, pp. 23–24; Freeman 1938; Gage 1978, p. 93).

Little has resulted from even the modest hypothesis-oriented conception of applied science. Research findings on teaching tend to be inconclusive if not contradictory, narrowly focused on a variable or two, hard to relate to complex practical situations, and so forth. Besides a historical overview of our "ineffective" attempts to identify a research base for effective teaching, I have tried to point out specific weaknesses with contemporary research approaches, namely, performance-based teacher education, the search for effective teaching behaviors, the study of aptitude-treatment interactions, and the model of direct instruction. The inability of researchers on teaching to make significant progress, I have argued, is due to a series of dubious assumptions commonly made by these researchers. First, they have assumed that teaching behavior is directly related to student learning, with influence flowing only in one direction. Second, they have mistakenly viewed teaching as a natural phenomenon whose stability makes possible the identification of enduring regularities and whose "giveness" justifies omitting from inquiry the human purposes that underlie teaching behavior. Third, for any technical problem of instruction they assume a one-best-solution, which is potentially discoverable prior to the act of teaching.

No researchers seriously argue that we currently have an applied science of education in the sense that clusters of confirmed hypotheses are available to guide our teaching efforts, though some researchers come very close to making this claim (see, for example, Brophy 1980; B.O. Smith 1980; Stevens & Rosenshine 1981). The major question for most researchers is whether such an applied science is possible. In recent years many researchers have become disenchanted with the behavioral research approaches that I have analyzed in earlier chapters, and some have abandoned the psychological behaviorism in which most of these behavioral approaches are grounded. Though behaviorally based research on teaching continues to thrive, an alternative, growing out of cognitive psychology, is now available: information-processing psychology. (ATI research, also related to the cognitive tradition, rarely entails any careful exploration of the cognitive processes involved in various interactions; see Resnick 1981, p. 689.)

Rather than imitating attempts by behaviorists to discover laws or dependable relationships among observable variables, information-processing psychologists focus on trying to understand the structure and function of the mind. The key questions for information-processing psychology are: How is the mind built? (structure), and How does the mind operate? (function) (Calfee 1981). The information-processing psychologist may observe behavior to draw inferences about mental processes, "but, in a dramatic departure from behaviorism, the mind, not behavior, is of central interest" (Floden 1981, p. 79).

Since information-processing psychology attempts to understand the mental processes involved in learning, it seems to avoid some of the objections I have already raised to the possibility of an applied science of teaching. For example, information-processing psychologists seem much less likely to assume teaching has a direct impact on learning, largely because of their interest in carefully examining the ways in which such factors as student beliefs and student schemata mediate the learning of content (Floden 1981, pp.

88–89). It is not clear, however, whether information-processing psychology can cope with the bidirectionality of teacher-student influence, since the information-processing perspective focuses largely on the student, especially on understanding how the student's ability to learn from his environment is "constrained by the intrinsic limitation of his ability to process information" (Shulman 1981). As an antidote to the student (and learning) bias of the information-processing perspective, there is an information-processing research tradition that explores the phenomenology of teaching; studies of how teachers experience teaching do indicate that there is wisdom in our commonsense notion that teachers differ substantially in how they interpret and react to a particular student behavior (Shulman 1981, pp. 95–97). It is likely, therefore, that information-processing psychology will be more sensitive than are behavioral approaches both to the bidirectionality of student-teacher influence and to the mediated nature of the teaching-learning process.

Information-processing psychology, however, does seem vulnerable to two of the dubious assumptions associated with behavioral approaches to research on teaching. First, the information-processing approach apparently assumes that the learning process is a natural phenomenon. That is, underlying information-processing psychology there appears to be a belief that ultimately we will find how the mind really works, not only the cognitive processes involved in memory, attention, selective perception, and so forth but also the structures that undergird cognition.

While it is possible that one day we may discover a general model of the mind, progress in this direction is thus far modest. Jenkins argues that we ought not attempt to build a general model of the mind because human beings are "universal machines" that "can become any kind of machine that they need to be in a given situation." As a result "the only work that we can do is to model their behavior in particular situations and particular environments, facing particular kinds of problems" (1981, p. 237). To the extent that Jenkins is correct that we humans adapt our thinking to the requirements of a particular task or environment we are mistaken in our assumption that learning is a natural phenomenon. Rather than existing independent from the teaching-learning situation and therefore being part of our "nature," our information-processing operations may well be constructed by us to deal with whatever situation is at hand. That is, information-processing operations may be adapted to the subject matter at hand, the level of knowledge already possessed by the student, the degree of student confidence with various processing strategies, and so forth. Learning may be a social or human construction no less than is teaching.

A second dubious assumption underlying behavioral approaches also seems relevant to information processing. Information-processing psychologists seem to believe that not only are they going to find out how the mind really works but in addition are going to discover there is a one-best-way to conceptualize the work of the mind. It is unusual for an information-processing psychologist to state the one-best-way assumption directly, but some of them come very close. Calfee, for example, concludes a review of recent studies of teachers' thinking by stating: "An important advance in research and practice in teacher education...would be the development of a simple and coherent framework for classroom teaching: there may be many ways to 'do it' but I suspect that a single conception will suffice for 'thinking about it'" (1981, p. 54). Similarly, Resnick, in commenting about the possibility of a new, cognitively based learning theory, says: "A breakthrough isn't just around the corner, but it certainly is in sight" (Schneider 1981, p. 6). Elsewhere, Resnick and Ford state that they "look forward to a true psychology of instruction, a psychology that explicitly attempts to link processes of learning to the design and conduct of teaching" (1981, p. 253).

As in the case of behavioral conceptions of teaching, there is neither compelling logical argument nor firm empirical evidence for believing that there is a one-best-way for processing material to be learned. Successful learning may well be obtainable through diverse cognitive paths. Even Jenkins' (1981) hypothesis that the mind is situationally adaptable does not necessarily lead to the conclusion that there is a best cognitive approach for each learning situation. There may be a variety of effective ways to adapt one's information-processing operations to any particular situation. Of course, those who want to search for the answer to the one-best-way by which humans process information should not be discouraged from making the attempt, but we ought to maintain a high degree of skepticism until substantial evidence is gathered in support of the one-best-way assumption. Further, even if the search for the secrets of information processing is successful, we still are not justified in employing these processes in teaching situations unless they are linked to learning goals we consider to be desirable (Floden 1981, pp. 85–86).

As a result of measuring information-processing psychology against the dubious assumptions underlying behavioral approaches to the study of teaching, I think it is possible that several of the assumptions also apply to information-processing psychology. In particular, information-processing psychology seems prone to search for the one-best-way by which the mind works, and this approach to psychology also seems to assume that learning is a natural phenomenon. However, information-processing psychology does appear to be much better able to account for the mediated nature of the teaching-learning process than are behavioral approaches, and it may also be more sensitive to the bidirectionality of student-teacher influence. In the end, though, our judgments concerning the relevance of various assumptions to information-processing psychology must be tentative, since this field is relatively young.

As the field matures, the optimism and enthusiasm expressed by many of its proponents may fade, especially if dramatic breakthroughs are not achieved. But even if no breakthroughs are achieved, the study of information-processing psychology still may have considerable impact on teaching. Information-processing psychology may encourage teachers to view their students less as behavers, a legacy of behaviorism, and more as thinkers. "Information-processing psychology restores the mind to humanity, and may eventually restore the pupil's mind in the eyes of the teacher" (Floden 1981, p. 102). But Floden also notes that information processing points to an analogy between computers and man, thereby causing educators to question the free will and human dignity we typically attribute to students. Even though speculation about how the information-processing perspective might affect our notions of students is fascinating, such speculation does take us beyond the realm of considering information-processing psychology as a basis for an applied science of teaching.

It is the generation of specific insights concerning the learning process that would establish information processing as a legitimate applied science of teaching. The previous quote from Resnick and Ford captures the goal of such an applied science of information processing; they note that a "true psychology of instruction" would be one that "explicitly attempts to link processes of learning to the design and conduct of teaching" (1981, p. 253). Though the information-processing literature is substantial and growing rapidly, there are not at this point adequate findings about the process of learning to provide specific guidance for choosing instructional strategies (Floden 1981, pp. 87–90). Whether an applied science rooted in information processing will ever be derived is open to question. Much depends, it seems to me, on whether learning is a natural phenomenon whose essence is stable and can be discovered or whether learning turns out to be a social construction in which the learner adapts his thinking to the task at hand.

Near the end of his philosophically oriented critique of information-processing psychology, Floden suggests that we should not be unduly disappointed if information-processing research fails to provide direction for our educational efforts. He suggests that social science probably makes a greater contribution through "the concepts it introduces and the methods it develops, than through the conclusions it draws" (1981, p. 105). Calfee seems to concur when he states that:

> Modern cognitive psychology may have its greatest impact on education not from empirical findings and microtheories, though these are important, but rather from an emerging set of notions about how to understand complex systems, notions that have resulted from analyses of intelligent thought and the creation of artificial intelligences. (1981, p. 33)

Based on current evidence, Floden and Calfee's expectations for the indirect impact of information-processing psychology seem more realistic than the expectations Resnick and Ford hold for finding direct ties between our knowledge of learning processes and the design and conduct of teaching. (For a general discussion of the impact of basic research on education, see Getzels 1978.) It would seem prudent for Resnick and Ford to rethink their "direct impact" conception of applied science, though such a change would reduce the appeal of the applied science metaphor.

If we return to Scheffler's analysis of a practical art—the starting point for the discussion of the applied science metaphor—we find that Scheffler favors a direct impact conception for science-based practical arts. The "rules" that are to improve the practitioner's performance of a practical art are to be derived from the scientific findings that underlie that art. In the case of the science-based practical art of teaching, these findings should come not only from psychology but also from such disciplines as sociology, anthropology, biology, political science, and economics. Even though Scheffler is careful to observe that the "rules of teaching" do not "exhaustively rule out failure" (1960, p. 71), he nevertheless stresses the potential for scientific findings to affect educational practice (see, also, Scheffler 1956). Komisar (1961) argues that Scheffler has excessive faith in the practical potency of the findings from the sciences underlying education, an interpretation whose validity I attempt to defend in this book.

TEACHING AS A CRAFT

In contrast to practical arts that are scientifically based, certain practical arts—for example, cooking and coaching—develop rules of practice from factual knowledge grounded in "the heritage of common sense, or folklore, or the accumulated experience of practitioners" (Scheffler 1960, p. 73). While many rules for teaching currently are derived from such craftlike sources as common sense and folklore, Scheffler urges us to develop a scientific basis for teaching so that one can increasingly "judge and choose procedures on the basis of theoretical understanding, rather than their mere conformity to cookbook specifications embodied in the lore transmitted by previous generations" (p. 74). Besides portraying a sense of the power and insight associated with scientific knowledge, Scheffler also suggests that craftlike sources of teaching knowledge are rules of thumb unthinkingly copied from prior generations.

This assumption that craft knowledge is composed of oversimplified prescriptions to be religiously copied by the beginning teacher is a widely held view of craft knowledge. In this section I highlight this conception of craft in order to clearly distinguish it from my own interpretations of craft and moral craft in Chapters 4 and 5. After examining a typical characterization of the craft-as-imitation perspective and looking briefly at the related idea of apprenticeship, I compare the results of this analysis with my conceptions of craft and moral craft.

A representative example of viewing craft as imitation is the description by Hartnett and Naish (1980) of the craft perspective in teacher education. They believe that it is possible to examine the professionalization of teachers from four distinctive perspectives, namely, ideological (a closed system of belief), technological (a focus on teaching technique), critical (an emphasis on the moral and empirical complexities of teaching), and craft. The craft perspective, according to Hartnett and Naish, stresses practical experience in the schools using the rationale that this experience provides insight into the interests of the students as well as knowledge of both the means and ends of education. In particular, its advocates see experience-based knowledge as being more practical than theoretical perspectives derived from the academic disciplines.

The conception of craft as imitation is usually viewed as an inadequate perspective for teacher education programming. In the first place, this perspective is basically conservative because past practice is accepted without criticism. Second, the craft perspective may oversimplify educational issues by focusing on the teacher's point of view; the student perspective, for example, may be slighted or be seen only as an object of teacher activity. Third, having more experience may not enlighten the teacher if she does not possess the concepts and ideas necessary to understand the significance of her experience. Fourth, the craft perspective may well be "indifferent to theory which does not grow fairly directly out of practice and hence be indifferent to the basic, intermediate, and even to the applied disciplines" (Hartnett & Naish 1980, p. 267). This litany of criticisms is indeed serious, and similar criticisms have been leveled by a variety of educators at the craft approach and its reliance on experience (see, for example, Brauner 1978; Broudy 1979; P. G. Smith 1973; Zeichner 1982).

The experiential emphasis of the craft-as-imitation approach naturally leads us to use teaching experience to obtain pedagogical expertise. The core of a training program, therefore, is seen as student teaching or internships. Furthermore, from a craft perspective, the emphasis in student teaching is on placing the novice teacher with a master teacher who exemplifies the best in teaching practice. The beginner's placement with a model teacher converts the entire activity into a type of apprenticeship in which "the heart of the training lies in the candidate's efforts to imitate the competent teaching that he has witnessed" (Arnstine 1975, p. 114). This system is sometimes disparaged by referring to it as "mere apprenticeship" (p. 114), a characterization that does little to clarify the concept of apprenticeship but does make one's attitude toward this mode of training clear.

Now, of course, if apprenticeship "merely" involves imitation of good practice, then the apprenticeship approach is difficult to defend as appropriate preparation for the intellectual and moral activity we call teaching. However, to restrict apprenticeship to the modeling of expert practice seems to be an unnecessarily narrow view of apprenticeship. Apprenticeship, in fishing, ceramics, or carpentry as well as in teaching, involves imitation of skilled practice, but it also entails the master craftsman's giving reasons for why she proceeded in a particular way, analyzing the initial trials of the novice, and providing other forms of verbal analysis. Moreover, the novice may quiz the master about a variety of topics associated with learning to teach. Apprenticeship is verbal and analytic just as much as it is modeling skilled performance.

Any overly narrow conception of apprenticeship reflects an underlying conception of craft that is also overly narrow, that is, craft as the imitation of expert practice. The reason that I went into such detail in my earlier comparison of fishing and teaching was to illustrate that a craft typically involves not only technical skill but also analytic knowledge and the ability to apply this analytic knowledge to specific situations. As a result of these analytic characteristics, it is not necessarily true that fishermen and other craftsmen are wedded to past practice, ignore the student perspective, lack concepts needed to analyze experience, or possess the simplistic characteristics often attributed to them. Certainly some craftsmen are rigid and simpleminded, but such craftsmen are generally not blessed with the title of master teacher or master fisherman.

To help ensure that the craftsman maintains a critical attitude toward his work I have added a moral outlook to the craft metaphor. Adding the moral perspective to the craft orientation helps alert us to the desirable ends at issue in teaching. Thus when we employ the moral craft metaphor—defined as a reflective, diligent, and skillful approach toward the pursuit of desirable ends—we have added a concern for desirable ends to craft analysis without losing sight of the need for skillful performance. The moral craft metaphor, therefore, does not reject the idea of skillful performance so much as it places skillful performance in a larger context. Further, the moral craft metaphor does not rule out the use of imitation or modeling to obtain skilled performance, so long as the model is consciously chosen.

The basic distinction between craft as imitation and the moral craft metaphor lies with the inability of the craft-as-imitation metaphor to provide an adequate account of craft activity. To focus teaching or any other craft on copying skilled performance is to vastly oversimplify these crafts and to overemphasize the modeling aspect of apprenticeship. Apprenticeship learning—and any craft conveyed through this form of instruction—needs to be analytic as well as imitative. Moreover, in the case of teaching, we need to supplement empirical analysis by a moral perspective, that is, we need to ground apprenticeship in reflection.

CONCLUSION

This chapter opened with an examination of how metaphors are used in educational thought. By transferring meanings usually associated with noneducational settings to educational settings, metaphors can provoke us into viewing educational phenomena in new ways. I suggested two possible questions whose answers might help us determine the soundness of various teaching metaphors. First, which metaphors alert the classroom teacher to perspectives he ought to attend to? Second, which metaphors lead researchers to conduct significant inquiry?

I examined the moral craft metaphor both to argue that this metaphor is not a combination of incompatible ideas and to illustrate that the differing emphases of the *moral* and *craft* terms can reveal dilemmas in our educational practice. A hypothetical example from classroom discipline illustrated how it can be difficult to concurrently maximize a craft and a moral concern, that is, to efficiently use a behavior modification approach and maintain a particular student-teacher relationship.

A classic case of the inappropriate application of a noneducational metaphor to teaching is the teaching-as-art metaphor. As a result of the dissimilarities between teaching and the fine arts, we should not think of the fine arts as a metaphor for teaching so much as a source of teaching strategies. But there is another arts-oriented metaphor for teaching: teaching as a practical art.

Some practical arts derive their rules for improving practice from an underlying science (or sciences). In this chapter I looked at a cognitively oriented approach labeled information-processing psychology. While the field of information-processing psychology is young and the outcome of its research is unclear, its major contribution may well be to encourage practitioners to take the mental life of students seriously, though few master practitioners ever ignored the life of the mind to the extent recommended by behavioristic psychologists.

In the last section, "teaching as a craft," attention is directed to those practical arts whose rules for improving practice are derived from folklore and the accumulated experience of practitioners. This conception of craft as imitation is radically different from the conception of craft that I developed in the prior two chapters. Certainly craft learning does involve technical skill that often is appropriately learned through imitation of a master craftsman, but craft also entails the mastery of analytic knowledge and the ability to apply this knowledge to specific situations. To accept a craft-as-imitation perspective, therefore, is to accept a simple-minded view of craft and an overly restrictive conception of the teaching-learning relationship entailed by apprenticeship.

Not only is craft as imitation not good craftsmanship but in addition craft perspectives tend to be restricted to empirical concerns. For this reason I have wedded a moral dimension to the craft one, with the result being the moral craft metaphor. This metaphor encourages us to favor a reflective, diligent, and skillful approach toward the pursuit of desirable ends. Such a stance toward teaching is much less like the craft-as-imitation approach described by Hartnett and Naish (1980) than it is like the perspective they label as *critical*, a perspective which stresses the moral as well as the empirical aspects of teaching issues, the importance of reflecting on what purposes education ought to serve, and the need to remember the limitations of current knowledge.

· PART III ·

IMPLICATIONS OF THE MORAL CRAFT METAPHOR

If it is fruitful to consider teaching as a moral craft, then the teacher logically ought to be called a moral craftsman. Immediately several questions come to mind. Assuming that a moral craftsman is a distinct type of teacher, then just what does he do? Is there a knowledge base of technical skills and analytic knowledge that each moral craftsman must master? If so, where is this knowledge base codified? When this knowledge base is applied to problems of teaching practice, is there a one-best-way of acting out one's role as a moral craftsman or are there many ways to fulfill one's responsibilities?

Before I begin to address these kinds of questions in the next two chapters I want to caution anyone interested in implementing the moral craft metaphor, partly because of my own limited experience in attempting to implement this metaphor and partly because of the complexities of teaching practice. I have found it hard to move from the abstract moral craft metaphor to the concrete realities of day-to-day teaching. There are at least four difficulties: the relatively recent derivation of this metaphor; the difficulty of using a "root metaphor" to prescribe specific courses of action; the tendency of teaching to develop an internal dynamic that resists theoretical ideas not consonant with this dynamic; and the difficulty in using my practical experience with the moral craft metaphor to draw conclusions someone else will find useful. Each of these issues is treated briefly to show the complications it presents for deriving practical implications from the moral craft metaphor.

Since I have only recently developed the moral craft metaphor from professional reading and from reflection on my own personal experience, I have not had much opportunity to try to use this metaphor to guide my day-to-day work with prospective and practicing teachers. Much of this book is an attempt to critique the applied science metaphor, especially its behavioristic version, that currently dominates educational thought, and to provide both a rationale for my moral craft metaphor and a rough idea of the components of this alternative metaphor. Nevertheless, I did engage in a variety of practical efforts while developing the idea of the moral craft metaphor; therefore, I can speak about the interrelationship between this evolving metaphor and educational practice.

But the task of deriving practical implications from the abstraction labeled *moral craft* raises a second caution. Bluntly stated, we must ask ourselves whether we can aspire to determine a practical course of action by appealing to a metaphor. Black (1944) forcefully argues against this expectation. He notes that many of our most influential educational theorists have used a single persuasive analogy—a "root metaphor" in his terms—around which to organize their educational thought. In particular he cites the use by Rousseau, Pestalozzi, and others of an analogy between the child and a natural biological organism. But this "child as biological organism" (or any other metaphor for the child) cannot tell educators exactly what to do in specific teaching situations:

> Too much must not be expected of the first principles of education, as of those of any other study. If they promote a preliminary organization of intentions (as the creation of an electric field facilitates motion along the established lines of force), they will have done all that can reasonably be expected of principles of the highest generality. (Black 1944, p. 290)

Others who have explored the relationship between the first principles or basic research in education and the practice of that field tend to agree with Black that the relationship is indirect (see Broudy 1976; Clifford 1973; Dewey 1929b; Glass 1971; James 1902, chap. 1; Kliebard 1982a). Yet this relationship can be potent. Basic research can lead to altered perceptions of the operation of the schools (Getzels 1978), and the acceptance by psychologists of certain root metaphors for human nature has channeled the practice of psychological research in directions compatible with these metaphors (Allport 1960, chap. 4).

That the first principles or root metaphors of a field of human study have a potent but indirect impact on practice is captured by Black's claim that such principles "promote a preliminary organization of intentions." As a result, it is reasonable to expect "that theoretic knowledge is unlikely to become practically useful except through the judgment, skill, and experience of the practitioner who applies the general concepts to the particular circumstance" (Getzels 1978, p. 517). Not everyone is happy with this state of affairs. Arguing from an applied science perspective, Glass complains that "metaphors are too inexact to serve as reliable guides to practice" (1971, p. 26) and that teachers are both resistant to basic research and prone to distort its meaning as they convert it into practice. As a result, he believes that educational research findings need to be embedded in books, curriculum materials, school architecture, and so forth, in order that "the behavior of schoolmen can be subtly shaped by rationally designed instruments of education" (p. 28). Thus Glass, an applied science proponent, shares a belief in the indirect impact of metaphors with Broudy, Dewey, Getzels, and others who rely more on the wisdom of practitioners than on the manipulation of practitioners by "rationally designed instruments of education."

There is a third difficulty facing me when I attempt to derive implications for practice from the moral craft metaphor. Teaching is not a form of practice under the firm control of the practitioner. Rather, teaching involves interaction between teacher and student in at least two different ways. In the most straightforward sense, the teacher tries to adapt her teaching tactics to whatever instructional problems she observes in the student. In turn, the student attempts to adapt his learning efforts to the tactics employed by the teacher. Teaching, therefore, is interactive in that it involves an unending string of attempts by teacher and student to adapt to each other's activities, though, of course, either party may choose to limit these adaptive efforts. This mutually adaptive form of interaction assumes that the teacher has certain preconceived goals toward which she is trying to move the student. Teaching may also be interactive in a second sense, namely, that "the ends it achieves are often created in process.... Teaching is a form of human action in which many of the ends achieved are emergent—that is to say, found in the course of interaction with students rather than preconceived and efficiently attained" (Eisner 1979, p. 154). This creation of teaching ends during the process of teaching involves interaction in the derivation of ends, while the mutual adaptation to one another's activities focuses interaction on the efficient achievement of preconceived ends. Of course, a whole variety of forces outside the classroom affects the ends and techniques of teaching and might therefore be said to "interact" with the teacher's efforts in the classroom.

All of these forms of interaction, as I noted when I introduced the topic of interaction in Chapter 2, tend to reduce the extent to which the teacher is in control of teaching practice. Teaching practice is less like a garden whose vegetables, planting schedule, and harvest time are largely determined by the gardener than it is like a baseball team whose strategy is influenced as much by the activities of the opposing team and the structure of the ballpark as it is the preferences of the manager. Teaching practice, I am suggesting, develops an internal dynamic of its own rather than simply being the product of teacher planning and decisions. As a result, the teacher employing the moral craft metaphor, or any other theoretical idea, is seeking to apply the idea to a moving target. Unless the theoretical idea is in tune with the internal dynamic of ongoing teaching practice—in all its interactions—then the hope of converting this idea into practice may be frustrated. Thus, even though teaching is a social construction and should apparently be quite amenable to reconstruction, in reality any attempt at reconstruction through the application of a theoretical idea to practice will have to cope with a complex system of ongoing interactions.

Of course, the theoretical idea, if it is a potent one, may be able to transform the way in which the teacher views and participates in the ongoing interactions. But limitations remain. Students will continue to act in light of their perceptions of the teaching situation. Moreover, one's colleagues may not be affected by the theoretical idea, a development of particular importance if team teaching or other forms of cooperation are employed. In addition we must remember that outside the classroom there are forces whose impact on teaching practice will persist, for example, legal mandates, community pressures, faculty norms, and so forth. In the end, a theoretical idea, even a potent one, may be inundated by a swirl of interactions.

A fourth problem involves my difficulty in knowing how to communicate to the reader what I believe I have learned from trying to implement the moral craft metaphor (or earlier versions of this idea). One option for me is to follow the lead of some recent researchers who have studied teaching through intensive case studies of a single class or of a small number of classes, most often by using participant-observation methodology. The outcome of such inquiries based on anthropological methods is not so much generalizations that might be appropriate across varied teaching situations as it is detailed "accounts of participants' interpretations in specific situations" and "explications of the assumptions that underlie these interpretations" (Bellack 1981, p. 69). These accounts, of course, cannot yield precise rules for practice, but they can alert the practitioner to how the participants in one situation construed and acted upon particular educational ideas.

Upon reflection, I have three reasons for not employing a participant-observer style of inquiry to examine my attempts at implementing the moral craft metaphor. First, my own experience as a practitioner convinces me that the key to wise action in a practical situation is not so much awareness of all the intricacies of the situation as it is the ability to know those aspects of a situation to attend to and those to ignore. Therefore, detailed accounts of practical action are as likely to be confusing and mystifying as enlightening, at least in so far as the purpose of these accounts is to help the reader identify those aspects of a situation to which attention ought to be given. Second, regardless of how a clinical effort turns out, I usually have an after-the-fact feeling that a number of avenues might have been pursued to arrive at the same outcome. That is, there is no more likely to be a one-best-way for implementing the moral craft metaphor than there is a one-best-way of effective teaching. The participant-observer approach, however, emphasizes the course of events actually pursued and the dynamics of this pursuit rather than attending to alternative courses of action, even though these alternatives may have been very seriously considered. In short, participant-observer methodology tends to take the "realities" of a situation too seriously, thereby suggesting a deeper logic in practical affairs than indeed is the case. Third, I often have trouble occupying a participant-observer role in that I usually am a central participant in the situation under study. Often I am responsible for grading other participants. As a result, many sources of data are closed off to me or filtered to take into account my status in the situation. Besides limiting access to "objective" data, my central role in the practical situations I am studying means that I rarely have the time or energy to conduct the interviews, take the field notes, and do the other forms of data gathering needed to construct detailed case studies.

The theoretical and pragmatic reasons mentioned here for not employing the participant-observer methodology to construct case studies should not blind us to one great advantage of this style of research. The detailed accounts that result from this research style give credibility to whatever interpretations are developed because the data cited illustrate that the researcher has observed the practical problems that daily face us. Anyone sensible enough to study the real world of practical events, we conclude, is not subject to the degree of naiveté of those who generalize about classroom events on the basis of experimental studies, especially when these studies focus on one or two variables or are done in highly controlled settings. This surface credibility of participant-observer studies, however, should not blind us to the real problems involved in generalizing from a participant-observer data base (Wehlage 1981b).

I want to be very clear that I do not aspire to generalize from my experience in the sense of identifying regularities one can expect when attempting to implement the moral craft metaphor. For now the needed research base is not available, a problem that faces most forms of research on schooling (Wehlage 1981b). As a result, many of the questions posed at the beginning of this introduction to Part III must be answered, at least for the present, in the negative, or answered with that old reliable phrase, "I don't know." In particular, there is no established knowledge base of technical skills and analytic knowledge each moral craftsman must master, a condition that suggests the need to explore a variety of ways of applying the moral craft metaphor to teaching.

What I think is reasonable is that I recount some of my key experiences with practical efforts based on the moral craft metaphor. The descriptions of these efforts will be more on the order of case examples than full-fledged case studies; I will provide detail and interpretation only for those aspects of my experience I believe deserve to be highlighted. The reader, then, may critically review my account to see if my insights can be transferred by analogy to other teaching contexts.

Wehlage identifies this approach as generalizing by analogy and notes that it differs from conventional approaches to generalization because the reader not the writer does the generalizing: "The task falls to the reader to be on the lookout for analogous situations in which insights can be applied. The use of the case as an analogy carries with it no rigorous logic of probability or deduction. . . . It is up to the consumer to decide what aspects of the case apply in new contexts" (1981b, p. 216). As the reader generalizes I urge her to keep in mind the cautions I raised earlier in this introduction about moving from the abstract moral craft metaphor to implications for daily practice.

As I deal with the practical implications of the moral craft metaphor, I will break this discussion into two sections. In Chapter 7, Working with Teachers, I examine how the moral craft metaphor can inform the work of someone who works directly with teachers on the improvement of classroom teaching. My experience with three forms of direct involvement with teachers is discussed: in-service teacher education, preservice teacher education, and supervision of classroom teaching. Emphasis is given not only to how the moral craft metaphor helped me preliminarily organize my intentions but also to other factors that affected my work in each of these three areas. I use case examples to help the reader attempt to generalize by analogy.

Chapter 8, Regulating and Studying Teaching, focuses on the guidance that the moral craft metaphor can provide for research on teaching and for policy issues related to the improvement of teaching. In particular, I analyze how the moral craft metaphor led me to question the validity of the standards of the National Council for Accreditation of Teacher Education, and I also discuss the extent to which this metaphor helped me formulate an alternate set of standards. The last part of the chapter looks at research on teaching and how current research strategies might be reformulated to make them more consistent with a moral craft perspective. Special attention is given to the need for inquiry that will help teachers be more reflective about their daily work.

·7·

WORKING WITH TEACHERS

This chapter is designed to illustrate how the moral craft metaphor can inform the work of those who see themselves as helpers of teachers. Such helpers may occupy a variety of roles, including school building administrator, college professor, department head, teacher center staff member, supervisor of instruction, central office personnel, fellow teacher. An experienced teacher himself may well be the best person to reflect on how the moral craft metaphor applies to his daily activities. It is ironic that in a profession committed to helping youngsters become autonomous adults so little concern is given to the self-development of the professional. Be that as it may, I am grouping together efforts at self-help with those efforts involving a helper. What unites the vast array of helping and self-help efforts is that all of them focus on a common function: the improvement of teaching. Further, all of these efforts require direct contact with or self-confrontation by teachers.

To illustrate how the moral craft metaphor can lead those who help teachers improve their instruction to a "preliminary organization of intentions," this chapter will provide three examples of my own use of the moral craft metaphor. These examples are drawn from three types of helping activities: in-service teacher education, pre-service teacher education, and direct supervision of classroom instruction. The purpose of all three of these activities is to improve teaching, and each activity involves direct contact between a helper and a teacher or a teacher's self-confrontation with his own teaching ideas.

In the first part of the chapter I relate the moral craft metaphor to the Master's Project, the last course in a degree program for experienced teachers. The moral craft metaphor enters into the Master's Project largely at the point of writing up the project experience, especially the section I call *analysis*. Considerable attention is given to instances of analysis to illustrate how analysis can have both a moral and a craft dimension. I also discuss how my approach to the Master's Project goes beyond the moral craft metaphor to take into account other considerations.

To illustrate how the moral craft metaphor can be applied to preservice teacher education, I discuss the evolution of the secondary professional semester, especially my attempt in 1981 to ground the content and structure of this semester in the moral craft metaphor. The majority of the 1981 professional semester syllabus is reproduced (see the Appendix), and I briefly examine how elements of this syllabus relate to the moral craft metaphor. But I also discuss why syllabus-based teaching is an incomplete instructional approach for beginning teachers and the difficulties a professional semester faculty can have in agreeing on a metaphorical basis for its curriculum.

The last example of relating the moral craft metaphor to helping activities involves my work in classroom supervision. After giving some background on my supervisory experience, I discuss several key points in my career as a supervisor, partly to show the intellectual origins of the moral craft metaphor and partly to show how the developing idea of the moral craft metaphor affected my work as a supervisor. Since I never have been very successful at introducing the moral perspective into classroom supervision, I finally came to believe that supervision by itself is too weak an intervention to direct teacher attention to the moral dimension. I conclude my discussion of supervision by attempting to describe several structural interventions that might make it possible to address the moral perspective through classroom supervision, especially in preservice programs.

THE MASTER'S PROJECT

Before I describe the Master's Project as an example of the use of the moral craft metaphor with in-service education, I need to provide some background about the program for which the project is the culminating experience. In the mid-1970s Washington University and Maryville College initiated a Master of Arts in Education in the Teaching-Learning Process, a program in which the students were to take half of the courses at each institution. The split structure is not the only way in which the program varies from conventional in-service programs; another difference is that only two of the ten courses are required: the Teacher as Learner (an introductory course) and the Master's Project.

The rationale for giving the experienced teacher an active role in the formulation and direction of her own program was twofold. On the one hand, a teacher ought to engage in a self-directed program experience because the program developers want the teacher to model this orientation with her own students. We assumed that a teacher who took considerable responsibility for her own education would be prone to encourage her students to do the same. On the other hand, designing one's own program, we assumed, would lead the teacher to become an active agent who establishes professional goals, explores alternatives, makes decisions, and reflects on the consequences of these decisions in light of original goals. This exploratory and purposeful behavior is what we believed a teacher needs to steer a steady course through the maze of contemporary educational issues. In summary, "the self-directed teacher can be both a model for her students and a problem solver of educational issues" (Finch & Tom 1978, pp. 3–4).

Having the teacher select most of the courses in her program makes self-direction possible, but we believed that many teachers— subject in the past to totally prescribed programs—were not necessarily prepared to move directly into an open-ended program. To make the best possible use of an open-ended structure, a teacher needs considerable insight into her own strengths and weaknesses (so she can make wise choices among courses), and she needs an overview of today's pressing educational issues (so she can break out of her own encapsulated job).

Thus was born the idea for the Teacher as Learner course, the introductory, required course in the Teaching-Learning Process program. This course was to have two major objectives: helping the teacher assess her strengths and weaknesses and expanding the teacher's horizon beyond her professional niche. To address the latter goal, the instructor of the Teacher as Learner course employs a series of guest speakers from a variety of school and other settings. Each speaker presents the currents shaping his own area of interest and places these developments within the context of contemporary education. In this way we attempt to expand the view of the experienced teacher beyond the boundaries of her professional role.

Along with this series of presentations, the other major objective of the course is implemented. This objective is a personal assessment of the individual's strengths and weaknesses and of her ability to set and achieve short- and long-range goals. The personal assessment objective is implemented through a variety of exercises designed to develop a heightened consciousness of the student's areas of strength as well as the areas that require more growth. The culmination of the Teacher as Learner course is a goal-setting exercise focusing on professional growth goals for the next five years. The teacher, in view of her assessed strengths and weaknesses, decides who and where she wants to be in five years' time.

Once a teacher makes specific decisions about her professional future, planning the remaining credit hours of her graduate program should be relatively straightforward. Courses, workshops, and seminars from both institutions are selected on the basis of the projected goals. A teacher's five-year plan, of course, may change, either as a result of experiences during the program or as a result of an evolving sense of professional identity.

Near the end of the Teaching-Learning Process program comes the second required course: the Master's Project. This project is the other major attempt to structure a self-directed program. However, unlike the Teacher as Learner course where the emphasis is on exposing the teacher to new perspectives and helping the teacher assess new directions for professional development, the Master's Project experience tries to provide closure for the teacher participant. The teacher is supposed to identify a project related to her work situation, and the overall purpose of the project is to encourage the teacher to synthesize the experiences she has had in the Teaching-Learning Process program with her job responsibilities. Typical project topics include: developing a drug education program for sixth graders; researching and writing up discipline guidelines for beginning teachers; creating a questioning guide to accompany a selected list of children's literature books; and developing a one semester psychology course with correlated individualized learning activities.

A general problem-solving model is used to guide the teacher's approach to a Master's project. (See Finch & Tom 1978 for an early version of the guidelines used to help the teacher participant think through her project experience.) The first step is to identify a problem in one's own work setting and to prepare a written proposal for the project instructor (each semester one university instructor works with all students doing projects). The proposal, one or two pages in length, is to explain why the teacher is interested in a particular project, to describe how the project is related to the teacher's job situation, to list specific objectives for the project, and to outline the nature of the final write-up of the project experience. The Master's Project instructor, then, either accepts, rejects, or suggests modifications in the project proposal. The project instructor's reactions can be directed at the topic of the project, the proposed project activity (as revealed in the project objectives), or the proposed content of the paper in which the project is to be summarized and evaluated.

My own experience as a project instructor, a role I have played every summer session since 1977, suggests that the initial reaction by the project instructor to a teacher's project proposal is critical to the ultimate success of the Master's Project. Frequently a teacher takes any questioning of his project proposal as implied criticism. As a result, I try to convey a sense that I can work inside the teacher's perspective. To illustrate this accepting tone, I quote from my current project guidelines:

> In past summers a few people have been concerned that I might not approve of the topic they are interested in. Let me assure you that I reject very few topics, because I believe that you are better able than I to select a job-related topic. I view my role as a friendly outsider who is trying to help you do the best possible job with the topic you have selected. As a result, I will react to your project proposal by requesting clarification of ambiguous points, by suggesting alternative ways of approaching your topic, by urging you to limit your effort if I feel your plans are too ambitious, or by making other comments/suggestions which I believe may improve the quality of your project.
>
> The only criterion I use when deciding whether to accept/reject a project topic is whether the project involves creative effort on your part. For example, a project in which you propose gathering a large amount of teaching materials for future use is likely to be rejected because no creative effort is involved, unless of course you plan to organize these materials for teaching purposes, develop specific teaching plans, and so forth. Adaptation of already existing teaching materials to your particular teaching situation is a legitimate project topic.

But my acceptance of most proposal topics does not mean that I am uninterested in the substance of these proposals. On the contrary, I am explicit in the project guidelines that the final write-up of a project must emphasize what I term *analysis*. Again to quote from my current project guidelines:

> In any project you would, of course, have an obvious final product, e.g., certain curriculum materials if you are developing a curriculum unit, the results of a survey if you are conducting a survey, and so forth. In addition to this "obvious" part of a final product, you also need to include in your Master's paper certain types of analysis, e.g., an assessment of whether you reached your objectives, a description and critical analysis of any problems (foreseen or unforeseen) which developed as you carried out your project, an analysis of what you would do differently if you were to do a similar project again, a discussion of what you

plan to do with the results of your project. *The reason that you are expected to go beyond the "obvious" final product is because the overall purpose of the project is to have you apply the inquiry and reflective skills you have learned in the Teaching-Learning Process Program to on-the-job responsibilities.*

The types of analysis noted in the guidelines are largely empirical; they stress issues of curriculum planning and evaluation.

As I work with teachers during the summer project experience I extend the concept of analysis to include more personal questions, questions that raise normative as well as empirical concerns. Among the personal reaction questions I introduce during an orientation session devoted to analysis are the following: What did you learn from this experience? Do you consider your project to be worth the effort you gave to it? What assumptions (about your students, yourself, or the topic of your project) are you making and what is your assessment at the end of the project of the validity of these assumptions? As I introduce these questions and give examples of how teachers have addressed the questions previously, I stress that I am interested in an analytical perspective that is normative as well as empirical.

I also emphasize that in evaluating the projects, I attend to the quality of the analysis as much or more than I do to the finished product itself, that is, the curriculum materials, a plan for a new classroom structure, or whatever tangible outcome results from the project. Returning again to my current project guidelines, I quote from the section on evaluating a project to illustrate the importance I attach to the analysis of the project experience:

> What I try to do is obtain an agreement—a contract—with you as to exactly what you are going to hand in at the end of the project experience. Then I concentrate my evaluation on whether you deliver what we agreed on.
>
> Above all I am interested in your ability to analyze the project experience. I am interested in your ability to analyze your project experience because I consider such an analysis to be consistent with the reflective skills which we are trying to develop through the Teaching-Learning Process program.... The "A" grade is reserved to a Master's paper that not only fulfills the contract but also contains a first-rate analysis.

In this way I attempt to establish the importance I attribute to the analysis.

Before I discuss the extent to which I believe I have been successful in encouraging the development of first-rate analyses, I want to quote extracts from several analyses. The first extract is by an intermediate teacher who was reassigned to kindergarten and wanted to develop a science program for five-year-olds:

> Looking back over my freshly completed project, I can sense a strong feeling of personal satisfaction and accomplishment. It was my intention to develop a series of learning activities which would introduce kindergarten students to the elementary concepts of science, while at the same time developing and strengthening their oral language skills. I feel I have succeeded in reaching these goals....
>
> Prior to my efforts on this project, I had felt somewhat fearful of approaching science as part of my kindergarten program. This fear of teaching science was undoubtedly a result of lack of experience as well as lack of self-confidence in the subject area. During my first year of teaching at the kindergarten level, I realized that children at this developmental stage felt no fear whatsoever towards their environment nor the lessons to be learned from exploring the world around them. My fears alone were standing in the way of progress as far as a science curriculum was concerned. Realizing now that the fear of science felt by myself was not shared by the children made the pursuit of this project a rational idea....
>
> I feel my interest in this subject area will be encouraged even further after I have begun to utilize it in the classroom. The major problem I encountered and found frustrating in doing my project resulted in the lack of a classroom with students to field test my ideas. I am left with only speculations as to how a class will react to the units I have developed. I'm sure if there had been an opportunity to field test my ideas, I would be better equipped to analyze my project.

A second extract, also a curriculum development effort, focused on a plan developed by an eighth-grade American history teacher to let a small number of her students do independent research on topics related to local and regional history:

> In the beginning, the students selected for the pilot project needed a great deal of encouragement to initiate and develop ideas, especially when they deviated from past notions of what a project ought to be—either a report or a model. This was probably a result of years of insisting on conformity and squelching creativity, an attitude not totally peculiar to Catholic schools. As the pilot program progressed, it became evident that some students lacked certain study skills and many were uncertain of what constituted an acceptable end product and how the products could be shared.

These deficiencies were too important to treat lightly. Resulting changes included establishing a whole-class project to teach/reinforce/review research skills, developing a list of possible kinds of acceptable end products, and fostering the ideal of thinking creatively *about something....*

Student reaction to the project was good. Only a limited number of replies have been returned for the student evaluation questionnaire, but they, plus conversations with students, indicate that the students liked the free time, the field trip, and the size of the group. They were uncomfortable with their uncertainty about acceptable end products in the beginning, but were far less concerned with the amount of time I spent with them than I was!

The pilot was a success from my point of view. The students studied areas on their own for which we could not afford more than minimal class time. The random learning of research skills will be refined with the revised program. Motivation and interest were high. Ideas for further modification and uses of the revised program are already surfacing. The library field trip described in the whole-class project will be in cooperation with our English teacher, who plans to work with the eighth grade early in the year on note-taking, outlining, and correct preparation of term papers and reports. This slight modification should reduce the amount of class time I must spend teaching process skills.

A third extract, again from a curriculum effort, is by a teacher who developed alcohol education materials for her sixth graders. In addressing the question of what she had learned from her project experiences, she stated:

My answer is three-fold. First, I learned a wealth of information on a subject and its inherent problems, about which I have been totally unaware. The process of alcohol-abuse prevention is continuous; therefore, a uniform program throughout a student's education is important.

Second, after examining past drug education programs in my own school district and in other districts, I found them to be irrelevant to today's alcohol-abuse problems....

The third aspect of my own education concerning the planning and teaching of an alcohol education program is that I have become emotionally sensitive toward the subject. Students who have an alcoholic in their family are having to cope with a serious problem at home. For such students, who tend to have emotional problems and conflicts, compassion is in order....

In conclusion, I have thoroughly enjoyed developing this program and look forward to implementing it during the coming school year. It is by no means finished; I plan to continue to update and add materials frequently.

This teacher concluded her analysis by saying that "as a result of my work on this project, I have contemplated becoming further involved in the field of alcohol education."

The three samples are from analyses I consider to be good ones, but the extracts are by no means atypical. It is common for teachers to reflect on ways the Master's Project stimulates them to improve their teaching craft, as the American history teacher did when she analyzed how she could improve the structure and operation of the independent research projects when she used the project approach next year. It is somewhat less common for a teacher to probe her personal reactions to the project experiences, as the kindergarten teacher did in some detail and the sixth-grade teacher did briefly. These personal reactions involve not only the craft elements of teaching but also upon occasion focus on the moral dimension of teaching.

Instances of analysis related to the moral dimension of teaching do not so much focus on the topic of the student-teacher relationship as they do on the question of what curricular content is worth mastering. For example, the kindergarten teacher indirectly discussed her relationship with the students when she noted that her assumption that her students feared science was a mistaken assumption; in the end she decided that it was she who was insecure about her ability to handle science instruction with very young children. But more important to the kindergarten teacher than her relationship with students was her concern about the value of science instruction for kindergarten youngsters. This concern included not only the "background in science I hope to create" but also science instruction as a means to the achievement of other ends, for example, as "a source for curiosity and imagination to thrive" and as one basis for her "reading and math readiness programs." In a similar way the sixth-grade teacher concerned with alcohol abuse was much more interested in the importance of the subject matter than she was in the relationship she established with her students. Other examples could be provided to illustrate that teachers, when they are concerned with the moral dimension of teaching, are more likely to focus on curricular rather than student-teacher relationship issues. This greater emphasis on curricular concerns is probably a reflection of the teachers' tendency to choose projects that involve the development of curriculum materials, and my own tendency, at least until recently, to place more emphasis on the curricular rather than the relational basis of the moral perspective. Perhaps it is more difficult for experienced teachers and teacher educators to see the student-teacher relationship as problematic than it is for us to see curriculum content as problematic.

Even though teachers often are open to rethinking curricular issues, I have had several notable failures in focusing teacher attention on the question of what content youngsters ought to learn. A brief recounting of one incident may suggest some of the difficulties involved in alerting teachers to the problematic basis of curriculum decisions. A business teacher proposed a project in which she would develop a curriculum guide and resource file for teaching a one-semester general business course for ninth and tenth graders. The most commonly used text in this subject area was, she believed, "very outdated" and needed a supplementary "curriculum guide for use in the classroom for more effective teaching of this course. I would like to develop role-play situations, case studies, and varied visual materials that would make this class more interesting to students as well as to teachers." I accepted her proposal but in my written reaction to her proposal asked what type of analysis she anticipated doing since she had not discussed this topic in her proposal.

Her failure to discuss what type of analysis she planned to do is a common omission from proposals, so I had no way of anticipating her conception that curriculum content is a "given" not in need of analysis, a belief that subsequently led to a conflict between the two of us. When I received a sample unit containing an overview of the American economy, I found that most of the resource materials and many of the teaching activities stressed the desirability of a laissez-faire view of capitalism. Frequently cited sources were from the American Manufacturers Association, Junior Achievement, the Chamber of Commerce of the United States, and other relatively conservative organizations. She made little use of groups that attempt to provide a balanced view of our economy (for example, the Committee for Economic Development or the Joint Council on Economic Education), and no use of pro-labor or other groups that might attempt to present a view of our economy not necessarily grounded in a laissez-faire philosophy. Since one of her objectives was to provide "a general knowledge of the American economy," I felt that I needed to question her reason for presenting a pro-business view of the economy as if this were a universally accepted conception of our economy.

During the course of two discussions I presented my concern about the one-sided nature of her introductory unit on the American economy. Rather than provide a rationale for her approach, she explained that the conservative approach was consistent with the text with which she was correlating her curriculum guide. Since I did not consider this explanation an adequate one—especially in light of her previous statement that the text was in some ways outdated—I pressed the need for her to be able to defend the curriculum guide in terms other than an appeal to the authority of a textbook. However, she kept returning to her desire to be able to better teach the text used by most school districts by supplementing it with interesting activities. I finally suggested removing the unit from the course, if she could not defend it other than in terms of its consistency with a commonly used general business text. In the end, she chose not to remove the unit the on American economy but rather to remove the objective that stated the unit would provide an overall knowledge of the American economy.

As I look back on this incident I believe I was never able to convince her that selection of curriculum content is a meaningful problem that cannot be resolved merely by appealing to the authority of a textbook. She kept returning to her desire to teach "an efficient, effective and successful general business course." To her the book was "very outdated" in the sense that it did not employ a variety of teaching techniques to convert the rather dull content of a general business text into activities that grabbed the attention of adolescents. Curriculum content for her was a given, a fact established by those who wrote textbooks. Her task, she believed, was to interest and engage students in the study of preordained content.

I should note that she was capable of rejecting the authority of the textbook when the issue was one of teaching methodology. She developed a variety of creative teaching activities that were not in the book and could be substituted for methodological suggestions contained in the text. Moreover, in her analysis she attended to such questions as whether her activities were varied enough to maintain student interest and where additional teaching activities might be needed. She was, therefore, able to see teaching methodology, the craft of teaching, as problematic at the same time that selection of content was not open to reconsideration. In a sense her Master's Project illustrates that reflection can occur in empirical terms and not necessarily in moral terms.

In most projects, however, I succeed in obtaining a relatively high level of analysis, which usually includes a moral as well as an empirical dimension. I cannot, of course, be sure that the cause of this analysis is the Master's Project experience. Perhaps those who analyze their projects are inclined to be analytic, and the project experience merely stimulates them to call forth an already developed skill. Neither do I know whether teachers continue to employ analytic perspectives once the project experience is over, since I lose contact with most of them at the conclusion of the Teaching-Learning Process program. But I believe I can speak with some assurance that teachers are capable of considerably more analytic thought than they are typically given credit for. (See Berlak & Berlak 1981, pp. 234–36, for a brief but thoughtful discussion of the tendency for some researchers to attribute to teachers conceptual simplicity and a largely intuitive approach to their work.)

I have introduced the Master's project experience to illustrate one approach to grounding in-service teacher education in the moral craft metaphor. As I seek to stimulate a teacher to think analytically, I continually have in the back of my head the moral craft metaphor; this metaphor helps remind me that I need to encourage the teacher to engage in normative analysis as well as in analysis from a craft or empirical perspective. In this way the moral craft metaphor leads me to a preliminary organization of my intentions (Black 1944).

I do not attempt to prescribe a particular approach to analysis. For example, I do not try to influence the teacher to conceptualize craft knowledge as being composed of mechanical skill, analytic knowledge, and the application of analytic knowledge to specific situations, as I argued in Chapter 5. It is far less important that the teacher think about craft knowledge as I do than it is that he reflect on his craft to see how he might improve it. Similarly, I do not attempt to prescribe a specific way of analyzing normative issues. Rather, in the guidelines and especially in conferences, I attempt to pose questions that will help the teacher reflect on what content ought to be taught to youngsters and what relationships he ought to establish with his students.

My reluctance to impose a particular approach to investigating moral and craft issues is partly motivated by my belief that such issues can be legitimately viewed from diverse points of view. In additon I believe that variations among individual teachers make it pedagogically desirable to approach different teachers in varying ways. For the teacher not predisposed to analyze his own teaching, any attempt to reflect on his craft may be a challenge; in such cases I try to support the teacher in his initial attempts, regardless of how the teacher reflects on his craft. On the other hand, many analytically inclined teachers are seeking out new ways of analyzing their craft experience and are open to my suggesting sophisticated approaches to looking at their craft. Openness to craft exploration, however, does not necessarily carry over to the moral domain, as is evident in the case of the business teacher. Considerable delicacy is often required when I raise moral concerns, perhaps because teachers are more likely to see their craft as problematic than to see the moral dimension of their work as in need of exploration. Moreover, if the probing of the moral dimension results in direct confrontation and argument —as in the instance of the business teacher—then the teacher often closes himself off to further probing. For this reason I have largely omitted the moral dimension from my discussion of analysis in the guidelines and have tried to introduce this topic in a personalized way through my direct interaction with the teacher.

No issue troubles me more than how hard I should press a teacher to be analytic. The danger of pushing too hard is that the teacher, in an attempt to please me and be evaluated well, substitutes a taken-for-granted view of analysis for a taken-for-granted view of practice. For example, a teacher once pulled me aside after I had made a strong pitch on the importance of analysis and said, "Now, I want you to tell me exactly what you want for the analysis so I can do it right." My enthusiasm for the value of analysis seemed to convince her that she had better do it my way if she hoped to receive an A. I countered her request for the correct way to conduct an analysis with an argument that there was no one right way to be analytic. On the contrary, I argued that there are many ways in which a teacher can reflect on his craft and the moral basis of his actions. He should, I continued, select those approaches relevant to his project.

It is important to remember that in addition to choosing the forms of analysis to be conducted, the teacher also selects the project to which the analytical perspective is to be applied. Further, the outline of the final product, including the nature of the analysis, is proposed to me by the teacher in the form of a contract. Of course, I must agree to the contract, but I have found that my reliance on teacher initiative in the selection, organization, and proposed analysis of the project opens the teacher to most suggestions I might have for extending the analysis. Latent in my conception of the Master's Project is a belief that the teacher is an active professional, a decision maker whose perspective may need to be broadened but who ought to be in control of how this perspective is to be expanded.

Thus we are back to the rationale for the Teaching-Learning Process program, a rationale that stresses the teacher as an active agent who establishes professional goals, explores alternatives, makes decisions, and reflects on consequences in light of the original goals. Analyzing the project experience is a concrete way of fostering the image of the teacher as decision maker. But I also try not to impose a particular conception of analysis on a teacher; the teacher is encouraged to develop her own approach to analyzing the moral and craft basis of her work. Essentially all I require is that the teacher assume and reflect on her decision-making responsibilities. (A related approach is John Elliott's concept of the self-monitoring teacher: Elliott 1976–77; Wehlage 1981a, pp. 109–12.)

It is difficult for me to judge the extent to which my approach to the Master's Project goes beyond the moral craft metaphor to take into account other considerations. I believe that my open-ended approach to analysis is consistent with the moral craft metaphor, but many of the mechanics of the project experience probably are derived from my practical experience conducting projects rather than from the metaphor itself. For example, my decision to delay and personalize the introduction of the moral dimension is a result of my experience with teachers who are often threatened by direct questions on the importance and/or wisdom of their teaching activities. Similarly, my tendency to give teachers considerable choice and control over the project experience is not the only approach that could be developed out of the moral craft metaphor, though the image of the teacher as decision maker inherent in such an approach seems consistent with the moral craft metaphor. But I also find, as I noted earlier, that providing teachers considerable choice and control over the project experience makes them open to suggestions I may have for extending their analyses. I conclude, therefore, that the moral craft metaphor does help me preliminarily organize my intentions but that other considerations are involved in moving from a metaphor to an in-service effort such as the Master's Project experience.

THE SECONDARY PROFESSIONAL SEMESTER

Not until 1980, the year that I formalized the moral craft metaphor (Tom 1980c), did I begin to think about how this metaphor could be applied to my work in our undergraduate secondary teacher education program. But before discussing my attempt to apply the moral craft metaphor to this program, I need to outline some steps that had been taken to restructure the professional courses in our secondary program.

In 1979, those of us involved in the secondary education program decided to reorganize the seven separate professional courses into a cluster of three introductory courses (Educational Psychology, American School, and the Education and Psychology of Exceptional Children) and a professional semester (a full-time semester of student teaching and related education course work). The primary reason for developing the professional semester was to try to better link education course work with teaching practice; the actual courses included in the professional semester were General Methods, Reading in the Content Areas, Specialized Curriculum and Methods (each student takes the appropriate course in his teaching area), and Student Teaching. A faculty team was in charge of supervision of student teaching as well as all professional semester course instruction (except the specialized curriculum and methods courses). By making the same faculty members responsible for both course work and supervision, we hoped we could both internally tie together courses as well as integrate ideas from these courses with student teaching. A similar effort by our colleagues in the elementary program had already been attempted and had proven to be fruitful (Cohn 1979, 1981).

Initial faculty and student reaction to our first professional semester in 1979 was positive. The students appreciated our attempt to make the course work they took along with student teaching directly related to their teaching experience while the faculty team felt that the team approach was a viable way to integrate course work and teaching practice, our basic reason for moving to a professional semester format.

But the fall-1979 version of the professional semester still was subject to many of the problems common to traditional teacher education programs. In particular, this professional semester was not grounded in a conception of good teaching; instead its major thrust was to link a melange of educational ideas with teaching practice, an atheoretic approach which is typical of contemporary teacher education (Brauner 1978). In the absence of a unifying vision of the nature of good teaching, the content focus of the professional semester tended to be diffuse, with many different pedagogical topics being introduced. However, we successfully confronted a variety of logistical issues, for example, which schools should we work with, how can we involve student teachers in selecting their school and teacher placements, how can on-site supervision follow through on ideas introduced in campus-based instruction. In my experience, logistical and other implementation issues tend to occupy huge amounts of staff time when a teacher education program is being initiated or reformulated, especially if the program has a significant field-based dimension as in the case of our professional semester (Tom 1976).

Besides not identifying a coherent content focus for the 1979 professional semester, we also restricted our planning efforts to the professional semester segment of the secondary program; no intellectual links were established between the professional semester and the other three courses in the certification sequence. Such linkages are not easy to make, for, as one of my colleagues is fond of noting, every instructor is his own teacher educator, each course is its own teacher education program. Nevertheless, a program constructed of intellectually disconnected courses and experiences does leave the entire task of intellectual integration up to the student, the very person who has all she can do to put into practice the pedagogical content of a teacher preparation program.

As a result of these considerations, I resolved to attempt a major rethinking of the professional semester when we next offered it in the spring of 1981. For the time being I decided not to tackle the question of how to connect the professional semester to the rest of the education courses. Instead I would try to ground the professional semester in a conception of good teaching, that is, the teacher as a moral craftsman. This moral craftsman conception, however, could not be built into one aspect of the professional semester: the special methods courses. With one exception, the five instructors for those courses were adjunct professors who were only loosely tied to the four members of the professional semester team. My efforts as coordinator for the professional semester team, therefore, were restricted to relating the moral craft metaphor to the remaining twelve hours of the professional semester.

As in the case of the Master's Project, I took into consideration other factors besides the moral craft metaphor as I redesigned the professional semester. For example, since our 1979 students liked playing a major role in the student-teaching placement process, I retained the placement process developed by the prior coordinator, that is, the students visited each of our four cooperating schools, selected a school, and often interviewed a specific teacher from the chosen school. Placing students, therefore, was to become a major activity in Phase I (the first two weeks of the semester). Another planning consideration not directly related to the moral craft metaphor was our decision to include a period of full-day student teaching in order that student teachers might sample what it means to be a career teacher. As a result, Phase III in the semester was to involve four weeks of full-day student teaching. In order to show the reader the overall structure of the 1981 professional semester and the ways in which the moral craft metaphor was embedded in it, I have reproduced in the Appendix the professional semester syllabus, except for the reading activities and requirements. The reader may want to consult the syllabus in order to obtain an overview of the five phases of the semester, the rationale for stressing the moral craftsman image, and the content themes of the professional semester.

As one looks at the specific topics included in the various phases of the semester, I believe it is fairly obvious how the moral and craft dimensions are built into the program. Typical craft items include lesson-planning skills, readability formulas, skills in analyzing teaching, approaches to test construction, varieties of questioning strategies. Moral-oriented concerns include such topics as the issue of establishing desirable classroom norms, expressive objectives as an alternative to behavioral objectives, the hidden curriculum, the question of what relationship a student teacher should develop with his cooperating teacher and with his students. The desegregation/integration theme could be either a craft or a moral topic, depending on whether the student argued a policy position or whether he restricted himself to understanding the dynamics of desegregation/integration in his school situation. For the most part, the "orientation to teaching" theme did not involve the direct achievement of either craft or moral ends but rather focused on activities instrumental to such ends. The student-teaching placement process and the job search skills, for example, are not important in themselves but rather are useful steps toward the realization of significant craft and moral goals. Most content in the professional semester, however, is directly tied to the moral craft metaphor.

As in the case of the Master's Project, I am illustrating one way that a teacher education program—or at least a portion of a program—can be grounded in the moral craft metaphor. However, a few comments about overall student reaction to the semester do seem to be useful in order to gain a general impression of the dynamics of the professional semester. Much of this information comes from the staff's observation of the student teachers' behavior, but we also conducted a formal evaluation of student reaction to the professional semester.

In general, the students appeared more interested and involved in the craft than the moral components of the professional semester, as might be suspected by anyone familiar with the "how to" orientation of the typical novice. Further, whatever success we had in raising moral concerns was less likely to be in the context of a formal curriculum presentation than it was in the context of a concrete issue or a specific event. That is, the abstract discussion of varying strategies for justifying curriculum content was not nearly so interesting to students as was the discussion of whether students ought to be compelled to learn certain basic "facts" of American history. Even more engaging were discussions of specific events and issues in which the novices were personally involved, for example, a pupil's disinterest in a student teacher's favorite topic as seen on videotape, or a student teacher's spontaneously raising a discipline problem that involved his authority relationship with students. Similarly, the analysis of craft concerns also seemed easier when there was a concrete event or issue that had personal meaning for the novice, for example, applying a readability formula to text materials currently being used by the student teacher, or seeing evidence from a videotape that a student teacher was having trouble gaining pupil attention at the beginning of a lesson.

My comments about the power of pedagogy that makes abstract

issues concrete and personal may seem to be a mundane observation, but this observation has widespread implications for the design of a professional semester. It is not enough to introduce abstract content in the campus sessions of the professional semester and expect it to be absorbed and used by novices in their teaching situations. Even in a well-designed professional semester program, content taught in campus-based courses may not be appropriately employed in student teaching (Cohn 1981). Introducing moral and craft content through concrete topics and issues may facilitate its retention and applicability to field situations, particularly if the novices have difficulty drawing connections between pedagogical ideas and classroom practice. But regardless of how the content is introduced by the professional semester faculty, each faculty member needs to keep in mind key ideas embodied in this content as she observes the classroom work of novices. Continual attention to these ideas—set induction, hidden curriculum, authority of the teacher, and so forth—enables the faculty member to bring to the attention of the novices classroom instances of these ideas. This capacity of a staff member to help student teachers draw relationships between previously introduced ideas and their particular teaching situations is referred to by Cohn (1981) as situational teaching.

What I am suggesting, therefore, is that the presentation of content based in a conception of good teaching is not enough to guarantee a coherent and effective professional semester. Direction needs to be built into more than the syllabus. In addition to relying on the syllabus, the faculty member must possess a conceptual map of the syllabus so that whenever a classroom teaching situation pertinent to that map does arise the faculty member is prepared to demonstrate the connection between previously introduced ideas and teaching practice. Teaching in a teamed professional semester might be said to occur in two stages: awareness of ideas through syllabus-based teaching and application of these ideas to classroom practice through situational teaching.

If anything, my account of the development of the secondary professional semester underplays some of the difficulties involved in the design and implementation of this effort. Remember that even after our second cycle in 1981, we were still attempting to integrate only twelve of the fifteen hours and that we had not yet constructed any significant intellectual links with other education courses in the secondary program. Perhaps the only major change I attempted in the second cycle was to build an explicit conception of good teaching into the professional semester, but I am not sure that the moral craft metaphor was internalized by other members of the professional semester faculty. While I believe that they were sympathetic to this idea, the overall design of the syllabus was mine and was agreed to by the professional semester faculty. I am not sure how much of the moral craft emphasis persisted in the springs of 1982 and 1983, since I did not participate in the third and fourth cycles of the professional semester.

The tendency for a professional semester program to change intellectual direction when new core faculty assume leadership should not be surprising. Individual teacher educators hold radically different ideas about the nature of good teaching. The history of our elementary professional semester is concrete evidence that wide philosophical swings can occur when staff leadership changes. In the short period of five years (1971 to 1976), the elementary program operated from three distinct philosophical orientations: an inquiry-personal commitment model, a model that gave primacy to the cooperative development of the program by school and university personnel, and a model of good teaching with considerable similarities to the moral craft metaphor. These three philosophical shifts can be clearly linked to the fact that a new person (or persons) assumed program leadership (Tom 1976).

I believe that if we explored the underpinnings of these three philosophical orientations, we would find some distinctive metaphor or combination of metaphors embedded in each of these programs. Even teacher education programs that are eclectic and appear not to be grounded in a coherent conception of teaching are in reality often based in an adjustment metaphor, that is, the task of a teacher education program is to prepare teachers to perpetuate schooling as it is currently constituted (Arnstine 1975; Brauner 1978). However, basing a program in a latent metaphor such as adjustment involves a different process than constructing a program in relationship to an openly stated metaphor. When a latent metaphor is used, the process of relating the content and structure of a program to this metaphor is likely to be loose and incomplete, since the latent metaphor is only partly a conscious consideration.

On the other hand an explicit metaphor, as we have seen with my experience with the moral craft metaphor, can provide considerable direction for developing the content and structure of a program. Nevertheless, even if I am correct in my argument that explicit metaphors provide more programmatic direction for preservice programs than latent metaphors, it is important to note several caveats, namely, that factors other than a metaphor do influence the design of a program, that metaphor-derived content needs to be internalized and used by the teacher educator at appropriate times as well as formalized in a syllabus, and that members of a faculty team may have considerable difficulty agreeing on a metaphor.

SUPERVISION OF CLASSROOM INSTRUCTION

Supervision of classroom instruction has been one of the central activities of my twenty-year career as a teacher educator. In my graduate student days at Madison, supervision of student teachers and interns helped finance my doctoral study. When I came to Washington University in 1966 to work in a federally funded curriculum dissemination project, I frequently led critiques in which experienced teachers analyzed one another's teaching of new social studies materials. A few years later, I had a one-year clinical professor appointment between the Ladue school district and Washington University. As clinical professor I concurrently held the roles of cooperating teacher and university supervisor. During the early seventies I administered a large-scale and relatively conventional student teaching program. After several years of observing our elementary staff experiment with field-based teacher education, I helped in 1979 to reorganize the secondary program into a professional semester format in which campus instructors were also the student teaching supervisors. More recently I have been working with principals in the St. Louis public schools to help them adapt ideas from clinical supervision to their current approaches to classroom observation and evaluation. Not only have these experiences been scattered over twenty years but in addition they have involved experienced teachers and principals as well as novice teachers, improvement of instruction as well as teacher evaluation, questions of curriculum implementation as well as of teaching technique, and experimentation with new supervisory roles and approaches as well as with conventional supervisory arrangements.

My supervision endeavors, moreover, have been among the most potent learning experiences in my professional career. Supervision has been a proving ground for a whole variety of my ideas, for example, ideas about disseminating new curricula, relating education course work and teaching practice, and changing other people's teaching behavior and ideas. Supervision, in brief, has been a crucible in which I could test ideas; it has kept me and my ideas connected to the reality of teaching practice

The analytical and critical perspective that I have gradually developed toward teaching practice, including my conceptualization of the moral craft metaphor, is largely the result of my supervisory experience. In the following section I will touch upon several key points in my supervisory career, partly to show the intellectual origins of the moral craft metaphor and partly to show how the developing idea of the moral craft metaphor affected my work as a supervisor. But before starting an analysis of my own work as a supervisor, I want to touch briefly upon the supervision I received as an intern teacher because this experience, unbeknownst to me, was a forerunner of the moral craft metaphor.

When I arrived at Two Rivers, Wisconsin, in the fall of 1962, I was perhaps more anxious than the typical beginning teacher. I had never student taught and was moving directly from being a teaching assistant in a college European history course to being an intern teacher responsible for four high school classes of World History. I was paired with an experienced teacher, Sid Sivertson, who in addition to watching over me also had five World History classes of his own. We regularly combined our classes to form one large group so I was able to watch Sid teach as well as to talk to him about various planning and teaching issues. My personal experience as an intern, with full classroom authority in a teaming situation, has made me doubt that the conventional student teaching arrangement is a necessary step in the induction of novice teachers.

Not only did the intern structure differ from that of student teaching but in addition there was a different supervisory relationship between Sid and me than between a cooperating teacher and a student teacher. Since Sid and I were teaching the same course to different classes of students, we frequently discussed how to approach certain topics or compared notes on how our plans had actually worked in our classes. Of course, we also jointly planned the topics of large-group instruction and watched each other teach large groups. When Sid offered advice about the craft of teaching, I felt free to accept or reject this advice, depending on whether I thought the advice was appropriate for my own classes. In a sense we were colleagues sharing a common task more than we were a master teacher and an apprentice. The intern structure—because it acknowledged my authority and autonomy—made it possible for Sid and me to establish a give-and-take supervisory relationship, a situation that differs considerably from the one-way relationship typical in student teaching.

In addition to my ongoing discussions with Sid, there were a few supervisory visits by a faculty member from Madison. Since Two Rivers is about three hours from Madison and since the supervisor had a variety of public relations tasks to perform while he was at the high school, he rarely had time to conduct a complete conference subsequent to his classroom observation. Therefore, after two of his three visits, he wrote letters to follow up his brief supervisory conferences, a fortuitous outcome that enables me to quote twenty-two years later exactly what he told me. After his first visit to observe a large-group presentation on the Middle East he wrote me:

Your lesson for the day—movie, lecture, film-strip—was an ambitious one inspired, as I understood the matter, by the need to cover a rather large section of history in a painfully brief period of time. . . . My comments on the lesson are these:

1. Movie could have used some introduction so that students would know what in particular they should be looking for.

2. Students might have been permitted, perhaps encouraged, to raise questions about the film.

3. As we discussed, the tone of the lecture was Western-Christian oriented, a position most of us take inadvertently. The impression was created of Muslims being on the bad side and Christians on the good side, an impression which obviously will not contribute to world understanding.

4. Again, no questions were encouraged. I understand that this is your mode of operating in the large group. However, a more timely moment may not arise for discussing some of the crucial issues which grow out of the Christian-Muslim conflicts of the middle ages, such as whether there was a right side and a wrong side in the Crusades, or whether one religion is better than another, etc.

5. One would hope that the next day's work would grow organically out of the previous day's. I couldn't be sure that this would happen judging from your assignment announced at the end of the hour.

His pattern of mixing together what I label craft and moral concerns continued when he returned a month later:

Your lecture-question-answer session gave every appearance of being well-planned. . . . In themselves, clear delivery and logical organization are insufficient to insure the understanding of your listeners. In the case of the listeners being relatively immature and uninterested high school students, one must take special pains to be certain that he has "engaged" his audience, i.e., got them involved or committed to the topic under discussion, and that the structure or bones of the presentation have been laid bare, not once, but a number of times. . . .

Towards the end of the period you led the class into an explication of the preamble to the Declaration of Independence. In general, I felt this work was well done. I kept hoping, however, that you would place the document in its modern setting (the relation of the document to currents of scientific development of the past had already been made). Do the "self-evident" truths still have relevance? Any *conflict* between American official belief and behavior? I believe that there was an opportunity for the clarification of democratic values—it is this clarification and the

> problems associated with this clarification which, to my mind, is
> central to the teaching of the social studies at the high school
> level.

Again my university supervisor raised topics and concerns that were partly craftlike and partly moral.

In retrospect I believe my university supervisor operated implicitly, if not explicitly, from a supervisory orientation with great similarity to the moral craft metaphor. Unfortunately I have little recollection of how I reacted to my supervisor's attempt to raise such moral topics with me as the Western bias of my lecture or the possibility of viewing the Declaration of Independence in a contemporary context. Perhaps all I have done in this book is to rediscover and articulate an orientation thrust upon me during my induction into secondary school teaching.

In any case, when I returned to graduate school after two years of high school teaching, I supervised student teachers with little regard for the moral dimension of their work. Indeed my most poignant memory from my initial supervisory experience is the fear I felt during a class observation that I would not know what to tell the student in the subsequent conference. My doctoral advisor counseled that I focus on a limited number of topics during each conference, a suggestion I tried to follow.

Gradually I became more confident of my analytic ability, and I developed a supervisory approach based on identifying a small number of key difficulties in a novice's teaching. What made a teaching problem a "key" difficulty was that this problem's presence retarded the development of teaching proficiency in several areas, not just in a single area. The tendency to ask several questions at one time, for example, might hamper one's ability to conduct several types of teaching activities, for instance open-ended discussions, drill exercises, guided discussions, application of a principle to a new situation. I saw my task as analyzing a novice's teaching to identify several key difficulties, documenting the importance of these items to the novice, and working with the beginner to plan a way to overcome these key difficulties. This focused style of supervision helped me to become adept at analyzing the teaching problems of a novice; I could usually figure out which teaching problems seemed to be the greatest barriers to the overall technical success of a beginner.

But still I was not satisfied with my supervisory approach. I was becoming skillful at analyzing teaching, but the person I was supervising obtained little practice in analysis; instead, the student teacher became the consumer of my inquiries. Over the short run, my approach might yield rather sizable improvements in the technical behavior of a novice, but over the long run my analytic ability was of little value to the first-year teacher who no longer had me around. Since the improvement of an experienced teacher's instruction is just as dependent on analytic ability as the beginner's, I decided to encourage the beginner to engage in self-analysis of teaching rather than to be the recipient of my analyses. A second problem with my key-difficulty approach to supervision was that the selected topics inevitably reflected my perspective. During my initial years of supervision, I gradually became aware that my suggestions, no matter how carefully derived, were not necessarily helpful to another person if that person saw the teaching situation differently than I did. I remember being deeply affected by Combs' (1958) idea that "people do not behave according to the facts as others see them; they behave in terms of what seems to them to be so" (1958, p. 21). I came to believe that my supervisory efforts could be potent only if I viewed the teaching situation from the perspective of the person being supervised.

In a sense I doubted my ability to be helpful to novice teachers in anything beyond a short-term and superficial way. Out of this crisis I developed an approach for student teacher supervision that I came to call selective supervision (Tom 1972). The essential characteristics of selective supervision are: maintain a short supervisory agenda, carry over agenda items from one supervisory session to another, encourage the novice to contribute agenda items along with the university supervisor. Generally, I began the process of selective supervision by asking the beginner to identify in writing an aspect of her teaching that would serve as a focal point for my classroom observations. Typically this topic was some kind of teaching problem that had been bothering the student teacher. After observing the beginner teach, I worked with the novice in our first conference to further clarify the problem, discuss some alternative solutions to the problem, and hopefully decide jointly on a plan of action to deal with the problem. During the next classroom visit I focused my observation on the identified problem and observed the success of the attempted resolution. In the subsequent conference we compared notes on what happened vis-à-vis the selected teaching problem. The outcome of this discussion might be a decision that a new plan of action was needed or a determination that the original problem needed to be reformulated more precisely. During this second conference I also might introduce a teaching problem of concern to me, and follow the same process during subsequent observation-conference cycles as with the novice's agenda item. An agenda item was pursued until the problem embedded in it was resolved to the satisfaction of both the student teacher and me.

The emphasis in selective supervision is less on the speedy resolution of a variety of teaching problems than it is on teaching the beginner a simple model for analyzing classroom teaching. The student teacher is expected to learn how to define a teaching problem with some precision, how to explore alternative solutions to that problem, and how to gather evidence on the effectiveness of a potential solution to a teaching problem. Although the supervisor plays an active role in the analytic process, the novice is generally asked to identify the first problem and is also expected to play an active role in all supervisory discussions. When the supervisor has the opportunity to start introducing teaching topics, he can take into account the perspective of the novice, as revealed by the teaching problem or problems already identified by the beginner.

In general I have felt that the use of the selective supervision approach—and permutations of this approach (see, for example, Hill 1968)—has helped student teachers become analytic about their teaching craft. Beginners are often able to analyze their own teaching by using the simple problem-solving model built into selective supervision. In addition, since the problems selected by the novice tend to reveal a great deal about personal anxieties and conceptualizations of the teaching role, I believe selective supervision gives me the information I need to understand the perspective of the beginner.

Despite experiencing success with selective supervision, I find many novices resistant to this approach, often because they want me to tell them what they need to do in order to be more effective teachers. Such beginners implicitly believe that there are certain potent techniques known to experts but not to beginners. The job of the supervisor, according to this type of student, is to communicate these technical secrets to the uninitiated. Beginners who place considerable faith in the efficacy of teaching technique usually have trouble realizing that the conditions under which a technique is used are as important as the nature of the technique, that the precise statement of the problem to be resolved is as important as knowledge of appropriate solutions, that so-called master teachers attend to an enormous range of factors besides technique as they practice their craft. To someone who believes that the potency of teaching techniques can be separated from the context in which they are employed, selective supervision can appear to be an evasion of the supervisor's responsibility, an attempt by the supervisor to withhold valuable technical advice from the novice.

However, even when a novice is willing and able to do the analysis of teaching built into the selective supervision approach, I have not been satisfied with the results. In my experience, as long as the supervisor responds primarily to the concerns raised by the novice, the analysis of teaching tends to be restricted to the craft domain. For the most part, novices do not seem to raise moral concerns spontaneously, an outcome understandable in light of Fuller's (1968) developmental model of teacher concerns. According to Fuller, teachers proceed through three major phases of concerns: about self, about self as teacher, and about pupils. The first phase, typical of students prior to teaching experience, is marked by conventional adolescent concerns: grades, parental relationships, choice of vocation, and self-identity. Concerns about self as teacher tend to arise during initial teaching experience or in anticipation of that experience. These concerns focus on such questions as: What is expected of me as a teacher? How adequate am I? How do pupils feel about me? The last, and most mature, level of concern is characteristic of experienced superior teachers. Examples of concerns about pupils are: Are pupils learning what I am teaching? Are pupils learning what they need? Of all these concerns, the only obviously moral one is the question of whether pupils are learning what they need. That is, the only moral concerns postulated by Fuller are a subgroup of the highest level of concerns. Fuller's findings probably reflect that teaching attracts those who tend to favor the status quo and that teacher educators are unable to develop professional preparation programs that "result in the analytic turn of mind one finds in other occupations whose members are trained in colleges and universities" (Lortie 1975, chap. 2; p. 231).

Moreover, my supervisory experience with veteran teachers suggests that they are as likely to focus on simplistic craft concerns as are beginners. I realize that such a claim is a sweeping one, but on the other hand I have had the opportunity to work with practicing teachers in a wide variety of settings, ranging from a curriculum dissemination project (Tom 1973a, 1973b) to consulting with school principals interested in using clinical supervision with their teachers.

It is not so much that teachers cannot thoughtfully address moral concerns as it is that a variety of environmental factors direct teacher attention away from moral issues. Not the least of these factors is the predilection of contemporary researchers on teaching to separate empirical and normative issues and largely ignore normative issues. Text materials and articles these researchers prepare for practitioners presume a gulf exists between moral and empirical issues, and give most attention to empirical research and its implications for practice. The idea that empirical issues are paramount is also reinforced by such potent educational movements as behavioral objectives and competency testing. In addition, status in the larger society is accorded to those who have practical know-how and technical expertise, though such recent social movements as the Moral Majority are challenging our reverence for technique. Furthermore, the way the tasks of teaching are currently organized—mutual isolation, vague but demanding goals, superficial in-service education, intensity of work environment—all discourage teachers from being reflective about fundamental educational issues (Lortie 1975, pp. 232–35).

My belief that many environmental factors direct teacher attention away from moral concerns plus my own inability to develop a supervisory approach that regularly moves novices beyond analyzing craft concerns are two reasons why I concluded that classroom supervision by itself is too weak an intervention to direct teacher attention to moral concerns. Remember also that my university supervisor's direct attempt to impress a moral perspective on me did not substantially affect my own initial supervisory efforts. The intervention I ultimately decided was potent enough to pose moral concerns to teachers is the professional semester, though one other supervisory experience occurred before I arrived at that decision. This experience, a clinical professorship, showed me the power that can result when three normally distinct supervisory and teaching roles are combined in one person.

In one way, my clinical professorship was a typical appointment, for I held a joint appointment between Ladue, a local school district, and Washington University. In fact, the existence of such a joint appointment is the only characteristic that was shared by the various clinical appointments made in the 1960s and early 1970s (Tom 1974a). My other responsibilities as a clinical professor were to teach two high school social studies classes daily, to supervise social studies student teachers who were placed with three teachers in my high school, and to develop in-service programming for my high school. Except for the development of in-service programming, I pursued my responsibilities with enthusiasm and at least some success. But the most fascinating and meaningful part of my clinical professorship fell outside my job description and involved me in an unanticipated opportunity to integrate methods instruction and student teaching.

Since two of our social studies students decided very late to become teachers, they had to take the general principles of instruction course, a prerequisite for student teaching, at the same time they were student teaching. The general principles course stressed such generic craft content as lesson planning, questioning strategies, and discipline, but it also included an examination of the role of the school in American society, a topic of potential moral import. I decided to keep these two students in my classroom so I could integrate the content from the general principles course with their daily teaching responsibilities. We worked as a team of three, planning lessons together, watching one another teach, and conducting group analysis of the teaching at the end of each morning's lessons. I fulfilled, at one time, three roles: methods instructor, cooperating teacher, and university supervisor.

This concentration of multiple roles in one person made possible an integrated approach to teacher education that I had never before experienced, either as a student or as an instructor. As cooperating teacher, I could control the structure of the classroom curriculum, keeping in mind the novices' need to experience a variety of teaching situations as well as the learning requirements of my high school seniors. Further, I could make direct ties between the content of the general principles course and the experience of classroom teaching, since I was in charge of both activities. Lastly, there was no conflict between the expectations of the cooperating teacher and those of the university supervisor since I held both roles. Of course this concentration of authority in one person placed great responsibility on me to balance the interests of high school students with those of student teachers and to illustrate links between pedagogical content and teaching experience. Despite the authority I exerted over the two novices, there was still a spirit of teaming among the three of us, not unlike the feeling I had experienced with Sid that we-are-all-in-this-together. Without doubt I was the teacher of the two classes, yet the three of us did operate basically as a teaching team as we planned lessons, taught them, and analyzed the results of our efforts. The sense of fulfillment I obtained from integrating university course work and classroom teaching led me to want to conduct the general principles–student teaching experience on a larger scale.

Yet not all aspects of my work as a clinical professor went smoothly, particularly my efforts related to the moral dimension. Even though my extended contact with the two social studies student teachers opened up many more possibilities than the typical university supervisor has for probing the moral dimension, I still found that my student teachers' most pressing concerns involved craft issues. Analysis of these craft topics plus planning for the next day frequently absorbed the entire hour we had available for discussion. But our daily hour-long discussions often did permit me to raise moral issues, especially those having to do with the purposes of social studies instruction.

Even though my interest in the moral dimension of supervision was less well-developed during my 1969–70 clinical professorship than it was at the time of the 1981 professional semester, the daily contact that accompanied the clinical professor structure made it easier to raise moral issues than was the case during the professional semester when visits to a student teacher occurred about once every two weeks. What strikes me as an exciting possibility would be to combine the two structures, that is, to create a professional semester format in which the cooperating teacher and university faculty roles are combined. With this structure, the supervisor-cooperating teacher-methods instructor would be able to daily engage in situational teaching (Cohn 1981), focusing on both the moral and the craft dimensions of the moral craft metaphor. As it stands now, the best we have been able to do in either our elementary or secondary professional semesters is to have the methods instructor-supervisor in the schools for one visit a week. The remainder of the time, supervision must be conducted by the cooperating teacher, a person whose primary instructional responsibilities are to youngsters and whose supervisory training and familiarity with the professional semester curriculum may be limited.

If I were to attempt to sum up what I have learned from my own supervisory experience I would say that classroom supervision, as conventionally conducted, can help a teacher improve the craft of teaching, but there are severe limits on the impact of traditional classroom supervision. Such supervision does not seem to be an effective means for raising issues from the moral domain, a conclusion I have drawn from my experience as both an intern and a supervisor of student teachers. However, I think it is possible through selective supervision, or some similar approach, to lead a teacher to be more analytic about her work, at least in relation to craft issues. In the end, though, I have been dissatisfied with my efforts to develop a traditional supervisory approach grounded in the moral craft metaphor. There are too many constraining factors, for example, the supervisor has intermittent contact with the student teacher, the supervisor's ability to operate from the teacher's perspective is limited, the supervisor may well be unfamiliar with the pedagogical content taught prior to student teaching.

In order to make potent supervision possible, I have come to believe that supervision must be part of a larger educational intervention. I have already mentioned that I would like to see a marriage between a clinical professorship (which combines the supervisor and cooperating teacher roles) and the professional semester (which combines the supervisor and methods instructor roles). Such a marriage would not only combine three roles in one person—thus eliminating many problems of coordination and concurrently maximizing the possibilities of situational teaching—but would also bring faculty and students together in an intense, one-semester relationship. Hopefully the length and intensity of such a semester program would make it possible to consistently raise moral issues without slighting craft issues. Such a program, of course, would be very demanding, both on the faculty team that concurrently taught young students and university students and on the university, which would have to either recreate the largely defunct campus laboratory schools or assume instructional responsibility for a portion of a local public school.

Somewhat less desirable, though more realistic, is a professional semester format in which a university faculty team works closely with a small number of schools and cooperating teachers. This arrangement does not require a university to maintain a school but does perpetuate the dual roles of university methods instructor-supervisor and cooperating teacher. Unless the cooperating teachers are knowledgeable about the professional semester curriculum and have released time to play a major role in the supervision of novices, then the existence of two supervisory roles (university faculty and school faculty) is likely to lead to confusion, misunderstanding, and even antagonism, rather than to a coherent program (Wehlage 1981a). Our experience with the professional semester format at Washington University suggests that it is very difficult to obtain significant teacher involvement in the professional semester process (Tom 1976, pp. 15–18). That teachers should have trouble playing a major role in a professional semester format should not be surprising; their time and energy is almost totally absorbed in teaching youngsters.

Even less desirable than such major interventions as the professional semester or the professional semester–clinical professorship combination are such interventions as an intern–experienced teacher team or a double placement in student teaching. While I found my internship pairing with Sid to be a collegial relationship in which I learned a lot, Sid was never able to make ties between my teaching experience and the pedagogical curriculum I had studied in Madison; he did not know the substance of that curriculum. The same problem generally exists when extended student teaching placements are used, since more student teaching does not necessarily make cooperating teachers more aware of the pedagogical curriculum. About the best that can be done under such low-power interventions as internship or extended student teaching is to try, as my university supervisor did, to introduce the novice to various issues, or to use a supervisory approach similar to selective supervision in an attempt to encourage self-analysis by the beginner.

CONCLUSION

At the beginning of this chapter I identified my task as providing insight into how I have used the moral craft metaphor to organize preliminarily my intentions in three areas of helping teachers: preservice teacher education, in-service teacher education, and supervision of classroom teaching. In the case of the Master's Project experience, I came to place special emphasis on the conduct of an analysis of the project, hopefully with some concern for the moral as well as the craft dimension of the project experience. Analysis is also key to the secondary professional semester, but in this instance analysis tends to involve the introduction of certain content and the situational application of this content to various teaching contexts. Lastly, analysis also is involved in classroom supervision, though I have found that the traditional structure under which supervision usually occurs places considerable constraints on the potency of supervisory analysis.

Underlying my emphasis on analysis is a belief that the moral craft representation of teaching entails a problematic view of teaching. The opposite view of teaching would be to view craft as imitation and moral as preordained values, but such conceptions of moral and craft are inconsistent with the socially constructed character of educational phenomena. Socially constructed phenomena are problematic in that they can be oriented in many different directions, depending on our human intentions.

Analysis or reflection seems to me to be a reasonable way of addressing the problematic character of socially constructed phenomena. Rather than take educational phenomena for granted and accept them as part of nature, we need to stand back and decide what educational ends are worthwhile and how we might practice our teaching craft to pursue these ends. Unfortunately many practitioners and researchers are willing to accept educational phenomena at face value and find the open-endedness of reflection to be disconcerting. They long for educational phenomena to be as real and enduring as a tree or a piece of furniture.

The very recognition that educational phenomena are problematic is a major step for many practitioners, especially since they are continually involved in the flow of "real" classroom events. It is for this reason that I have increasingly come to believe that training programs must represent a major intervention in the life of a novice or an experienced practitioner, if we are to shake the practitioner loose from accepting at face value the ongoing realities of practice. In addition, the difficulty of establishing the problematic character of educational phenomena has led me to employ relatively simple models of analysis, including asking straightforward questions, using situational teaching, or the self-identification of problems as in selective supervision. More elaborate models of analysis do exist, but complex models seem as likely to confuse as to enlighten, particularly when the practitioner is a beginner.

I have tried to identify some of the salient aspects of my experiences as I worked to implement the moral craft metaphor in teacher education and classroom supervision. Hopefully, the case examples I described and interpreted have provided the reader with insights that can be transferred by analogy to other helping contexts. Of course the reader may come up with dramatically different approaches as she tries to relate the moral craft metaphor to contexts of interest to her, and will of necessity need to consider a variety of factors external to the metaphor. I wish the reader good fortune in her creative efforts at generalization.

·8·

REGULATING AND STUDYING TEACHING

In the prior chapter I tried to show how the moral craft metaphor guided my own work with teachers. Now I want to step back from my direct involvement with teachers and consider what guidance the moral craft metaphor can provide for research on teaching and for policy issues related to the improvement of teaching.

The policy area I have chosen to explore is the accreditation of teacher education programs, particularly the standards that are used to judge whether programs are to be nationally accredited. The responsibility for national accreditation is held by the National Council for Accreditation of Teacher Education (NCATE), a private group composed of representatives from the American Association of Colleges for Teacher Education, the National Education Association, and other professional groups with an interest in teacher preparation. While NCATE accreditation is voluntary and is possessed by less than half of the institutions preparing elementary and secondary teachers, there is some prestige associated with having the imprimatur of NCATE and there is the tangible benefit that some states recognize teacher preparation conducted in other states if this preparation is NCATE approved. At the same time, NCATE, from its inception in 1952, has been embroiled in controversy concerning its structure, procedures, and standards (Bush & Enemark 1975; Mayor & Swartz 1965, chap. 6).

After explaining how I became interested in NCATE's approach to accreditation, I proceed in the first section of this chapter to analyze the ways in which NCATE standards are flawed. I give special attention to the vagueness of the standards, the overemphasis on procedural concerns, and the establishment of these standards through consensual decision making. I believe that development of the moral craft metaphor made it easier for me to question the validity of the NCATE standards, especially the tendency of the standards to focus on the process of teacher education rather than on its substance.

However, just because the moral craft perspective helps me expose the flimsy nature of the current standards does not necessarily mean that this perspective will lead us to see how these standards ought to be revised. In order to formulate alternative standards grounded in an appropriate vision of educational quality, other considerations must be added to the moral craft metaphor. Central to these additional considerations is the need to ensure that accreditation judgments are reliable as well as valid and the need to avoid an overly narrow definition of educational quality. The last part of the NCATE discussion focuses on why such considerations as reliability and educational quality ought to be taken into account as new standards are developed.

The second section of this chapter focuses on the implications of the moral craft metaphor for research on teaching. Initially I review the major shortcomings of the applied science metaphor—its narrow conception of teaching, its simplistic view of causality and of teaching phenomena as natural, and its assumption that knowledge ought to control teacher behavior. These shortcomings cripple our efforts at inquiry, I argue, only if the purpose of teaching inquiry is seen as developing before-the-act knowledge of effective teaching practices. But within the context of a democratic, pluralistic society the purpose of teaching inquiry—and the knowledge and theory derived from this inquiry—ought to be to help the teacher to be more reflective about her work. In short, teaching theory ought to be more a source of insight and enlightenment rather than a source of specific rules or general prescriptions.

Over the years, a number of educators have argued that teaching theory ought to help teachers be reflective, but these attempts have largely been unsuccessful. This lack of success is partly the result of insight-oriented theory not being rooted in the day-to-day activities of teaching. As a consequence, I believe that insight-related topics need to be studied in such a way that these topics are tied to classroom life. To help understand how to make these ties, I draw upon the concept of generative theory developed by Kenneth Gergen. Generative theory is theory which fosters reconsideration of that which is taken for granted. I examine three instances of such inquiry: the use of the concrete problems of teaching as a focal point for discipline-based inquiry (Peters 1977), the dilemmas of teaching framework (Berlak & Berlak 1981), and the search for alternative ·metaphors such as the moral craft metaphor.

NCATE STANDARDS

My interest in the nature of the NCATE standards dates back to a visit by a NCATE team to our campus in the fall of 1979. My department chairman asked me to mastermind preparation for the visit, especially the conduct of the institutional self-study that culminates in writing an institutional report.

The essential task of the report is to document the extent to which the programs in a department or school of education are consistent with NCATE standards. The standards—approximately twenty-five—are grouped into six domains, namely, program governance, curricula, faculty, students, resources and facilities, and program evaluation and planning. While NCATE has developed an elaborate set of procedures for conducting its accreditation activities (Olsen 1979), the heart of the accreditation process is the evaluation of programs against the standards (Larson 1979; Tom 1980a). A program that meets NCATE standards is accredited; one that does not meet these standards is denied accreditation.

My experience preparing for our NCATE visitation in 1979 led me to conclude that the standards are seriously flawed. Not only are there over twenty distinct standards but in addition each standard often contains dozens of individual test conditions (Larson 1979). Further, most of these numerous test conditions are vaguely stated, since key terms frequently lack operational definitions. In addition, the test conditions are grounded neither in a substantial research base nor in a conception of good teaching (Tom 1980a).

What the test conditions composing the standards really do is "focus far too much on irrelevant considerations and on the institutionalization of an outmoded professional education curriculum" (Tom 1980b, p. 25). An example of an irrelevant consideration is the overriding concern in the standards with procedural issues rather than with NCATE's self-proclaimed purpose of ensuring that programs "meet national standards of quality" and that graduates of these programs be "well-prepared school personnel" (NCATE 1979, intro.). Key procedural issues in the standards include such topics as whether the professional curriculum is systematically designed and whether professors of education govern teacher education programs. By focusing attention on *how* programs must be governed and conducted, the standards direct attention away from *what* constitutes quality preparation and, in effect, reify established approaches to teacher preparation.

Underlying these specific criticisms of the standards—their vagueness, their lack of attention to the issue of quality, and their commitment to present forms of programmatic organization—is my concern that professional consensus is not an adequate basis for the development of accreditation standards. The problem with using consensus is that in the attempt to make it as broad as possible—an avowed goal of NCATE (Gubser 1980)—the standards are prone to become a hodgepodge of test conditions, with each interest group lobbying for its "pet" criteria and against criteria viewed as inimical to its concerns. Controversial test conditions tend to fall by the wayside, and the final collection of standards is likely to lack coherence. In brief, the political process of establishing standards by consensus is likely to yield a patchwork quilt of test conditions.

Of course, if the interest groups involved in establishing standards implicitly share a conceptual orientation, then there may well be an unarticulated coherence to the test conditions contained in the standards. Such a situation does seem to prevail in the case of the current NCATE standards; underlying these standards is a craft perspective, with a tinge of the applied science metaphor. For example, when one looks at the curriculum domain, these standards emphasize areas of professional study that have been predominant in the craft of teacher preparation for at least fifty years (Monroe 1952), that is, humanistic and behavioral studies; teaching-learning theory, usually divided into general and special methods; and practicum (NCATE 1979). Indeed, throughout the standards there is an emphasis on maintaining the structure and content of the conventional teacher education program and on regulating such traditional concerns as procedures and criteria for student admissions, adequacy of physical resources, use of part-time faculty, and so forth. While new standards are occasionally introduced or old standards supplemented, there has been an amazing continuity in the substance of the standards; over the years the major change in these standards has been their increasingly detailed specification (Tom 1981, p. 48).

Key to this apparent continuity is the already-mentioned use of professional consensus to derive the standards. Gubser, a recent director of NCATE, explicitly states that NCATE attempts to use a "broad professional consensus" in order to develop "standards which represent the broadest possible base of professional knowledge and consensus" (1980, p. 119). In this way, the standards have come to prescribe that accredited teacher education programs imitate whatever the constituents of NCATE believe is the best of past practice.

This imitation of past practice is the core of the oversimplified conception of craft I critiqued in Chapter 6.

This mindless conformity to accepted programmatic practices is best exemplified by that recurrent question central to all accreditation decisions: Does the program meet NCATE standards? Not asked are such questions as: Has the faculty based its program on a coherent and defensible conception of educational quality? Are the prospective teachers alert to the moral dimensions of their teaching responsibility as well to its empirical dimensions? Does the curriculum and the program's structure concurrently help the novice deal with the school system as it is now constructed *and* help her decide how she might work to reconstruct this system? These and similar questions on the substance of educational quality simply cannot be confronted when programs are judged by accreditation standards devoted to enforcing consensually based visions of best practice. Rather, the use of consensually derived standards directs one's attention toward making sure that a program is in tune with the melange of standards that has evolved over the years.

I believe that the development of the moral craft metaphor prompted me to ask questions that challenged the validity of the NCATE standards. If one is primarily concerned about past political struggles between professors of education and those in arts and sciences, then it is perfectly reasonable to ask whether education professors control the governance of a teacher preparation program. But if we are concerned about the preparation of moral craftsmen, then the governance process per se is not an important issue. Similarly, a focus on the moral craftsman metaphor does not suggest that a teacher preparation program must be systematically developed, with attention to detailed objectives as well as general ones. The level of specificity of programmatic objectives is much less important than the content of these objectives. The overall effect of the moral craft metaphor is to direct our attention to the substance rather than the process of teacher preparation.

However, using the moral craft metaphor as a stimulus to expose irrelevant and tradition-bound test conditions in the current standards does not necessarily lead us to know what test conditions ought to be included in a revised set of NCATE standards. Just as in other instances of applying the moral craft metaphor to a problem of practice, we must rely on considerations beyond this metaphor as we formulate a reasonable approach to accreditation policy. Among these additional considerations are the following: make sure that accreditation judgments are reliable as well as valid and avoid an overly narrow definition of quality.

To prescribe in the NCATE standards a rigid definition of

educational quality runs the risk of converting the standards into substance-oriented dogmas just as stultifying as the current procedure-oriented dogmas. While I am enthusiastic about the moral craft metaphor, I fully realize that other visions of educational quality are both possible and defensible. There are, for example, a variety of metaphors similar to the moral craft metaphor, for instance, teaching as hypothesis making (Coladarci 1959), teaching as inquiry (Bagenstos 1975; Schaefer 1967), teaching as interesting and honest work (Clements 1975), reflective teaching (Zeichner 1981, 1982), teaching as inquiry-personal commitment (Tom 1976, pp. 4–5; Wirth 1975). In addition, there are the metaphors I have critiqued in this book—namely, teaching as an applied science, art, or craft—as well as a metaphor I may have prematurely dismissed: teaching as growth (Feiman-Nemser 1980). To use the NCATE standards to compel adherence to a particular metaphor is tempting but unwise; there may well be a variety of metaphorical paths that lead to responsible teacher preparation.

But if no single vision of quality is to be sanctioned by the NCATE standards and these standards are not to prescribe certain procedures for organizing and conducting programs, some educators may see no need for any standards at all. However, I do see a significant role for national accreditation; some agency must ensure that the faculty of a higher education institution has available to it the resources and work environment needed to formulate and conduct a quality program:

> National accreditation . . . should concentrate on making sure
> that the higher education institution has the inputs necessary to
> develop a quality program, regardless of how quality is defined.
> Institutions of higher education have been known to starve
> programs for resources, admit academically weak students,
> tolerate mediocre teaching, and not reward faculty involvement
> in the schools. NCATE accreditation does have an important role
> to play in ensuring that institutions of higher education provide
> the preconditions essential to the development of quality
> programs. (Tom 1981, p. 49)

Implicit in this statement is the idea that four key preconditions to quality programming are "adequate financial support, selective admission standards, a vigorous faculty, and faculty involvement in the schools" (p. 51).

Since there is considerable evidence that NCATE has trouble reliably applying its current qualitative standards (Tom 1983; Wheeler 1980), I favor converting the four preconditions into quantitative standards whenever possible. The development of quantitative standards, of course, compels us to make complex professional judgments. For example, how much support is an "adequate" amount, or how "selective" must admission standards be for a program to merit accreditation. There is also the professional judgment of whether the four input standards I favor really are preconditions to quality programming, regardless of how quality might be defined. But I would rather have the complex professional judgments be made during the development of the standards than as part of a team's campus visit. Indeed, if the standards were to be quantified, institutional reports could be shortened, visiting teams could be reduced in size, and the team's visit could be brief and focused on verifying the data presented in the institutional report. Let us redirect our effort away from convincing a visiting team and the NCATE council that our programs meet vaguely stated standards and toward debating which standards are really important pre-conditions to quality and deciding how these standards are to be operationalized.

In the end, however, I doubt that any serious attempt will be made to consider which standards might address either the sub-stance of quality preparation or the preconditions for quality prep-aration. Those most closely involved in NCATE seem unaware that a consensus-building approach to deriving standards tends to reify conventional teacher education programming. The lockstep approach to teacher training that was condemned fifty years ago by Counts is still prevalent. "From state to state over the entire land," noted Counts, "the curricula of the public normal schools and teachers colleges are as like as peas in a pod" (1935, p. 6). Counts' language is a bit out of date, since these institutions are now regional universities, but his characterization of teacher preparation in the mid-1930s has a contemporary ring to it—and Counts could well have included private and major public institutions as well as normal schools and teachers colleges. Whether teacher educators will have the courage to rethink the standards that prop up conventional teacher preparation is unclear. Stinnett may well be right when he claims that "all accreditation tends to become a power struggle for control over the nature and content of education" (1970, p. 26).

I have gone into some detail concerning my general orientation toward national accreditation—and my reaction to NCATE stan-dards in particular—in order to illustrate the role that the moral craft metaphor played in my thinking. This metaphor underlies my criticism of the validity of the NCATE standards, though my concern about the ambiguity of the standards is not related to the moral craft perspective. Indeed, the open-ended nature of the standards has long been criticized by educators of many different metaphorical persuasions. The role of the moral craft metaphor is even more limited when I am determining what standards might replace those currently in effect. Other important considerations are the need to make reliable accreditation decisions and the need to decide whether certain metaphorical orientations ought to be excluded by NCATE standards.

In the end, I think it is fair to conclude that the moral craft metaphor helped me launch my critique of the procedurally oriented standards but that this metaphor is only one of several factors involved in any reconstruction of the NCATE standards. The major contribution of the moral craft perspective to rethinking the standards is that it kept my vision focused on the issue of quality—or, perhaps more accurately, preconditions to quality.

RESEARCH ON TEACHING

On the surface, the implications of the moral craft metaphor for research on teaching appear to be more direct than for accreditation policy. For example, the moral craft metaphor does provide inquiry with an underpinning that is dramatically different from the applied science orientation so common among researchers, especially among researchers who study teaching. Several of these researchers have told me that they believe acceptance of the moral craft metaphor literally destroys the rationale for research on teaching. Why conduct research in an attempt to develop scientific knowledge about teaching, they ask, if teaching is nothing more than a craft, particularly a craft with ambiguous moral overtones? Scientific rigor, they suggest, is inconsistent with the problematic conception of teaching inherent in the moral craft perspective.

In this section, I want to speak directly to the continuing need for inquiry on teaching, both to discuss the purpose of inquiry on teaching and to identify promising examples of such inquiry. But first I will summarize the major themes of my critique of the applied science metaphor.

The weaknesses in the teacher effectiveness perspective can be condensed into three categories of shortcomings: the teacher effectiveness perspective's narrow conception of teaching, its epistemological simplemindedness, and its assumption that knowledge ought to control teacher behavior. Of the three shortcomings, the most obvious one is the extraordinarily limited definition of teaching adopted by researchers working in the teacher effectiveness tradition. Teaching is conceived of as the efficient and effective achievement of student learning. That is, good teaching is defined strictly in empirical terms: whatever teaching practice can be shown experimentally to produce student learning is seen as a desirable teaching practice that ought to be included in teacher education programs (Gage & Giaconia 1981; Howsam et al. 1976). We assume the goals of teaching are to raise achievement test scores on standardized tests or to improve some student attitude, but which content or attitudes ought to be promoted by teachers is not seen as an issue amenable to systematic inquiry. Such teacher decisions are viewed as value judgments that fall outside the purview of scientific inquiry.

A few researchers, however, suggest that an empirical knowledge base could resolve some of the normative issues in teaching. Dunkin and Biddle, for example, believe that teaching ideologies develop basically because we do not know much about the nature of effective teaching: "We have interpreted these competing ideologies to be altogether human and understandable responses to our lack of scientific knowledge about the teaching field" (1974, p. 29). Gage's (1980) position on the potency of research-derived generalizations is more typical. He argues that teaching inherently involves artistry because the relationships among variables are complex and interactive and are, therefore, statistical generalizations rather than lawlike statements. Anticipating all the "twists and turns" that teaching may take is impossible, and the teacher, as he applies research-derived knowledge in teaching situations, must use "judgment, sudden insight, sensitivity, and agility to promote learning" (Gage 1978, p. 15). Note, though, that Gage's conception of teaching artistry focuses entirely on technique and does not include the normative issue of what content ought to be taught.

In brief, teacher effectiveness researchers do agree that the normative elements of teaching must be clearly separated from the empirical aspects of teaching. In addition, they see the technical or empirical components of teaching as having considerable potency, possibly capable of reducing our need to attend to the normative dimension of teaching. More common, however, is the belief that normative issues are outside the purview of the researcher. The unwillingness of teacher effectiveness researchers to entangle themselves in the normative dimension of teaching is understandable in light of the behavioristic orientation of many of these researchers (Sanders 1978). In addition, cognitively oriented researchers also exclude the normative dimension from their study of teaching.

Teaching, however, is normative as well as technical. Teaching inevitably involves the teacher attempting to influence the student to learn content that the teacher thinks is valuable (Peters 1965), and the student-teacher relationship itself is inherently moral in that one person temporarily has considerable control over the life of another

(Hawkins 1973). Moreover, the process of schooling is embedded in a particular set of political and social contexts that tend to be either maintained or transformed by the activities of teachers (Berlak & Berlak 1981). To ignore the normative dimension—content priorities, student-teacher relationship, cultural reproduction and/or cultural transformation—is to seriously distort the character of teaching. And to base teacher education on a concept of teaching as "any activity on the part of one person intended to facilitate learning on the part of another" (Gage 1978, p. 14) is to provide the teacher with an overly technical perspective.

The second problem with applying the teacher effectiveness perspective to teacher education involves epistemological weaknesses in this orientation. Two of the major weaknesses are: an overly simplified view of causality and the belief that the phenomenon of teaching is natural. I will briefly review each of these weaknesses.

Within the teacher effectiveness tradition there is widespread consensus that an empirical tie exists between teacher behavior and student learning. To establish the strongest possible causal link between teacher behavior and student learning, many teacher effectiveness advocates believe that experimental research should be stressed. "In experiments," note Gage and Giaconia, "we actively manipulate the level of one variable and then ascertain whether the level of another variable changes. If it does, then we have evidence that the manipulated, or independent, variable is a cause or determiner of the level of the other, or the dependent, variable" (1981, p. 3). Gage works in only one of the teacher effectiveness traditions—the so-called process-product approach—but assumes the causal link between teacher behavior and student learning exists in other traditions, for example, in the aptitude-treatment interaction approach. While no researchers claim that we can totally explain student learning in terms of teacher behavior—many variables other than teacher behavior are recognized as affecting student learning— process-product and aptitude-treatment interaction researchers maintain a persistent faith that they will eventually show that changes in teacher behavior "cause" specific changes in student learning. This assumed direct tie between teaching behavior and student learning is what I have termed the billiard ball hypothesis.

Since teacher effectiveness research has not revealed these causal links, the continued faith in their ultimate discovery is puzzling. One could attribute this faith to the inability of teacher effectiveness researchers to learn new ways of conceptualizing their research problems, but the belief is equally held by the most productive and gifted as well as the mediocre and unimaginative researchers. Neither can we attribute the persistence of this staunch belief to impending methodological breakthroughs. The most likely explanation for the continued search for a teacher behavior–student learning empirical link is the behaviorism that typically underlies teacher effectiveness research. This empirical link, as Sanders notes, "could be considered as simply a special case (although a complicated one) of the fundamental S-R connectionism presupposed by behaviorism—with teaching as the 'complex stimulus' and student outcomes as the 'complex response'" (1978, p. 184).

Unfortunately the connectionist conception of causality embedded in behaviorism—even in a sophisticated form—vastly over-simplifies any possible causal ties between teacher behavior and student learning. The student is not a passive receptacle whose learning is solely determined by teacher behavior and other input variables. Rather the student is an active, purposeful being so that "the activities the student engages in when confronted with instructional tasks are of crucial importance in determining what he will learn" (Anderson 1970, p. 349). Recognition of the student's active participation in the learning process, including the student's impact on teacher behavior, does not negate the impact of teacher behavior on student learning, but such recognition demands that learning be reconceptualized as student-teacher interaction, mediated by such factors as subject matter and student perceptions. In short, learning is "caused" by the intersection of teacher and student with subject matter, not by the teacher and other forces acting on the student. This interactive and mediated conception of learning also raises questions about some of the assumptions underlying the cognitive information-processing perspective, especially the presumption that we can ultimately discover how the mind really works and that this discovery will entail identifying the one-best-way of conceptualizing the work of the mind.

A second epistemological problem in the teacher effectiveness tradition is the mistaken belief that the activities of teaching are natural phenomena. So "natural" is this belief that it is often not even stated or, if stated, is not felt to need extensive defense (Dunkin & Biddle 1974; Kerlinger 1968).

Viewing teaching—and for that matter other educational phenomena—as natural makes it possible for teacher effectiveness researchers to attribute stability to the relationships among teaching-learning variables. Stability is assumed because natural phenomena are basically independent of man and his changing social purposes, much as the phenomena of physics and chemistry exist apart from man. The importance of stable relationships is that they make it possible for teacher effectiveness researchers to aspire to find statistical or even lawlike relationships among teaching-learning variables. In this manner, the postulate of natural teaching phenomena and its attendant assumption of stability of relationships among variables make possible the search for the "laws" of teacher effectiveness.

But teaching is not a natural phenomenon. On the contrary, teaching is intimately bound up with man and his social purposes (Ebel 1967, 1982). In a sense, I argued this point when the three normative bases of teaching were identified: choice among content priorities, the student-teacher relationship, and cultural reproduction/transformation. The centrality of these normative concerns to teaching practice is most obvious when an attempt is made to derive a teaching practice from a research finding. Such a derivation, Phillips convincingly argues, requires "linking premises involving value judgments...whether the researcher is aware of them or not" (1980, p. 19). The need for value-laden premises to link research results to teaching practices is present for both information-processing and behavioristic inquiry.

To the extent that we pretend that teaching is a natural phenomenon, we are perpetuating the blindness of researchers to the normative concerns central to teaching practice. How much better it would be if we were to apply the same systematic attention to the premises that link empirical theory to practice as we do to the creation of empirical theory itself. Such attention might be possible if we acknowledged more openly the socially constructed nature of teaching; then we would be guided to attend to the normative as well as the empirical dimensions of teaching practice.

Implicit in viewing the activities of teaching as a process of social construction is the idea that choice making is an integral part of teaching. A key question becomes: How do we decide if the argument made for goal X, or teaching practice Y, or educational policy Z is a good case? The reality of choice and the need for considered judgment in making choices are in direct conflict with the underlying assumptions of contemporary behavioral science. Modern behavioral scientists strive to understand human behavior, hopefully to predict this behavior, and ultimately to control it. As participants in the behavioral science tradition, teacher effectiveness researchers share in these guiding motives that emphasize making practice conform to research findings.

Thus we arrive at the third major shortcoming of the applied science basis of the teacher effectiveness tradition. While teacher effectiveness researchers aspire to understand and control teaching behavior, a major issue facing teachers is making choices among options, a problem that cannot be reduced to strictly empirical terms. I shall identify these two uses of a knowledge base as *knowledge for control* and *knowledge for liberation*—a designation with properly loaded words so that my personal position should be clear.

Teacher effectiveness researchers, however, may well accept these weighted labels and argue that they belong in the liberation camp. Do not teacher effectiveness research findings help liberate the teacher from the tyranny of the trial-and-error "knowledge" embodied in the craft tradition? And is not the analytic and experimental ethos that permeates behavioral science research a good antidote to the traditionalism so characteristic of our normal school heritage? Empirical research may well mark an advance over the educational theory of an earlier era—what R. S. Peters once called "undifferentiated mush" (1977, p. 169)—but teacher effectiveness researchers, findings can be applied just as dogmatically as allegedly craft knowledge was used during the normal school era. Indeed, the very epistemology of the teacher effectiveness orientation leads to the use of knowledge for purposes of behavioral control. That is, since teaching behavior is seen as natural and, in principle, lawful, it becomes the responsibility of the teacher to behave in accord with any theory verified by teacher effectiveness researchers.

Teachers not guided by empirical theory are presumed to be acting in an inefficient manner—a logical deduction if indeed empirical theory is of supreme importance to the conduct of teaching practice. Note, for example, Cronbach's discussion of how teachers adapt instructional method to the individual student:

> The significant thing about these adaptations is their informality. The teacher picks up some cues from the pupil's test record and his daily work, and other cues from rather casual observation of his social interactions. The teacher forms an impression of the pupil from the cues, usually without an explicit chain of reasoning. He proceeds on the basis of the impression to alter the instruction; the adaptation too is intuitive, without any explicit theory. No doubt the decisions tend to be beneficial, but there is reason to think that intuitive adaptations of this kind will be inefficient and occasionally may be harmful. (1969, p. 29)

Cronbach uses terms that suggest the adaptations are haphazard, for example, *informality, casual observation, an impression, usually without an explicit chain of reasoning, intuitive.* He concludes by charging that these intuitive adaptations are probably inefficient and may occasionally be harmful, an outcome he believes occurs because "it is very likely that teachers overdifferentiate" as they adapt their teaching to individual differences (p. 29). In the end, however, Cronbach admits that there is no research aimed directly at the topic of overdifferentiation: "I know no research on impressionistic adaptation of instruction" (p. 29). Other teacher effectiveness researchers are rarely as candid as is Cronbach, but their work is saturated with the idea that practice is impotent unless there is strong guidance from empirical theory.

It is, therefore, not difficult to see why teacher effectiveness researchers will continue to aspire to control the activities of the teacher. The teacher effectiveness epistemology is rooted in the assumed supremacy of theory over practice. As a result, the task of the practitioner is to behave in ways consistent with the empirical theory discovered by the researcher, with the researcher continually pursuing the elusive goal of the one-best-way to teach each youngster. The sense that teaching involves choice making as well as effective practice either is outside the perspective of the teacher effectiveness tradition or is tangential to the focus on the development of empirical theory.

If the teacher effectiveness tradition is inadequate because it ignores the normative dimension of teaching, because it is epistemologically simplistic in its conception of causality and its view of teaching as a natural phenomenon, and because it focuses on controlling teacher practices, what possible form of inquiry on teaching can avoid all these errors? Some have concluded that when we attend to interaction effects and acknowledge the socially constructed nature of teaching, we destroy the possibility of developing knowledge about teaching. Gage, for example, contends:

> In principle, this [interactive] view of teaching means that we can never have anything substantive, and the only thing that lasts beyond a given moment with its unique combination of teacher, pupil, subject matter, classroom, and time is a set of behavioral science methods of measurement, design, observation, appraisal, and statistical analysis. Research methodology has some lasting value, but nothing else does. (1980, pp. 11–12)

This pessimistic view of the prospects for research on teaching has a certain surface validity, if we assume that the purpose of research on teaching is before-the-act knowledge of effective teaching practices.

The problem with Gage's analysis is not that his logic is faulty but rather that his assumed purpose for research on teaching is wrongheaded. Prediction and control of behavior are perfectly appropriate criteria if one's purpose is technical, that is, to achieve agreed upon goals efficiently. But if phenomena are socially constructed and partly normative, then a predominant technical orientation is appropriate only if teaching is directed toward either indoctrination or maintenance of the status quo.

Using a technical perspective to guide research on teaching in a democratic, pluralistic society is a mistake. Over fifty years ago Bode observed that scientific analysis does not reveal the proper function of education in a democracy. Since "education is a tool that can be made to serve many masters," Bode believed that "it is of primary importance that our teachers should have a definite conception of their function in the social order" (1927b, p. 524). "The function of theory is not to prescribe for the prospective teacher what he is to believe, but to assist him in clarifying his understanding of what is meant by democracy and how the conception of democracy relates to the content and method of teaching" (pp. 523–24). Similarly, Bayles (1959) argues for educational theory that helps us clarify our thinking about democracy and what this thinking means for keeping school. Other teacher educators do not envision theory as linking a conception of democracy to teaching but do believe educational theory should help the teacher reflect on the meaning of her work. Broudy (1963) sees educational theory as an "interpretive" map to place teaching problems in context, and Peters views theory as a way of helping the teacher to reflect on what she is doing (1977, pp. 135–38).

None of these proposed conceptions of educational theory stresses the efficient production of learning, as might be done when theory is conceived of as a system of universal statements or, in the style of teacher effectiveness researchers, as individual laws or generalizations (Nagel 1969). On the contrary, rather than seeing theory as something from which specific teaching practices are deduced, these educators view educational theory as helping the teacher thoughtfully consider her purposes, her role as a socializing agent, and her behavior and its effects on students. Underlying these reflective purposes is the assumption that educational theory is a source of insight or enlightenment rather than a source of specific or general prescriptions. Proposing that educational theory should serve to make the practitioner more reflective is reminiscent of Fenstermacher's (1982) advice that the results of teacher effectiveness research be used as evidence for testing the beliefs of the teacher or as schemata for helping the teacher see classroom events in new ways. This view of educational theory is consistent with Nagel's fourth sense of theory as "any more or less systematic analysis of a set of related concepts," an analysis whose adequacy is "determined only in a secondary or peripheral way by considerations of empirical data" (1969, pp. 10, 11).

As the quote from Bode illustrates, there is nothing particularly new in the suggestion that theory ought to be more a source of insight and enlightenment than a source of rules and prescriptions. In teacher education, this conception of educational theory can be traced back at least to Dewey's (1904) classic discussion of theory and practice. Over the years, moreover, thousands of teacher educators—often from the so-called foundational areas of educational philosophy, history, sociology—have urged their students to probe epistemological issues, to relate education to the broader social context, to think rigorously about the purposes of general education, and so forth.

Such efforts, however, have not been particularly successful. The difficulties in using theory for enlightenment purposes are varied, including the tendency for such instruction to come early in teacher education programs so that it is separated from teaching practice, the inclination of novices to ignore pedagogical instruction not related to their survival concerns, the use of instructional materials that fail to tie "foundational" issues to the day-to-day activities of the teacher. A telling example of the capacity to remove foundational issues from the realm of day-to-day teaching occurred in my own teacher training when Henry's *Modern Philosophies and Education* was used as a text in a philosophy of education course. Each chapter of this text develops the educational implications of a school of philosophy, for example, Thomist, realist, idealist, and so forth. The fact that we novices did not consider ourselves realists, idealists, or whatever gave the epistemological and other issues raised by the text an Alice-in-Wonderland quality. The concepts introduced in Henry's book are not, in Nagel's (1969) terms, "systematically analyzed," particularly as these concepts relate to the world of teaching practice.

In short, enlightenment issues disconnected from the daily life of teachers are not likely to enlighten. All such disjointed instruction does is to convince beginning teachers that educational theory is irrelevant to classroom teaching, a belief already prevalent among experienced teachers. An enlightenment-oriented research strategy, therefore, must lead to outcomes that can be linked to teaching practice. Unless the socially constructed nature of teaching, the normative dimension of teaching, and other enlightenment-oriented characteristics are explored in relation to classroom life, there is little hope of conducting teaching inquiry whose results can be productively tied to teaching practice.

Before outlining several examples of enlightenment-oriented inquiry that are grounded in teaching practice, I want to relate this approach to educational inquiry to the contemporary dispute over the means and ends of social scientific research. Such comparison is possible because the critique of the conventional approach to the scientific study of human behavior is more advanced in several fields outside education than it is in the case of teaching. (Note, however, such exceptions as Berlak & Berlak 1981; Popkewitz, Tabachnick, & Zeichner 1979.) I will draw upon the epistemological reformulations of Kenneth Gergen, both because his critique is unusually insightful and because he is concerned with social psychology, a sister discipline to educational psychology, which is central to research on teaching. As we will see, Gergen's conception of the purposes of social psychological theory can be used to suggest parallel purposes for educational theory.

For over ten years, Gergen has been expressing doubt about the possibility of developing social psychological theory of transhistoric validity, about the predictive value of general theory, and even about our ability to verify any kind of theory or hypotheses. Gergen (1978) contends that since the dominant positivist-empiricist paradigm has not yielded a body of highly reliable propositions, we should try an approach to theory construction that does not give preeminent attention to the verification of theory. Instead we may want to "consider competing theoretical accounts in terms of their *generative capacity*" by which Gergen means *"the capacity to challenge the guiding assumptions of the culture, to raise fundamental questions regarding contemporary social life, to foster reconsideration of that which is 'taken for granted,' and thereby to furnish new alternatives for social action"* (p. 1346). Generative theory, therefore, is not circumscribed by "what now exists" but rather helps us consider alternative arrangements and evaluate the advantages and disadvantages of these arrangements. To those social psychologists who may object to generative theory because its social activism necessitates value commitments, Gergen answers that the traditional attempt to remain ethically neutral is in reality a value stance that tends to favor perpetuation of the status quo.

In a subsequent paper, Gergen (1980a) identifies three interrelated functions that are appropriate to the scientist facing a world of continuous change: the scientist as a conceptual constructionist, as a change agent, and as a prognosticator. The functions of conceptual constructionist and social change agent seem especially relevant to practicing educators. Conceptual constructionists attempt to supply us with varied conceptual schemes, each of which provides a lens through which an aspect of the shifting social world is made salient. Such conceptual constructions help us interpret the world. Gergen uses the term *vivification* to refer to the various types of interpretation, that is, transforming perception, sensitizing to a new idea, reconstructing one's experience, or questioning dominant assumptions. An example of a conceptional construction is Kohlberg's theory of moral development. While the suppositions of this theory, as well as its implications for action, are open to question, the theory does challenge some commonly held interpretations of the nature of moral judgment. The theory, therefore, can vivify by causing a person to reconsider his conception of the basis of moral judgment.

In addition to the interpretive role of the scientist, Gergen postulates a change agent role. He argues that such a role is inevitable, even for the scientist who only describes and analyzes society. For example, the widespread acceptance of social exchange theory can lead the general populace to view social life as a marketplace and human behavior as a commodity to be bought and sold. Instead of denying that social science research necessarily brings about changes in society, Gergen advocates that "theory...be formulated for the purpose of furthering valuational goals to which the scientist is committed. In the formulation of theory the scientist becomes a moral or ideological change agent" (1980a, p. 260). Such a stance toward the interrelationship of theory and valued goals is intellectually more honest than the belief that theory can be devoid of impact on societal goals.

Adapting Gergen's analysis to teaching, we can see at least two approaches to the pursuit of insight-oriented theory. First, educational theory can be developed to help teachers interpret teaching phenomena in new ways. Such interpretive uses of theory could include challenges to commonly held assumptions about teaching, alternatives to conventional teaching wisdom, suggestions for handling day-to-day teaching problems in more humane or effective ways. If theory directed at interpretation is fruitful, this theory will vivify the teacher's world. (See also the discussion of schemata by Fenstermacher 1982.) Second, theory can be created to sustain and promote desired teaching goals. While the researcher-advocate needs to be cautious about unduly influencing others over whom he has some kind of power, open recognition of the change agent role is certainly superior to the pretense of neutrality maintained by teacher effectiveness researchers. The researcher-advocate does need to be able to provide reasoned argument for the ends he is pursuing, a responsibility teacher effectiveness researchers should also assume. Both the interpretive and advocate functions employ theory in a generative or reconstructive sense rather than in an explanatory and predictive sense.

Since the generative conception of the purpose of educational theory is so at variance with the typical emphasis on verification and control, there is a relatively limited amount of teaching inquiry directed at the creation of generative knowledge and theory. I will briefly discuss three examples of inquiry designed to develop generative theory; these examples tend to fulfill an interpretive rather than an advocacy function. The examples include: Peters' use of concrete problems of teaching as a focal point for discipline-based inquiry, the Berlaks' interpretive framework of the dilemmas of teaching, and the search for alternative metaphors of teaching.

The proposals of R. S. Peters for the study of teaching seem to be based on an interpretive use of theory. He believes that the impact of theory on practice is indirect because teaching is not a technology in which theoretical findings can be easily applied to practice. Rather, the impact of educational theory on practice is "the gradual transformation of a person's view of children, of himself, and of the situation in which he is acting" (1977, p. 163). During initial teacher preparation the major function of educational theory is "to remove certain naiveties that students bring to the educational situation, through having only participated in it at the consumer end, and gradually to restructure their view of the situation" (p. 164). Subsequent theoretical training should be more rigorous, making increased use of the various disciplines—for example, philosophy, psychology, sociology, history—whose differentiated forms of thinking are necessary to foster the development of clearheaded and informed solutions to the problems of teaching. All through Peters' writing on teacher preparation is an emphasis on the teacher as a self-directed, critical, experimental person. For Peters, therefore, theory appears to have primarily an interpretive purpose, since theory is supposed to sensitize the teacher to new ways of seeing students and teaching.

The sensitization occurs in relation to the concrete problems of teaching. Illustrative problems include: Should children be punished at school? What is the educational significance of play? Can morality be taught? Such concrete problems supposedly provide a means for integrating the philosophical, psychological, historical, and sociological components of educational theory, and these problems can be returned to again and again during a teacher's career. Peters specifically objects to ideological instruction designed to provide answers to the concrete problems of teaching (1977, pp. 164–67). It is the student who must use theory to think about these problems; the theory cannot tell the teacher what to do, particularly in the area of methodology.

The knowledge base implicit in Peters' proposals is more concerned with identifying and exploring problems than with providing answers to these teaching problems. Questions about the substance of the knowledge base remain, however. In particular, which concrete problems are important to the enterprise of teaching? There are also questions about how to apply the disciplines to the study of educational problems. For example, how can the curriculum be structured so that the study of these problems through the relevant disciplines does not result in isolated courses in the various disciplines? On the other hand, how far must one go into the type of thought characteristic of a discipline so that the analysis of a problem profits from the rigor of the discipline? Peters acknowledges these and related issues but does not provide much guidance toward resolving them. He seems not so much concerned about prescribing the content of the knowledge base or about specifying how disciplines are to be applied to this content as he is interested in identifying the general terrain on which the knowledge base is to be constructed, that is, on the problems of teaching.

Berlak and Berlak (1975, 1981) propose a much more specific framework for interpreting classroom life. Drawing upon the research tradition of symbolic interactionism which emphasizes the meanings an individual takes from situations, the Berlaks conceptualize sixteen dilemmas that attempt to capture the complexities and contradictions they observed in English primary schools. Each dilemma represents the polar opposite ways in which a particular teaching issue can be resolved, for example, whether a teacher views knowledge as given or as problematic. In addition to dilemmas that deal with classroom control and curriculum, there is a set of dilemmas labeled *societal*; these dilemmas focus on issues of equality, justice, and social relations among people of different ages, sexes, and ethnic and racial groups. An example of a societal dilemma is equal versus differential allocation to students of such resources as materials and teacher time. Stone and Wehlage (1982) have developed a dilemma framework that has some similarities to the work of the Berlaks.

Key to the Berlaks' approach is the question of how teachers resolve the various dilemmas of teaching. What appear on the surface to be "apparent inconsistencies in a teacher's behavior and language could be explained if we hypothesized that the teacher is drawn to some degree toward both poles of a dilemma" (1975, p. 223). That is, in the case of the dilemma "intrinsic versus extrinsic motivation" the teacher is drawn "to the idea that the impetus for learning comes—and should come—primarily from within the learner and, on the other hand, to the idea that some kind of action by the teacher or others is required for learning to be initiated and sustained by a child" (pp. 231–32). In particular, the Berlaks are interested in the *patterns* of dilemma resolution because knowledge of these patterns gives insight into the trade-offs a teacher makes and the conditions under which particular trade-offs are made.

The Berlaks (1981) believe that the dilemma language can empower a teacher by providing a way to conceptualize her current patterns of teaching choices, consider alternative patterns for making these choices, and examine the consequences of present and/or future patterns of dilemma resolution on the lives of children. In addition, the dilemma language helps a teacher identify the origins of patterns of dilemma resolution, including an awareness of the realities that constrain her ability to change her behavior. This use of the dilemma framework to analyze and reconceptualize behavior is central to what the Berlaks consider the purpose of teacher education programs: helping a teacher become aware of political, cultural, and moral choices involved in teaching practice.

The purposes the Berlaks hold for teacher preparation programs suggest that they are interested in using educational theory for purposes of advocacy as well as interpretively (they would probably object to the separation of these two functions). They are, however, careful to note that a teacher's interpretive awareness of an alternative way of resolving a particular dilemma is not necessarily a sufficient basis for behavior change. Awareness of an alternative must be accompanied by the craft knowledge needed to implement this alternative. For example, in the process of instituting a program in which children read self-selected books (in order to give increased emphasis to intrinsic motivation and holistic learning), a teacher may discover she tends to sacrifice other valued beliefs (that learning is social and that the teacher should maintain control over standards). The craft problem, therefore, becomes learning how to develop a reading program that maintains an emphasis on social learning and teacher standards while it gives increased attention to intrinsic motivation and holistic learning. Such a task is enormously complicated, particularly since we know so little about how teachers develop craft knowledge (Berlak & Berlak 1981).

Teacher effectiveness researchers could make a real contribution to the advancement of a teacher education knowledge base if they turned their attention to the exploration of craft knowledge. It is the absence of appropriate craft knowledge that often frustrates teacher efforts to implement desired alternatives. While it is true that two traditions of research on teaching—ethnographic and cognitive information processing—attend to some aspects of craft knowledge such as teacher planning or classroom control, these two traditions are relatively new entrants in the arena of teaching research. In addition, practitioners of both of these traditions tend to share most of the questionable assumptions associated with the teacher effectiveness orientation, for example, teaching is a natural phenomenon, teaching is the efficient production of learning, and empirical theory ought to control practice. Generally, however, they do have a more sophisticated conception of causality because they attend to the context of teaching and to the teacher's purposes and perceptions more than do the dominant traditions within the field of teacher effectiveness. It is not clear whether these newer approaches can help codify craft knowledge or whether the inquiry of such perceptive teachers as Herbert Kohl is a more promising route. For now, I think it is clear that Kohl's work is considerably more sophisticated and provocative than the work of the research establishment.

In contrast to the Berlaks' elaborate dilemma framework and their parallel concern for craft knowledge, there is a third approach that represents a more general style of inquiry. This approach involves the search for new metaphors that challenge the dominant view of teaching. Early in the twentieth century, Rice's accountability metaphor—that is, the idea that teaching should be judged by its results—was an alternative conception that challenged the assumptions then prevalent about the nature and the purposes of teaching. Today, I believe that the moral craft metaphor has the same "generative" capacity as Rice's embryonic applied science metaphor had at the turn of the century. In a sense, therefore, this book—especially Parts II and III—is an example of generative inquiry.

Gergen considers the development of alternative metaphors as an appropriate way to create generative theory. He notes that "many commonly accepted explanations for human action are tied to prevailing metaphors within the culture" (1980b, pp. 267–68). The power of a metaphor, Gergen observes, is in the potency of its visual image, which may be so great as to deflect attention from approaches to social action grounded in other metaphors. The domino theory of American foreign policy, for example, was based on a metaphor that so fascinated policy makers in the 1960s that alternative conceptions of foreign policy were not seriously entertained. In order to challenge the domino theory or any other potent metaphor, a theorist tries to create a "novel visualization that may unify a range of diverse experiences" (p. 269).

The moral craft metaphor certainly does bring together diverse experiences; in fact, many educators would say that the moral and craft elements that are unified through this metaphor are in conflict. Craft is commonly associated with the skillful achievement of practical ends while moral entails the question of what ends are worthwhile. How can a metaphor unite a concern both with what ends are desirable and with what means are reasonable paths to these desirable ends? How can we focus concurrently on the empirical and normative dimensions of teaching? Such a combination is conceivable, as I argued in Chapter 6, and leads us to view moral craft as a reflective, diligent, and skillful approach toward the pursuit of desirable ends. What is striking about the moral craft metaphor is that it encourages us to break down the dualism in teaching between empirical and normative concerns that is perpetuated by the dominant applied science metaphor.

As I introduced the topic of alternative metaphors, I said that this approach to developing generative theory was a more general style of inquiry than the Berlaks' sophisticated dilemma framework. The level of abstraction of metaphors, for instance, is considerably higher than the sixteen dilemmas in the Berlak framework. Moreover, as I noted in Chapter 6, metaphors typically are compact, leaving much to our imagination, our past experiences, and our personal way of using language. As a consequence, metaphors usually need to be explored in some detail, often requiring us to make numerous linkages and comparisons. Such was the case with my discussion of the moral and craft basis of teaching, and the resultant moral craft metaphor was seen to provide only rough guidance for my work in teacher education and supervision of instruction.

From the preceding analysis, I conclude that the derivation of alternative metaphors is a promising approach to the development of generative theory but that alternative metaphors serve more to reorient one's thinking than to suggest specific courses of educational action. (See Kliebard 1982a, for a thoughtful discussion of the relationship of metaphor and theory.) No form of generative theory is going to tell us what to do in particular teaching situations. The socially constructed nature of teaching phenomena magnifies the choice-making element of teaching and requires us to reflect on how we want to approach any particular situation.

There is the broader question regarding the extent to which the three approaches to developing generative theory—using concrete teaching problems as a focal point for discipline-based inquiry, employing a dilemmas-of-teaching framework, and creating alternative metaphors—avoid the shortcomings associated with the teacher effectiveness perspective. These three approaches appear to avoid an overly narrow definition of teaching, since all three approaches assume inquiry on teaching should be centrally concerned with the normative as well as empirical dimension of teaching. These three approaches also seem consistent with a socially constructed view of teaching, though it is not clear whether they avoid the overly simplified conception of causality characteristic of the teacher effectiveness tradition. For the most part, however, causality is not a central concern of generative theories, since their focus is more on reflection and reconstruction than on explanation and prediction. Lastly, there is legitimate reason to worry that generative theories can lose their power to enlighten and to prompt reconsideration of taken-for-granted ideas, especially if such theories become dominant and are accepted as unquestioned truths. In this regard, the history of the applied science metaphor is instructive; a once generative idea is now assumed to be true. It may well be that each generation of researchers must rethink its guiding metaphors if it is to avoid having its research behavior—as well as the behavior of teachers—controlled by whatever metaphor happens to be dominant.

CONCLUSION

When I began in 1980 to be critical of NCATE standards, I had several people challenge me to provide a better alternative. Usually these people admitted that there were fundamental problems with the standards, especially with applying the standards in a reliable way to teacher education programs. But these people argued, appropriately I believe, that it is very difficult to decide what substance—what specific view of quality—the standards should endorse if the standards were to abandon their long-standing focus on procedures. Despite these difficulties, I was sorely tempted to argue that all programs must be grounded in the moral craft metaphor or in a specific interpretation of that metaphor.

In the end, however, I decided that the new focus for NCATE standards ought to be on preconditions to quality, regardless of how quality might be defined. This decision raises as many problems as it resolves, for it is not at all obvious whether the four preconditions I favor really are the most appropriate preconditions. Certainly we need vigorous debate over which preconditions are the most desirable, but I believe that a specific vision of quality ought not be prescribed, even if this debate thereby becomes harder to conduct. Each group of people responsible for a program ought to be held responsible for the design of that program.

In order for us to take a generative perspective—in teacher education program design or in any other "regulated" area of teaching practice—we must not respond primarily to externally imposed criteria. It is hard enough to assume a generative stance in the absence of such criteria; our inclination seems to be to assume that teaching phenomena are natural rather than socially constructed. All that externally imposed criteria do is to magnify the sense in which we feel we must respond to our environment rather than create it.

Perhaps the aspect of teaching inquiry most antithetical to the development of generative theory is our conviction that the task of theory is to verify how the teaching-learning process works. As long as we adhere to a verification view of theory, we are restricted from taking personal responsibility for the direction of the teaching-learning process. It is indeed more comfortable to believe that one is in tune with the regularities of teaching than to realize that one's real task is to create these very regularities. (See van Manen 1982, for a similar view of the nature and purpose of educational theory.)

In a fundamental sense, inquiry into teaching must always be out of tune with the dominant conceptions of teaching. It is the task of researchers on teaching to remind each generation of practitioners that what appears to be a natural process occurring within the context of a natural institution is in reality a socially constructed process occurring in a socially constructed institution. For now, I believe that conceiving of teaching as a moral craft helps alert us to the artificial nature of teaching phenomena.

APPENDIX

SECONDARY PROFESSIONAL SEMESTER, SPRING 1981
WASHINGTON UNIVERSITY

The secondary professional semester is a full-time experience that runs from January 19 to May 15. Twelve of the fifteen hours in this experience are team taught by four faculty members: Bill Connor, Vivian Gellman, Dick Nault, and Alan Tom. The twelve hours include instruction on reading in the content areas and general principles of teaching as well as student teaching. The last three hours is a curriculum and instruction course and is conducted by one of the following instructors: Lloyd Klinedinst (foreign languages), Richard Lodholz (mathematics), Hal Zimmerman (psychology and social studies), Melba James (science), or Bernetta Jackson (English). While not tightly integrated with the remaining twelve hours, the curriculum and instruction courses are designed to give the student the specialized help he/she needs to teach in his/her chosen subject area. All of the curriculum and instruction courses are offered Wednesday evening, 4:00–6:30 P.M.

The remaining twelve hours of course work and experience occur during the day, typically between 8:30 A.M. and 3:30 P.M. The January 19–May 15 time period is divided into five phases:

1. *Phase I: Two Weeks* (January 19–January 30)
   a. *Location:* Most instruction is on campus, with several visits to schools where student teaching placements will be made.
   b. *Activity/Purpose:* Phase one is designed to start instruction on the craft of teaching, to help each student select a school, and to provide an opportunity for a student to meet with a teacher (in the selected school) to arrange a mutually acceptable placement.

2. *Phase II: Seven Weeks* (February 2–March 20)
   a. *Location:* In the mornings the student will be working with

his/her cooperating teacher (for at least three class periods, one of which can be a free period). On Monday, Wednesday, and Friday afternoons from 1:00–3:00 P.M. the WU (Washington University) staff will have the students in class; Tuesday and Thursday afternoons are not scheduled.

b. *Activity/Purpose:* To continue instruction on the craft of teaching and to introduce the normative elements of teaching at the same time as the student is gaining classroom teaching experience. WU staff will begin supervisory visits.

3. *Phase III: Four Weeks* (March 23–April 17)
   a. *Location:* Full-day student teaching (except for Friday afternoons when the WU staff will meet with the students).
   b. *Activity/Purpose:* Phase three is designed to give the student a realistic picture of what is involved in being a career teacher. Supervisory visits by WU staff will continue.

4. *Phase IV: Two Weeks* (April 20–May 1)
   a. *Location:* Same daily schedule as in phase two—half-day student teaching with afternoon sessions with the WU staff. Supervisory visits by WU staff will be completed by May 1, the last day students are in the schools.
   b. *Activity/Purpose:* Continuation of WU staff's attempt to articulate our instruction with the classroom experience of the student teachers.

5. *Phase V: Two Weeks* (May 4–May 15)
   a. *Location:* Some scheduled sessions with WU staff, but most of the time will be unscheduled.
   b. *Activity/Purpose:* The unscheduled time should enable students to complete projects/papers assigned in the curriculum and instruction courses as well as projects/papers concerning reading in the content areas and general principles of teaching. The scheduled time will be used for observation and analysis of videotapes, evaluation of the overall professional experience, and other topics to be selected later.

At the end of this seventeen-week experience we hope that each student will be prepared to assume teaching responsibility in his/her own classroom.

Before outlining the content/requirements of the professional semester, it is appropriate to give a brief rationale for our conception of the good teacher. This conception is what provides coherence to the content/requirements which compose the professional semester.

The good teacher, we believe, is a moral craftsman. The good teacher is a craftsman because he/she is involved in an activity that requires special skills and can be improved through careful observation and analysis. Both of these attributes of teaching (specialized skill and improvement through observation/analysis of past efforts) are central to crafts and, therefore, justify the characterization of teaching as a craft. But the good teacher is more than a skilled craftsman. Unlike many of the traditional crafts (for instance, ceramics, cooking, gardening), teaching involves the practitioner directly with people, rather than with material or animals. In addition, the student-teacher relationship is an unequal one in which the teacher has considerable power over the student. Since teaching does involve a human relationship among people of unequal power and authority, teaching is of necessity a moral endeavor. The teacher's control over the lives of students means he/she must be cautious concerning what he/she insists they learn and how he/she treats them. That is, the teacher must be morally sensitive. To sum up, the good teacher is both a craftsman (who has specialized skill that can be improved through observation and analysis) and a moralist (who must think carefully about what his/her relationship to students should be and about what these students ought to be taught).

A teacher education program designed to develop "moral craftsman" teachers needs content relevant both to the craft element of teaching (basic teaching skills and observation/analysis skills) and to the moral element of teaching (the student-teacher relationship and the issue of what knowledge/skills are important for students to learn). In addition to these two themes of content, the teacher in contemporary America must also be well-informed about a variety of societal forces that affect his/her daily teaching. Examples of such societal forces are court-ordered busing, public demands for teacher accountability, declining enrollments, and public concern about sexist curriculum materials. The "good" teacher needs to be aware of these societal forces and their implications in day-to-day teaching situations.

A fourth theme of content involves orienting the prospective teacher to teaching and to the occupation of teaching. Such orientation includes finding an appropriate student-teaching placement, learning about the expectations of the cooperating teacher, learning about what it feels like to teach all day, understanding whether teaching is the right career for a person, and organizing a job search strategy. Unless there is careful attention to orientation, a teacher education program is not really providing either a realistic training experience or a sound preparation for the first teaching job.

In our program we organize the four content themes so the following content is included:

1. *Craftsmanship*
   a. Generic teaching skills.
      1. Planning skills—lesson and unit planning.
      2. Interactive skills—questioning, classroom discussion, maintaining control, etc.
   b. Reading in the content areas, for example, readability formulas, cloze passages, directed reading activities.
   c. Observation/analysis skills (also included in the Educational Psychology course).
      1. Direct analysis of teaching (videotapes or live observations).
      2. Reflective skill, for example, student teacher awareness of his/her own concerns and motives.

2. *Moral Sensitivity*
   a. The student-teacher relationship.
      1. Teacher establishment of norms.
      2. The teacher as an authority.
      3. Effect of school organization on the student-teacher relationship.
   b. Justification of content taught to students.
      1. Typical strategies for justifying content.
      2. Hidden curriculum, that is, teaching attitudes/ideas we are not aware we are teaching.

3. *The Classroom and Societal Forces* (also included in the American School course).
   a. While many different types of content could be included under the "societal forces" theme, we are concentrating on the desegregation/integration controversy currently unfolding in the metropolitan St. Louis area.
   b. Accountability—particularly testing youngsters in the "basic skills" and testing teachers as a prerequisite for certification. This topic is discussed, but in not nearly as much detail as desegregation/integration.

4. *Orientation to Teaching:* as an activity and an occupation.
   a. Student-teaching placement process.
      1. Selection by student of a school.
      2. WU student-teacher interview.
   b. Student teacher and cooperating teacher relationship.
      1. Making this relationship a strong and positive one.
      2. The limits on student teacher authority.
   c. What is it like to teach?
      1. Full-day student teaching.
      2. The teacher's relationship with other school professionals, for example, counselors, principals, central office personnel, colleagues.
      3. Match between a student's interests and the rewards of a teaching career.
   d. The job search.
      1. Preparing a teaching file.
      2. Gaining interviewing skill through simulated interviews.

The content outlined above is integrated into our seventeen-week program.

The best way to see the overall flow of the semester is to outline the content for each of the seventeen weeks. The most detail is given for the first two weeks when the students are with us most of the time; instructional topics are provided for most of the remaining fifteen weeks. Daily objectives are not given because this would take too much space.

   Phase I: January 19–January 30
   Monday, January 19
      9:30–10:30:   Introduction to the professional semester (Tom)

11:00–12:00: Overview for "reading in the content areas" (Gellman)

1:00– 2:00: Effective learning experiences (Tom)

2:30– 3:30: Introduction to Tuesday school visits (Tom)

Tuesday, January 20

9:00–10:15: Visit to Brittany Middle School

10:45–12:00: Visit to Webster Groves High School

1:00– 2:00: Overview on lesson planning—focus on objectives and set induction (Tom)

2:30– 3:30: Directed reading activity (Gellman)

Wednesday, January 21

10:30–12:00: Matching materials and readers (Gellman)

1:00– 1:30: Introduction to Thursday school visits (Tom)

1:45– 3:00: Development of a lesson plan based on one of the specialized reading strategies (Gellman)

3:00: Staff meeting

Thursday, January 22

9:00–10:15: Visit to University City High School

10:30–11:45: School visit (tentative)

1:00– 2:00: Reflections on these school visits (Tom)

2:30– 3:30: Teach a mini-lesson based on a specialized reading strategy. Mini-lessons to be discussed in terms of clarity, direction giving, and "presence" (Gellman)

Friday, January 23

9:00–10:00: Completion of mini-lessons based on specialized reading strategies (Gellman)

10:00–11:00: Introduction to video equipment (Connor)

11:00–12:00: Informal work with videotape continues while students talk with staff about school preferences.

1:00– 3:00: Observation/analysis of teaching, including the viewing a videotape or two (Tom)

3:00: Staff meeting

Monday, January 26

9:00–10:30: National policy on school desegregation (Nault)

11:00–12:00: Lesson planning: teaching strategies and evaluation (Tom)

1:00– 3:00: Lesson planning: a workshop in which each person will create a lesson with specific objectives, set induction, appropriate teaching strategies, and an evaluation plan (Tom)

Tuesday, January 27

9:00–10:30: School desegregation: the local scene (Nault)

11:00–12:00: Interviewing for a student-teaching placement (Tom)

afternoon: Open to visit schools for interviews with teachers

Wednesday, January 28

9:00–10:30: Do exercise to discover one's concerns as a student teacher, relate to Frances Fuller's research on teachers' concerns, and discuss the implications of the teacher concern literature for the design of teacher education programs (Tom)

11:00–12:00: Effective instruction: matching what we want to teach with the concerns of our students? If so, why do we talk of teachers "motivating" students? (Tom)

afternoon: Open to visit schools for interviews

3:00: Staff meeting

Thursday, January 29

9:00–10:00: Establishment of norms: moving from beliefs to norms; norms as an instance of behavior modification? (Tom)

10:30–11:30: Analysis of teaching (transcripts/tapes) in terms of norms (Tom)

afternoon: To be determined (available for school interviews if necessary)

Friday, January 30

9:00–12:00: To be determined

1:00– 1:30: Jill Hill—setting up a teaching file

1:30– 2:00: Establishing a good working relationship with your cooperating teacher (Tom)

2:00: Staff meeting

Phase II: February 2–March 20 (half-day student teaching) WU sessions 1:00–3:00 P.M.

Monday, February 2: Discipline—a general structure (Tom)

Wednesday, February 4: Student-teacher relationship (Tom)

Friday, February 6: Analysis of videotapes.

Monday, February 9: Alternative teaching strategies (Tom)

Tuesday, February 10: Reception for cooperating teachers at 4 P.M.

Wednesday, February 11: Special focus on discussion as strategy (Tom)

Friday, February 13: Analysis of videotapes

Monday, February 16: No class

Wednesday, February 18: Teaching for integration (Nault)

Friday, February 20: Workshop for designing desegregation/integration papers (Nault)

Monday, February 23: Evaluation, especially grading (Tom)

Wednesday, February 25: Test construction workshop (Tom)

Friday, February 27: Analysis of videotapes

Monday, March 2: Lesson planning revisited—expressive objectives (Tom)

Wednesday, March 4: Lesson planning revisited—matching teaching and learning styles (Tom)

Friday, March 6: Analysis of videotapes

Monday, March 9: Strategies revisited—questioning (Tom)

Wednesday, March 11: Strategies revisited—workshop on sharing strategies (Tom)

Friday, March 13: Analysis of videotapes

Monday, March 16: Strategies for justifying content (Tom)

Wednesday, March 18: Open

Friday, March 20: Reading assignments on directed reading activity due. Reading workshop, including teaching students how to study (Gellman)

Phase III: March 23–April 17 (full-day student teaching) WU sessions 1:00–3:00 P.M.

Friday, March 27: Agenda to be determined (Gellman)

Friday, April 3: Agenda to be determined—(University City Spring vacation)

Friday, April 10: The teacher's relationship with other school professionals—report of interview findings (Tom)

Friday, April 17: Agenda to be determined— (Webster Groves Spring vacation)

Phase IV: April 20–May 1 (half-day student teaching)

Monday, April 20

Wednesday, April 22

Friday, April 24   Sessions will be held on Teaching as a

Monday, April 27   Career, Job Interviewing, Accountability,

Wednesday, April 29   Hidden Curriculum

Friday, May 1

Phase V: May 4–May 15 (largely unscheduled)

Friday, May 8: Reading assignment due

Tuesday, May 12: Desegregation/integration paper due

Friday, May 15: Determination by staff of final grades

Requirements/Grading

The student will receive four separate grades for the professional semester experience:

1. Curriculum and instruction course: Course requirements and grade determined by the instructor of that course
2. Reading: Evaluated by Vivian Gellman according to reading assignments
3. Principles of teaching: Grade to be determined by equally weighing the student's performance on three activities/tasks:
   a. Out-of-class assignments related to the moral craftsman themes of the professional semester—evaluated by Alan Tom
   b. Desegregation/integration paper—evaluated by Dick Nault and Bill Connor (see paragraph at the end of this section)
   c. Class participation evaluated in relation to the moral craftsman themes of the professional semester—to be done by the entire staff

4. Student teaching: The grade (pass or fail) is contingent on the student:
   a. Meeting the expectations of your host school for teaching performance.
   b. Demonstrating your ability to analyze your teaching, including sensitivity to the teacher-student relationship and an awareness of the need to be able to justify content to be taught to students, as well as the observation of craft-related skills.
   c. Demonstrating that you can successfully teach a secondary class for a sustained period of time.

   The pass/fail judgment is made by your supervisor in consultation with your cooperating teacher and other members of professional semester staff.

Guidelines for Desegregation/Integration Paper

During the course of the semester it is our hope that you will become more adept at managing effective classroom instruction and that you will become more familiar with issues that are likely to affect your career as a teacher. The desegregation/integration paper is directed at the second goal. An environmental issue that is likely to be at the forefront of concern in your school will be the legal efforts to include the county public schools in the desegregation of the city schools.

No later than May 12, you are asked to submit to Dick Nault a ten page (or less) paper on a broad topic related to school desegregation (for example, Should busing be used to desegregate schools? Should the county schools be included in the city desegregation efforts?) or on the impact of this litigation on your student teaching site (for example, An analysis of the school board's response to the city suit. An appraisal of race relations within your school). Three class sessions will be devoted to this overall topic, and one Friday session will be set aside for discussion of your paper plans. The following criteria will be used to assess your paper: ability to clearly define your paper topic, thorough analysis, application of appropriate analytic perspectives (research data, information gathered within your district), and the organization of your paper.

REFERENCES

Adams, K. A., & M. Q. Patton. 1981. Performance-based teacher education: Does it work? *Phi Delta Kappan* 62:660–62.

Adler, S. M. 1972. Painting and teaching. *Art Education* 25:5–7.

Allport, G. W. 1960. *Personality and social encounter*. Boston: Beacon.

Anderson, R. C. 1970. Control of student mediating processes during verbal learning and instruction. *Review of Educational Research* 40:349–69.

Andrews, T. E. 1972. Certification. In *Competency-based teacher education*, ed. W. R. Houston & R. B. Howsam. Chicago: Science Research Associates.

Apple, M. W. 1979. *Ideology and curriculum*. London: Routledge & Kegan Paul.

――――― 1982a. *Education and power*. Boston: Routledge & Kegan Paul.

――――― ed. 1982b. *Cultural and economic reproduction in education*. London: Routledge & Kegan Paul.

Arendt, H. 1968. The crisis in education. Ch. 5 in *Between past and future*. rev. ed. New York: Viking.

Arnstine, D. 1970. Aesthetic qualities in experience and learning. In *Aesthetic concepts and education*, ed. R. A. Smith. Urbana, IL: University of Illinois Press.

――――― 1975. Apprenticeship as the miseducation of teachers. *Philosophy of Education: Proceedings* 31:113–23.

Atkin, J. M. 1973. Practice oriented inquiry: A "third approach" to research in education. *Educational Researcher* 2:3–4.

Ayres, L. P. 1912. Measuring educational processes through educational results. *School Review* 20:300–09.

Bagenstos, N. T. 1975. The teacher as an inquirer. *Educational Forum* 39: 231–37.

Bagley, W. C. 1930. Teaching as a fine art. *Educational Method* 9:456–61.

Bantock, G. H. 1961. Educational research: A criticism. *Harvard Educational Review* 31:264–80.

Barr, A. S. 1929. *Characteristic differences in the teaching performance of good and poor teachers of the social studies.* Bloomington, IL: Public School.
———— 1931. *An introduction to the scientific study of classroom supervision.* New York: D. Appleton.
———— 1939. The systematic study of teaching and teaching efficiency. *Journal of Educational Research* 32:641–48.
———— 1948. Wisconsin studies of teaching ability. *Journal of Educational Research* 41:710–17.
———— 1958. Problems associated with the measurement and prediction of teacher success. *Journal of Educational Research* 51:695–99.
———— 1960. *Characteristics of good and poor teachers.* Available in A. S. Barr's papers located in the archives of the State Historical Society of Wisconsin.
———— 1961a. Foreword to the Wisconsin studies of the measurement and prediction of teacher effectiveness. *Journal of Experimental Education* 30: ii.
———— 1961b. Wisconsin studies of the measurement and prediction of teacher effectiveness. *Journal of Experimental Education* 30:5–156.
Barr, A. S., W. H. Burton & L. J. Brueckner. 1938. *Supervision.* New York: D. Appleton-Century.
———— 1947. *Supervision.* 2d ed. New York: D. Appleton-Century.
Barr, A. S., T. L. Torgerson, C. E. Johnson, V. E. Lyon, & A. C. Walvoord. 1935. The validity of certain instruments employed in the measurement of teaching ability. In *The measurement of teaching efficiency,* ed. H. M. Walker. New York: Macmillan.
Bayles, E. E. 1959. Present status of educational theory in the United States. *School and Society* 87:5–8.
Beardsley, M. C. 1970. Aesthetic theory and educational theory. In *Aesthetic concepts and education,* ed. R. A. Smith. Urbana, IL: University of Illinois Press.
Belkin, G. S. 1974. Communion in teaching. *Educational Theory* 24:170–82.
Bellack, A. A. 1981. Contrasting approaches to research on teaching. In *Studying teaching and learning,* ed. B. R. Tabachnick, T. S. Popkewitz, & B. B. Szekely. New York: Praeger.
Bennett, R. D. 1934. A basis for selecting the content of required courses in education. *Educational Research Bulletin* 13:113–19; 132.
Berger, P. L. & T. Luckmann. 1966. *The social construction of reality.* Garden City, NY: Doubleday.
Berlak, A., & H. Berlak. 1981. *Dilemmas of schooling.* London: Methuen.
Berlak, A., H. Berlak, N. T. Bagenstos, & E. R. Mikel. 1975. Teaching and learning in English primary schools. *School Review* 83:215–43.
Berliner, D. C. 1976. A status report on the study of teacher effectiveness. *Journal of Research in Science Teaching* 13:369–82.
———— 1980. Studying instruction in the elementary classroom. In *The analysis of educational productivity,* ed. R. Dreeban & J. A. Thomas. vol. 1. Cambridge, MA: Ballinger.
———— 1982. On improving teacher effectiveness: A conversation with David Berliner. *Educational Leadership* 40.12–15.

Bernal, J. D. 1956. *Science in history.* 2d ed. New York: Cameron.

Berson, R. 1975. The educational situation and the realm of values. *Educational Theory* 25:125–30.

Black, M. 1944. Education as art and discipline. *Ethics* 54:290–94.

———— 1979. More about metaphor. In *Metaphor and thought,* ed. A. Ortony. Cambridge: Cambridge University Press.

Blaisdell, H. F. 1969. *The philosophical fisherman.* Boston: Houghton Mifflin.

Bloom, B. S. 1971. Mastery learning and its implications for curriculum development. In *Confronting curriculum reform,* ed. E. W. Eisner. Boston: Little, Brown.

Blumer, H. 1962. Society as symbolic interaction. In *Human behavior and social processes,* ed. A. M. Rose. Boston: Houghton Mifflin.

Bobbitt, F. 1924. Discovering and formulating the objectives of teacher-training institutions. *Journal of Educational Research* 10:187–96.

Bode, B. 1924. Why educational objectives? *School and Society* 19:533–39.

———— 1927a. *Modern educational theories.* New York: Macmillan.

———— 1927b. The place of educational theory in teacher training. *The Ohio State University Bulletin* 32:523–24.

Borich, G. D. 1979. Implications for developing teacher competencies from process-product research. *Journal of Teacher Education* 30:77–86.

Borrowman, M. L. 1956. *The liberal and technical in teacher education.* New York: Bureau of Publications, Teachers College, Columbia University.

Bossert, S. T. 1981. Understanding sex differences in children's classroom experiences. *Elementary School Journal* 81:255–66.

Brauner, C. 1978. Accustoming: The hidden concept in training. *Philosophy of Education: Proceedings* 34:162–72.

Brophy, J. E. 1976. Reflections on research in elementary schools. *Journal of Teacher Education* 27:31–34.

———— 1979. Teacher behavior and its effects. *Journal of Educational Psychology* 71:733–50.

———— 1980. *Recent research on teaching* (Occasional Paper No. 40). East Lansing, MI: Institute for Research on Teaching, College of Education, Michigan State University. ED 204 280.

Brophy, J. E., & C. M. Evertson. 1976. *Learning from teaching.* Boston: Allyn and Bacon.

Broudy, H. S. 1956. Teaching—Craft or profession? *Educational Forum* 20: 175–84.

———— 1963. Can we save teacher education from its enemies and friends? In *Strength through reappraisal.* 16th yearbook of the American Association of Colleges for Teacher Education. Washington, DC: AACTE.

———— 1972. *A critique of performance-based teacher education.* Washington, DC: American Association of Colleges for Teacher Education. ED 063 274.

———— 1974. Teaching as acting—Perhaps, but. In *Teacher education as actor training,* ed. A Bagley. Occasional paper no. 3. Minneapolis: Society of Professors of Education, College of Education, University of Minnesota.

———— 1976. The search for a science of education. *Phi Delta Kappan* 58: 104–11.

_____ 1979. Options for teacher education. In *Alternative images of the future: Scenarios for education and the preparation of teachers.* Cedar Falls: College of Education, University of Northern Iowa. ED 181 015.

Buchmann, M. 1981. Personal communication. February 12.

Bullock, T. H. 1973. Seeing the world through a new sense: Electroreception in fish. *American Scientist* 61:316–25.

Bush, R. N., & P. Enemark. 1975. Control and responsibility in teacher education. In ed. K. Ryan, *Teacher education*, 74th yearbook of the National Society for the Study of Education, part 2. Chicago: University of Chicago Press.

Calfee, R. 1981. Cognitive psychology and educational practice. In *Review of research in education*, ed. D. C. Berliner. vol. 9. American Educational Research Association.

Callahan, R. E. 1962. *Education and the cult of efficiency.* Chicago: University of Chicago Press.

Charters, W. W. 1918a. The inadequacy of principles of teaching. *Educational Administration and Supervision* 4:215–21.

_____ 1918b. The administration of methods of teaching. *Educational Administration and Supervision* 4:237–44.

_____ 1924. Principles underlying the making of the curriculum of teacher-training institutions. *Educational Administration and Supervision* 10: 337–42.

_____ 1929a. What teachers ought to do. *Educational Research Bulletin* 8: 32–33.

_____ 1929b. A university curriculum study. *Educational Research Bulletin* 8:261–62.

_____ 1939. Does anybody use activity analysis? *Educational Research Bulletin* 18:133–34, 144.

_____ 1951. Professional and scientific objectives of graduate study in education. In *Graduate study in education*, ed. N. B. Henry. 50th yearbook of the National Society for the Study of Education, part 1. Chicago: University of Chicago Press.

Charters, W. W., & D. Waples. 1929. *The Commonwealth teacher-training study.* Chicago: University of Chicago Press.

Chase, A. 1983. The last bears of Yellowstone. *The Atlantic Monthly* 251: 63–73.

Clegg, A. 1979. Craftsmen and the origin of science. *Science and Society* 43: 186–201. Letters of response: 44:86; 44:480–81.

Clements, M. 1975. Alternatives in teacher education. *Curriculum Theory Network* 5:161–67.

Clifford, G. J. 1973. A history of the impact of research on teaching. In *Second handbook of research on teaching.* ed. R. M. W. Travers. Chicago: Rand McNally.

Cohen, D. 1977. *Ideas and action: Social science and craft in educational practice.* Chicago: Center for New Schools.

Cohn, M. 1979. The interrelationship of theory and practice in teacher education: A description and analysis of the LITE program (Doctoral dissertation, Washington University). *Dissertation Abstracts International* 40:3965–A. (University Microfilms no. 8002441.)

―――― 1981. A new supervision model for linking theory to practice. *Journal of Teacher Education* 32:26–30.

Coker, H., D. M. Medley, & R. S. Soar. 1980. How valid are expert opinions about effective teaching? *Phi Delta Kappan* 62:131–34; 149.

―――― 1981. The problem still remains. *Phi Delta Kappan* 62:738.

Coladarci, A. P. 1959. The teacher as hypothesis maker. *California Journal for Instructional Improvement* 2:3–6.

Collingwood, R. G. 1950. *The principles of art.* Oxford: Clarendon.

Combs, A. W. 1958. Seeing is behaving. *Educational Leadership* 16:21–26.

Confrey, J. 1981. Subject-matter specialists. Review of *Time to learn,* ed. C. Denham & A. Lieberman. *Elementary School Journal* 82:88–94.

Costin, F., & T. T. Hewett. 1971. Teaching and magic. *Educational Forum* 36: 43–45.

Counts, G. S. 1935. Break the teacher training lockstep. *The Social Frontier* 1:6–7.

Cremin, L. A. 1962. *The transformation of the school.* New York: Alfred A. Knopf.

Cronbach, L. J. 1967. How can instruction be adapted to individual differences? In *Learning and individual differnces,* ed. R. M. Gagné. Columbus, OH: Charles E. Merrill.

―――― 1975. Beyond the two disciplines of scientific psychology. *American Psychologist* 30:116–27.

Cronback, L. J., & R. E. Snow. 1969. *Individual differences in learning ability as a function of instructional variables.* Stanford, CA: School of Education, Stanford University. ED 029 001.

―――― 1977. *Aptitudes and instructional methods.* New York: Irvington.

Cruickshank, D. R., & J. H. Applegate. 1981. Reflective teaching as a strategy for teacher growth. *Educational Leadership* 38:553–54.

Cruickshank, D. R., J. Kennedy, E. J. Williams, J. Holton, & D. E. Fay. 1981. Evaluation of reflective teaching outcomes. *Journal of Educational Research* 75:26–32.

Cusick, P. A. 1973. *Inside high school.* New York: Holt, Rinehart & Winston.

Dearden, R. F. 1976. *Problems in primary education.* London: Routledge & Kegan Paul.

de Castell, S., & H. Freeman. 1978. Education as a socio-practical field: The theory/practice question reformulated. *Journal of Philosophy of Education* 12:13–28.

Denham, C., & A. Lieberman, eds. 1980. *Time to learn.* A publication of the California Commission for Teacher Preparation and Licensing. Washington, DC: U.S. Government Printing Office.

Dennison, G. 1969. *The lives of children.* New York: Random House.

Dewey, J. 1904. The relation of theory to practice in education. In *The relation of theory to practice in the education of teachers,* ed. C. A. McMurry. 3d yearbook of the National Society for the Scientific Study of Education, part 1. Chicago: University of Chicago Press.

———— 1929a. *The quest for certainty: A study of the relation of knowledge and action.* New York: Minton, Balch.

———— 1929b. *The sources of a science of education.* New York: Liveright.

———— 1956. *The child and the curriculum.* Chicago: University of Chicago Press.

Dickson, G. E. 1975. The future of CBTE. In *Topics in teacher education,* ed. R. J. Seibel. Bloomington, IN: School of Education, Indiana University.

———— 1979. CBTE revisited: Toledo's program remains strong. *Journal of Teacher Education* 30:17–19.

Domino, G. 1971. Interactive effects of achievement orientation and teaching style on academic achievement. *Journal of Educational Psychology* 62: 427–31.

Dornbusch, S. M. 1976. *The collegial evaluation program for faculty.* Stanford, CA: Stanford Center for Research and Development in Teaching, School of Education, Stanford University.

Doyle, W. 1977. Paradigms for research on teacher effectiveness. In *Review of research in education,* ed. L. S. Shulman. vol. 5. Itaska, IL: F. E. Peacock.

———— Research on classroom contexts. *Journal of Teacher Education* 32:3–6.

———— 1982. Stalking the mythical student. *Elementary School Journal* 82: 529–33.

Doyle, W., & G. A. Ponder. 1977–78. The practicality ethic in teacher decision-making. *Interchange* 8:1–12.

Dunkin, M. J., & B. J. Biddle. 1974. *The study of teaching.* New York: Holt, Rinehart & Winston.

Dunn, T. G. 1980. Understanding and coping with CBTE limitations. *Journal of Teacher Education* 31:27–33.

Ebel, R. L. 1967. Some limitations of basic research in education. *Phi Delta Kappan* 49:81–84.

———— 1982. The future of educational research. *Educational Researcher* 11: 18–19.

Eisner, E. 1977. On the uses of educational connoisseurship and criticism for evaluating classroom life. *Teachers College Record* 78:345–58.

———— 1979. *The educational imagination.* New York: Macmillan.

Elam, S. 1971. *Performance-based teacher education.* Washington, DC: American Association of Colleges for Teacher Education.

Elliott, J. 1976–77. Developing hypotheses about classrooms from teachers' practical constructs: An account of the work of the Ford Teaching Project. *Interchange* 7:2–22.

Feiman-Nemser, S. 1980. Growth and reflection as aims in teacher education: Directions for research. In *Exploring issues in teacher education: Questions for future research,* ed. G. E. Hall, S. M. Hord, & G. Brown. Austin: Research and Development Center for Teacher Education, The University of Texas. ED 189 046.

Fenstermacher, G. D. 1982. On learning to teach effectively from research on teacher effectiveness. *Journal of Classroom Interaction,* 17:7–12. (Reprinted from *Time to learn,* ed. C. Denham & A. Lieberman, chap. 6.)

Feuerstein, R. 1980. *Instrumental enrichment.* Baltimore: University Park Press.

Fiedler, M. L. 1975. Bidirectionality of influence in classroom interaction. *Journal of Educational Psychology* 67:735–44.

Finch, M. E., & A. R. Tom. 1978. *Maryville College-Washington University Master of Arts in Education.* St. Louis: Maryville College and Washington University. ED 168 977.

Fisher, C., R. Marliave, & N. N. Filby. 1979. Improving teaching by increasing "academic learning time." *Educational Leadership* 37:52–54.

Floden, R. E. 1981. The logic of information-processing psychology in education. In *Review of research in education,* ed. D. C. Berliner. vol. 9. American Educational Research Association.

Freeman, F. N. 1930. Teaching as an applied science. *Journal of Educational Method* 9:448–55.

———— 1938. Concluding comments and remarks on the province of scientific inquiry. In *The scientific movement in education,* ed. F. N. Freeman. 37th yearbook of the National Society for the Study of Education, part 2. Bloomington, IL: Public School.

Freire, P. 1970. *Pedagogy of the oppressed,* trans. M. Bergman Ramos. New York: Seabury.

Fuller, F. F. 1969. Concerns of teachers: A developmental conceptualization. *American Educational Research Journal* 6:207–26.

Gage, N. L. 1963. Paradigms for research on teaching. In *Handbook of research on teaching,* ed. N. L. Gage. Chicago: Rand McNally.

———— 1974. Evaluating ways to help teachers to behave desirably. In *Competency assessment, research, and evaluation,* ed. W. R. Houston. Multi-State Consortium on Performance-Based Teacher Education.

———— 1978. *The scientific basis of the art of teaching.* New York: Teachers College Press.

———— 1980. New prospects for educational research. *Australian Educational Researcher* 7:7–25.

Gage, N. L., & R. Giaconia. 1981. Teaching practices and student achievement: Causal connections. *New York University Education Quarterly* 12:2–9.

Gage, N. L., & P. H. Winne. 1975. Performance-based teacher education. In *Teacher education,* ed. K. Ryan. 74th yearbook of the National Society for the Study of Education, part 2. Chicago: University of Chicago Press.

Gagné, R. M., & L. J. Briggs. 1974. *Principles of instructional design.* New York: Holt, Rinehart & Winston.

Gall, M. D. 1979. Competency-based teacher education meterials: How available? How usable? How effective? *Journal of Teacher Education* 30:58–61.

Gergen, K. J. 1973. Social psychology as history. *Journal of Personality and Social Psychology* 26:309–20.

———— 1978. Toward generative theory. *Journal of Personality and Social Psychology* 36:1344–60.

———— 1980a. The challenge of phenomenal change for research methodology. *Human Development* 23:254–67.

———— 1980b. Toward intellectual audacity in social psychology. In *The development of social psychology*, ed. R. Gilmour & S. Duck. London: Academic.

——— 1982. *Toward tranformation in social knowledge.* New York: Springer-Verlag.

Getzels, J. W. 1978. Paradigm and practice: On the impact of basic research in education. In *Impact of research on education: Some case studies*, ed. P. Suppes. Washington, DC: National Academy of Education.

Glass, G. V. 1971. Educational knowledge use. *Educational forum* 36:21–29.

——— 1972. The wisdom of scientific inquiry on education. *Journal of Research in Science Teaching* 9:3–18.

Glick, O. 1968. The educational process in the classroom. *School Review* 76: 339–51.

Good, T. L. 1979. Teacher effectiveness in the elementary school. *Journal of Teacher Education* 30:52–64.

Good, T. L., D. Grouws, & H. Ebmeier. 1983. *Active mathematics teaching.* New York: Longman.

Good, T. L., & C. N. Power. 1976. Designing successful classroom environments for different types of students. *Journal of Curriculum Studies* 8: 45–60.

Gordon, D. 1980. The immorality of the hidden curriculum. *Journal of Moral Education* 10:3–8.

Gowin, D. B. 1960. Teaching—Its logic and its language. *Elementary School Journal* 61:179–90.

——— 1970. The structure of knowledge. *Educational Theory* 20:319–28.

——— 1981. *Educating.* Ithaca, NY: Cornell University Press.

Gray, F., P. S. Graubard, & H. Rosenberg. 1974. Little brother is changing you. *Psychology Today* 7:42–46.

Green, T. F. 1971. *The activities of teaching.* New York: McGraw-Hill.

Griffin, D. R. 1981. *The question of animal awareness.* rev. ed. New York: Rockefeller University Press.

Grumet, M. R. 1983. The line is drawn. *Educational Leadership* 40:28–38.

Gubser, L. 1980. NCATE's director comments on the Tom critique. *Phi Delta Kappan* 62:117–19.

Haggerty, M. E. 1929. Review of *The Commonwealth teacher-training study*, by W. W. Charters and D. Waples. *Elementary School Journal* 29:627–28.

Hall, R. 1959. The scholar and the craftsman in the scientific revolution. In *Critical problems in the history of science*, ed. M. Clagett. Madison: University of Wisconsin Press.

Haller, E. J. 1967. Pupil influence in teacher socialization: A socio-linguistic study. *Sociology of Education* 40:316–33.

Harap, H. 1929. Review of *The Commonwealth teacher-training study*, by W. W. Charters and D. Waples. *School Review* 37:467–70.

Hartnett, A., & M. Naish. 1980. Technicians or social bandits? Some moral and political issues in the education of teachers. In *Teacher strategies: Explorations in the sociology of the school*, ed. P. Woods. London: Croom Helm.

Hawkins, D. 1973. What it means to teach. *Teachers College Record* 75:7–16.

Hayes, H. E. 1977. Curriculum development as a moral enterprise. *Curric-*

ulum Inquiry 6:229–35.

Heath, R. W., & M. A. Nielson. 1974. The research basis for performance-based teacher education. *Review of Educational Research* 44:463–84.

Hendley, B. 1978. Martin Buber on the teacher-student relationship: A critical appraisal. *Journal of Philosophy of Education* 12:141–48.

Hersh, R. H., J. P. Miller, & G. D. Fielding. 1980. *Models of moral education*. New York: Longman.

Highet, G. 1950. *The art of teaching*. New York: Alfred A. Knopf.

Hill, W. M. 1968. I-B-F supervision. *Clearing House* 43:180–83.

Hirst, P. H., & R. S. Peters. 1971. *The logic of education*. New York: Humanities.

Hopkins, C. D. 1974. Electric communication in fish. *American Scientist* 62:426–37.

Houston, W. R. 1974. Competency based education. In *Exploring competency based education*, ed. W. R. Houston. Berkeley, CA: McCutchan.

Howsam, R. B., D. C. Corrigan, G. W. Denemark, & R. J. Nash. 1976. *Educating a profession*. Washington, DC: American Association of Colleges for Teacher Education.

Hudgins, B. B. 1971. *The instructional process*. Chicago: Rand McNally.

Hunt, D. E. 1976. Teachers' adaptation: 'Reading' and 'flexing' to students. *Journal of Teacher Education* 27:268–75.

Hurn, C. 1978. *The limits and possibilities of schooling*. Boston: Allyn & Bacon.

Jackson, P. W. 1968. *Life in classrooms*. New York: Holt, Rinehart & Winston.

———— 1970. Is there a best way of teaching Harold Bateman? *Midway* 10:15–28.

James, W. 1902. *Talks to teachers*. New York: Henry Holt.

Jenkins, J. J. 1981. Can we have a fruitful cognitive psychology? In *Nebraska Symposium on Motivation*, ed. H. E. Howe, Jr., & J. H. Flowers. vol. 28. Lincoln: University of Nebraska Press.

Jonçich, G. 1968. *The sane positivist: A biography of Edward L. Thorndike*. Middletown, CT: Wesleyan University Press.

Kalb, M., & M. S. Propper. 1976. The future of alcohology: Craft or science? *American Journal of Psychiatry* 133:641–45. Letters of response: 133:1345–46; 133:1467–68.

Kay, P. M., & B. Rosner. 1973. Are teachers colleges really prepared to handle competency based teacher education? *Journal of Research and Development in Education* 7:47–53.

Kazamias, A. M. 1961. A note concerning "Practice in Teaching" by Judson T. Shaplin. *Harvard Educational Review* 31:449–51.

Kerlinger, F. N. 1968. The doctoral training of research specialists. *Teachers College Record* 69:477–83.

Kilbourn, B. 1982. Thoughts on conceptual analyses of teaching. *Journal of Educational Thought* 16:64–72.

Kilgore, A. M. 1980. PBTE: A follow-up study. *Journal of Teacher Education* 31:55–60.

Kirschner, J. 1966. Education as technology: Functional analysis in the writings of W. W. Charters, 1904–1925. (Doctoral dissertation, Rutgers University). *Dissertation Abstracts International* 27:374–A. (University Microfilms no. 66–6776, 164.)

Klein, A. J., ed. 1941. *Adventures in the reconstruction of education.* Columbus, OH: College of Education, Ohio State University.

Klein, S. S. 1971. Student influence on teacher behavior. *American Educational Research Journal* 8:403–21.

Kliebard, H. M. 1970. The Tyler rationale. *School Review* 78:259–72.

————— 1972. Metaphorical roots of curriculum design. *Teachers College Record* 73:403–04.

————— 1977. Curriculum theory: Give me a "for instance." *Curriculum Inquiry* 6:257–69.

————— 1982a. Curriculum theory as metaphor. *Theory into Practice* 21:11–17.

————— 1982b. Education at the turn of the century: A crucible for curriculum change. *Educational Researcher* 11:16–24.

Koeller, S., & E. Thompson. 1980. Another look at lesson planning. *Educational Leadership* 37:673–75.

Kohl, H. 1976. *On teaching.* New York: Schocken.

Komisar, B. P. 1961. Review of *The language of teaching* by I. Scheffler. *Teachers College Record* 62:422–23.

Kozol, J. 1981. *On being a teacher.* New York: Continuum.

Larson, R. W. 1979. Examining standards: An important task for those involved in accreditation. *Action in Teacher Education* 1:11–20.

Leopold, A. 1949. *A sand county almanac.* New York: Oxford University Press.

Lillard, P. P. 1980. *Children learning.* New York: Schocken.

Linzey, A. 1976. *Animal rights.* London: SCM.

Lorber, M. A. 1979. From traditional to competency-based teacher education and back again: An eight-year "experiment." *Phi Delta Kappan* 60:523–24.

Lortie, D. C. 1975. *Schoolteacher.* Chicago: University of Chicago Press.

Macdonald, J. B. 1971. Responsible curriculum development. In *Confronting curriculum reform*, ed. E. W. Eisner. Boston: Little, Brown.

McKeachie, W. J. 1974. The decline and fall of the laws of learning. *Educational Researcher* 3:7–11.

McPherson, G. H. 1972. *Small town teacher.* Cambridge, MA: Harvard University Press.

Mager, R. F. 1962. *Preparing instructional objectives.* Palo Alto, CA: Fearon.

Mahoney, M. J. 1976a. The truth seekers. *Psychology Today* 9:60, 65.

————— 1976b. *Scientist as subject: The psychological imperative.* Cambridge, MA: Ballinger.

Martin, J. R. 1976. What should we do with a hidden curriculum when we find one? *Curriculum Inquiry* 6:135–51.

Martin, R. J. 1978. Craftsmanship and schooling. *Journal of Thought* 13:187–95.

Mayor, J. R., & W. G. Swartz. 1965. *Accreditation in teacher education.* Washington, DC: National Commission on Accrediting.

Medley, D. M. 1972. Early history of research on teacher behavior. *International Review of Education* 18:430–39.

———— 1973. Closing the gap between research in teacher effectiveness and the teacher education curriculum. *Journal of Research and Development in Education* 7:39–46.

Medley, D. M., & H. E. Mitzel. 1963. Measuring classroom behavior by systematic observation. In *Handbook of research on teaching*, ed. N. L. Gage. Chicago: Rand McNally.

Mergendoller, J. R. 1981. Personal communication. March 21.

Mitzel, H. E. 1977. Increasing the impact of theory and research on programs of instruction. *Journal of Teacher Education* 28:15–20.

Monroe, W. S. 1937. Progress toward a science of education. *Bulletin of the School of Education* (Indiana University) 13:43–51.

———— 1951. How has educational research contributed to the development of teacher education? *Journal of Teacher Education* 2:60–63.

———— 1952. *Teaching-learning theory and teacher education, 1890 to 1950.* Urbana: University of Illinois Press.

Mueller, L. 1976. Will computers tell us when to fish? *Outdoor Life,* 158:92, 94, 96, 130–31.

Nagel, E. 1969. Philosophy of science and educational theory. *Studies in Philosophy and Education* 7:5–27.

National Council for Accreditation of Teacher Education. 1979. *Standards for accreditation of teacher education.* Washington, DC: NCATE.

Needleman, C. 1979. Potter's progress: Self-understanding and the lessons of craft. *Psychology Today* 13:78, 81–82, 85–86.

Noble, C. G., & J. D. Nolan. 1976. Effect of student verbal behavior on classroom teacher behavior. *Journal of Educational Psychology* 68: 342–46.

Noble, G. L. 1971. Joseph Mayer Rice: Critic of the public schools and pioneer in modern educational measurement. (Doctoral dissertation, State University of New York at Buffalo). *Dissertation Abstracts International* 31:4503–A. (University Microfilms no. 71–6100, 342.)

Oliver, D. W., & J. P. Shaver. 1966. *Teaching public issues in the high school.* Boston: Houghton Mifflin.

Olsen, H. C. 1979. Accreditation of teacher education is alive and kicking. *Action in Teacher Education* 1:1–10.

Olson, D. R., & J. S. Bruner. 1974. Learning through experience and learning through media. In *Media and symbols: The forms of expression, communication, and education*, ed. D. R. Olson. 73d yearbook of the National Society for the Study of Education, part 1. Chicago: University of Chicago Press.

Ortony, A. 1975. Why metaphors are necessary and not just nice. *Educational Theory* 25:45–53.

Palmer, J. 1980. Personal communication. December 4.

Peck, R. F. 1976. Needed R and D in teaching. *Journal of Teacher Education* 27:18–21.

Peters. R. S. 1965. Education as initiation. In *Philosophical analysis and education*, ed. R. D. Archambault. New York: Humanities.

———— 1977. *Education and the education of teachers.* London: Routedge & Kegan Paul.

Peterson, P. L. 1979. Direct instruction reconsidered. In *Research on teaching,* ed. P. L. Peterson & H. L. Walberg. Berkeley, CA: McCutchan.

Phillips, D. C. 1980. What do the researcher and the practitioner have to offer each other? *Educational Researcher* 9:17–20, 24.

———— 1981. Perspectives on teaching as an intentional act. *Australian Journal of Education* 25:99–105.

Popkewitz, T. S., B. R. Tabachnick, & K. M. Zeichner. 1979. Dulling the senses: Research in teacher education. *Journal of Teacher Education* 30: 52–60.

Popkewitz, T. S., & G. G. Wehlage. 1973. Accountability: Critique and alternative perspective. *Interchange* 4:48–62.

Popper, K. 1979. Creative self-criticism in science and in art. *Encounter* 53: 10–14.

Pratte, R. 1981. Metaphorical models and curriculum theory. *Curriculum Inquiry* 11:307–20.

Provus, M. M. 1975. *The grand experiment.* Berkeley, CA: McCutchan.

Raths, L. E., M. Harmin, & S. B. Simon. 1966. *Values and teaching.* Columbus, OH: Charles E. Merrill.

Resnick, L. B. 1981. Instructional psychology. *Annual Review of Psychology* 32:659–704.

Resnick, L. B., & W. W. Ford. 1981. *The psychology of mathematics for instruction.* Hillsdale, NJ: Lawrence Erlbaum.

Rice, J. M. 1893. *The public-school system of the United States.* New York: Century.

———— 1897. The futility of the spelling grind. *Forum* 23:163–72, 409–19.

———— 1914. *Scientific management in education.* New York: Hinds, Noble & Eldredge.

Richek, M. A. 1979. "Spiteful tracts compete against bloodless surveys": The use of reading research. *Curriculum Inquiry* 9:45–57.

Rives, F. C., Jr. 1979. The teacher as a performing artist. *Contemporary Education* 51:7–9.

Rollin, B. E. 1981. *Animal rights and human morality.* Buffalo, NY: Prometheus.

Rosenshine, B. 1979. Content, time and direct instruction. In *Research on teaching,* ed. P. L. Peterson & H. J. Walberg. Berkeley, CA: McCutchan.

Rosenshine, B., & N. Furst. 1971. Research in teacher performance criteria. In *Research in teacher education: A symposium,* ed. B. O. Smith. Englewood Cliffs, NJ: Prentice-Hall.

Rubin, L. 1981. The artist teacher. *Journal of Education* 63:135–43.

Russell, B. 1979. *Second wind: The memoirs of an opinionated man.* New York: Random House.

Sandefur, J. T. 1982. Teacher competency assessment plans "Little short of phenomenal." *AACTE Briefs* 3:8–9, 11.

Sanders, J. T. 1978. Teacher effectiveness: Accepting the null hypothesis. *Journal of Educational Thought* 12:184–89.

Scates, D. E. 1947. Fifty years of objective measurement and research in education. *Journal of Educational Research* 41:241–64.

Schaefer, R. J. 1967. *The school as a center of inquiry.* New York: Harper & Row.

———— 1970. Teacher education in the United States. In *Current problems of teacher education*, ed. A. Yates. Hamburg, Germany: Unesco Institute for Education.

Scheffler, I. 1956. Science, morals, and educational policy. *Harvard Educational Review* 26:1–16.

———— 1960. *The language of education.* Springfield, IL: Charles A. Thomas.

Schmuck, R. A., & P. A. Schmuck. 1983. *Group processes in the classroom.* 4th ed. Dubuque: Wm. C. Brown.

Schneider, E. J. 1981. Another "back to the basics" push isn't going to help today's schools. *Educational R & D Report* 4:2–7.

Schrag, F. 1977. The child in the moral order. *Philosophy* 52:167–77.

———— 1980. Personal communication. November 13.

Schwab, J. J. 1973. The practical 3: Translation into curriculum. *School Review* 81:501–22.

Schweitzer, A. 1923. *Civilization and ethics*, trans. J. Naish. London: A. C. Black.

———— 1949. *Out of my life and thought*, trans. C. T. Campion. New York: Henry Holt.

Shaplin, J. 1961. Practice in teaching. *Harvard Educational Review* 31:33–59.

Sherman, T. M., & W. H. Cormier. 1974. An investigation of the influence of student behavior on teacher behavior. *Journal of Applied Behavior Analysis* 7:11–21.

Shulman, L. S. 1974. The psychology of school subjects: A premature obituary. *Journal of Research in Science Teaching* 11:319–39.

———— 1981. Recent developments in the study of teaching. In *Studying teaching and learning*, ed. B.R. Tabachnick, T. S. Popkewitz, & B. B. Szekely. New York: Praeger.

Simon, H. A. 1981. *The sciences of the artificial.* 2d ed. Cambridge, MA: MIT Press.

Singer, P. 1981. *The expanding circle: Ethics and sociobiology.* New York: Farrar, Straus & Giroux.

Smith, B. O. 1971. Introduction. In *Research in teacher education*, ed. B. O. Smith. Englewood Cliffs, NJ: Prentice-Hall.

———— 1980. *A design for a school of pedagogy.* U.S. Department of Education. Washington, DC: U.S. Government Printing Office.

Smith, L. M. 1977. Effective teaching: A qualitative inquiry in aesthetic education. *Anthropology and Education Quarterly* 8:127–39.

Smith, L. M., & W. Geoffrey. 1968. *The complexities of an urban classroom.* New York: Holt, Rinehart & Winston.

Smith, P. G. 1973. The philosophical context. In *The elementary school in the United States*, ed. J. I. Goodlad and H. G. Shane. 72d yearbook of the National Society for the Study of Education, part 2. Chicago: University of Chicago Press.

———— 1976. Knowledge and values. *Educational Theory* 26:29–39.

Smith, R. A. 1971. Is teaching an art? In *Aesthetics and problems of education*, ed. R. A. Smith. Urbana, IL: University of Illinois Press.

Snow, R. E. 1977. Individual differences and instructional theory. *Educational Researcher* 6:11–15.

—— 1980. Aptitude, learner control, and adaptive instruction. *Educational Psychologist* 15:151–58.

Soar, R. S. 1968. Optimum teacher-pupil interaction for pupil growth. *Educational Leadership/Research Supplement* 2:275–80.

Soar, R. S., & R. M. Soar. 1976. An attempt to identify measures of teacher effectiveness from four studies. *Journal of Teacher Education* 27: 261–67.

Stallings, J. 1980. Allocated academic learning time revisited, or beyond time on task. *Educational Researcher* 9:11–16.

Stanley, J. C. 1966. Rice as a pioneer educational researcher. *Journal of Educational Measurement* 3:135–39.

Stephens, J. M. 1960. Spontaneous schooling and success in teaching. *School Review* 68:152–63.

—— 1967. *The process of schooling.* New York: Holt, Rinehart Winston.

Stevens, R., & B. Rosenshine. 1981. Advances in research on teaching. *Exceptional Education Quarterly* 2:1–9.

Sticht, T. G. 1979. Educational uses of metaphor. In *Metaphor and thought*, ed. A. Ortony. Cambridge: Cambridge University Press.

Stinnett, T. M. 1970. Accreditation of teacher education institutions and agencies. *Phi Delta Kappan* 52:25–31.

Stone, C., & G. Wehlage. 1982. Four persisting school dilemmas. *Action in Teacher Education* 4:17–29.

Strung, N. 1982. All I know about hunting. *Field & Stream* 87:23, 25.

Superka, D. P., C. Ahrens, J. E. Hedstrom, L. J. Ford, & P. L. Johnson. 1976. *Values education sourcebook.* Boulder, CO: Social Science Education Consortium. ED 118 465.

Suppes, P. 1974. The place of theory in educational research. *Educational Researcher* 3:3–10.

Tanner, D., & L. N. Tanner. 1975. *Curriculum development.* New York: Macmillan.

Taylor, F. W. 1911. *The principles of scientific management.* New York: Harper & Bros.

Thorndike, E. L. 1910. *Educational psychology.* rev. ed. New York: Teachers College, Columbia University.

—— 1912. The measurement of educational products. *School Review* 20: 289–99.

—— 1922. The psychology of arithmetic. New York: Macmillan.

—— 1923. *Educational psychology: Briefer course.* New York: Teachers College, Columbia University.

Tidyman, W. F. 1915. A critical study of Rice's investigation of spelling efficiency. *Pedagogical Seminary* 22:391–400.

Tobias, S. 1976. Achievement treatment interactions. *Review of Educational Research* 46:61–74.

—— 1981. Adapting instruction to individual differences among students. *Educational Psychologist* 16:111–20.

————— 1982. When do instructional methods make a difference? *Educational Researcher* 11:4–9.

Tom, A. R. 1970. *An approach to selecting among social studies curricula.* St. Ann, MO: Central Midwestern Regional Educational Laboratory.

————— 1972. Selective supervision. *The Teacher Educator* 8:23–26.

————— 1973a. Implementing new social studies curricula: A model and its field trial. *Indiana Social Studies Quarterly* 26:30–39.

————— 1973b. Teacher reaction to a systematic approach to curriculum implementation. *Curriculum Theory Network.* No. 11:86–93.

————— 1973c. Three dilemmas: School-university ventures. *The Clearing House* 48:7–10.

————— 1974a. The clinical professorship: Failure or first step. *The High School Journal* 57:250–57.

————— 1974b. The case for pass/fail student teaching. *The Teacher Educator* 10:2–8.

————— 1976. *Field based teacher education: Implementation issues.* Paper presented at the National Teacher Education Conference, Indianapolis. ED 150 124.

————— 1980a. NCATE standards and program quality: You can't get there from here. *Phi Delta Kappan* 62:113–17.

————— 1980b. Chopping NCATE standards down to size. *Journal of Teacher Education* 31:25–30.

————— 1980c. Teaching as a moral craft: A metaphor for teaching and teacher education. *Curriculum Inquiry* 10:317–23.

————— 1981. An alternative set of NCATE standards. *Journal of Teacher Education* 32:48–52.

————— 1983. Should NCATE be disaccredited? The Washington University-Maryville College experience. *Texas Tech Journal of Education* 10: 73–86.

Tom, A. R., & J. R. Applegate. 1969. *The teaching workshop; An approach to implementing new social studies curricula.* St. Louis: Graduate Institute of Education, Washington University. ED 040 894.

Travers, R. M. W. 1975. Empirically based teacher education. *Educational Forum* 39:417–33.

————— 1979. Training the teacher as a performing artist. *Contemporary Education* 51:14–18.

Tyler, R. W. 1950. *Basic principles of curriculum and instruction.* Chicago: University of Chicago Press.

————— 1953. The leader of major educational projects. *Educational Research Bulletin* 32:42–52.

van Manen, M. 1977. Linking ways of knowing with ways of being practical. *Curriculum Inquiry* 6:205–28.

————— 1982. Edifying theory: Serving the good. *Theory Into Practice* 21: 44–49.

Vlaanderen, R. B. 1982. Teacher competency testing: Status report. *Educational Measurement: Issues and Practice* 1:17–20, 27.

Wallace, D., ed. 1980. *Getting the most from your garden.* Emmaus, PA: Rodale.

Waller, W. 1932. *The sociology of teaching.* New York: John Wiley.

Waples, D. 1953. W. W. Charters: The man and the educator. *Educational Research Bulletin* 32:29–36.

Wehlage, G. G. 1981a. Can teachers be more reflective about their work? A commentary on some research about teachers. In *Studying teaching and learning*, ed. B. R. Tabachnick, T. S. Popkewitz, and B. B. Szekely. New York: Praeger.

―――― 1981b. The purpose of generalization in field-study research. In *The study of schooling*, ed. T. S. Popkewitz & B. R. Tabachnick. New York: Praeger.

Weisskopf, V. F. 1979. Art and science. *American Scholar* 48:473–85.

Westbury, I. 1980. Review article—Ideology and curriculum. Review of *Ideology and curriculum* by M. W. Apple. *Educational Theory* 30:169–75.

Wheeler, C. W. 1980. *NCATE: Does it matter?* East Lansing, MI: Institute for Research on Teaching, College of Education, Michigan State University. Research series no. 92. ED 195 552.

Willis, P. E. 1977. *Learning to labour*. Farnborough, England: Saxon House.

―――― 1981. Cultural production is different from cultural reproduction is different from social reproduction is different from reproduction. *Interchange on Education Policy* 12:48–67.

Wilson, F. R., H. D. Gideonse, J. H. Johnston, & J. Schultz. 1981. How startling are the Coker, Medley, and Soar findings? A critique. *Phi Delta Kappan* 62:736–38.

Winne, P. H., & R. W. Marx. 1977. Reconceptualizing research on teaching. *Journal of Educational Psychology* 69:668–78.

Wirth, A. G. 1975. PBTE: A question of values. In *Regaining educational leadership*, ed. R. A. Smith. New York: John Wiley.

Wise, A. E. 1978. Teacher: Automaton or craftsperson. In *The in-service education of teachers*, ed. L. Rubin. Boston: Allyn & Bacon.

Zahorik, J. A. 1975. Teachers' planning models. *Educational Leadership* 33: 134–39.

Zeichner, K. M. 1978. Group membership in the elementary school classroom. *Journal of Educational Psychology* 70:554–64.

―――― 1981. Reflective teaching and field-based experience in teacher education. *Interchange* 12:1–22.

―――― 1982. *Activating teacher energy through "inquiry-oriented" teacher education*. Paper presented at the annual meeting of the Association of Teacher Educators, Phoenix.

INDEX

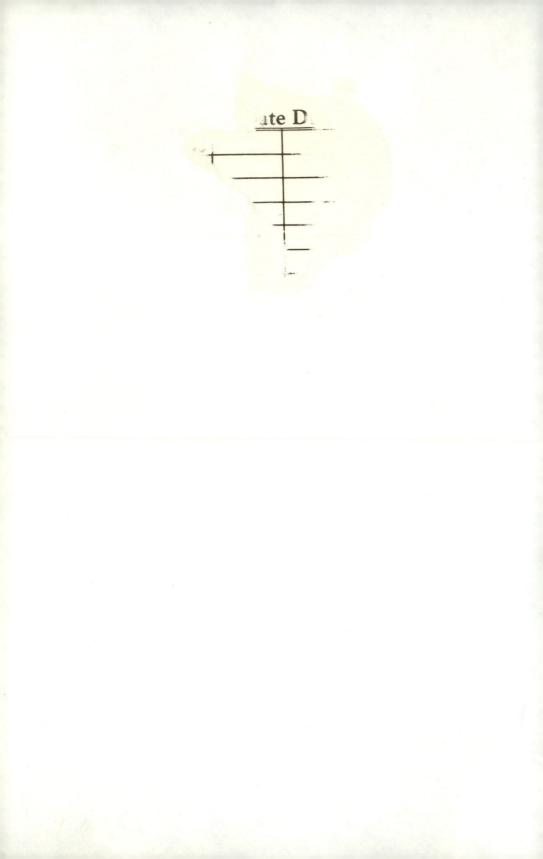

ate D